European International Relations 1648–1815

Jeremy Black

palgrave

First published 2002 by
PALGRAVE
Houndmills, Basingstoke, Hampshire RG21 6XS and
175 Fifth Avenue, New York, N.Y. 10010
Companies and representatives throughout the world

PALGRAVE is the new global academic imprint of
St. Martin's Press LLC Scholarly and Reference Division and
Palgrave Publishers Ltd (formerly Macmillan Press Ltd).

ISBN 0–333–96450–0 hardback
ISBN 0–333–96451–9 paperback

This book is printed on paper suitable for recycling and made from fully
managed and sustained forest sources.

A catalogue record for this book is available from the British Library.

Library of Congress Cataloging-in-Publication Data
Black, Jeremy.
    European international relations, 1648–1815/Jeremy Black.
        p. cm.
    Includes bibliographical references and index.
    ISBN 0–333–96450–0 (cloth)—ISBN 0–333–96451–9 (paper)
        1. Europe—Foreign relations. 2. International relations.
3. Europe—History—1648–1789. 4. Europe—History—
1789–1815. 5. Europe—Military policy.   I. Title.
D273.7 .B53 2002
327′.094′0903—dc21   2001045866

10 9 8 7 6 5 4 3 2 1
11 10 09 08 07 06 05 04 03 02

Printed in China

European International Relations
1648–1815

Contents

Contents

vi

Preface

This study will aim to provide an up-to-date, comprehensive and analytical account of international relations in Europe from the Peace of Westphalia to the Congress of Vienna. It will also cover the colonies and those areas affected by European power. The analytical framework will come first, in order to provide guidance to the chronology that follows. Throughout, the approach will be 'open-ended', drawing attention to methodological problems and conceptual issues, and making it clear where there is debate and uncertainty. This extends to the very coverage of the book. Given the constraints of space, it is necessary to be selective in deciding what to include, and this problem and process will be emphasized in order to focus attention on what was important both at the time and in hindsight. This book is informed by an awareness of the extensive and excellent work of numerous scholars on the period, some of which is cited in the endnotes, but also seeks an individual voice. This approach is anti-deterministic and wary of schematic accounts. In addition, insights gained from archival research in Paris, Nancy, The Hague, Darmstadt, Dresden, Hanover, Munich, Marburg, Osnabrück, Florence, Genoa, Modena, Parma, Turin, Venice, Vienna, and in British and American archives have been useful. I am most grateful to Linda Frey, Marsha Frey, Munro Price, Chris Storrs and an anonymous reader for commenting on an earlier draft.

JEREMY BLACK

List of Abbreviations

AE	Paris, Archives du Ministère des Relations Extérieures
AN	Paris, Archives Nationales
AST. LM	Turin, Archivio di Stato, Lettere Ministri
BL. Add.	London, British Library, Additional Manuscripts
Bayr. Ges.	Bayreuth Gesandtschaft
CP	Correspondance Politique
HHStA	Vienna, Haus-, Hof-und Staatsarchiv
MD	Mémoires et Documents
Munich	Munich, Hauptstaatsarchiv
Naf.	Nouvelles acquisitions françaises
Polit. Corresp.	*Politische Correspondenz Friedrichs des Grossen* (46 vols, Berlin, 1879–1939)
PRO	London, Public Record Office
SP	State Papers

Note: years given in brackets after individual monarchs, etc., are regnal years.

For Pam and John West
good friends

Europe in 1815 after the Congress of Vienna changes

Faroe Is.

Shetland Is.

Orkney Is.

NORWAY
Bergen
Christiania

Stavanger

SWEDEN

Göteborg

ATLANTIC
OCEAN

Edinburgh

UNITED KINGDOM

NORTH
SEA

DENMARK
Copenhagen   Malmö

Dublin

Manchester

Heligoland   Lubeck
FREE CITY   POMER
Hamburg
FREE CITY
Bremen   Stettin
FREE CITY
HANOVER   Berlin

Norwich   Amsterdam
Bristol   London

UNITED NETH.

Minden
WEST-   Hanover   BRANDENBURG
PHALIA

SAXONY

English Channel   Calais
Channel Is.

Antwerp
Cologne

Leipzig
Erfut   K. OF
SAXONY

LUX.

BOHEMIA
Frankfurt   Prague
FREE CITY

Paris

PAL.

Nuremberg
BAVARIA   A U S

Orleans

Strasbourg   Stuttgart

BADEN

Nantes   Tours

Basle

Munich   Salzburg

FRANCE

Berne
Geneva   SWITZERLAND   Innsbruck

La Coruña

Limoges

Lyons   SAVOY

ILLYRIA

Bordeaux

Grenoble

Milan
Turin   LOMBARDY-VENETIA   Trieste
PIEDMONT
Genoa   Venice

Toulouse

Braganzá
Oporto   Burgos   Pamplona
Valladolid

ANDORRA

Nice
Marseilles   MONACO   LUCCA
Florence

SAN
MARINO

Bologna

PARMA

MODENA

TUSCANY   PAPAL
STATES

SPAIN   Saragossa

Lisbon
Madrid
Toledo

Barcelona

CORSICA
Ajaccio

Rome

PORTUGAL

SARDINIA

Valencia

Balearic Is.

Pontecorvo
Benevento
Naples

Seville

Cartagena
Granada

Cagliari

Tangier   Gibraltar

Palermo
MEDITERRANEAN SEA

K. OF THE

Melilla

Oran

Algiers

Bona

ALGIERS

Tunis

TUNIS

Malta

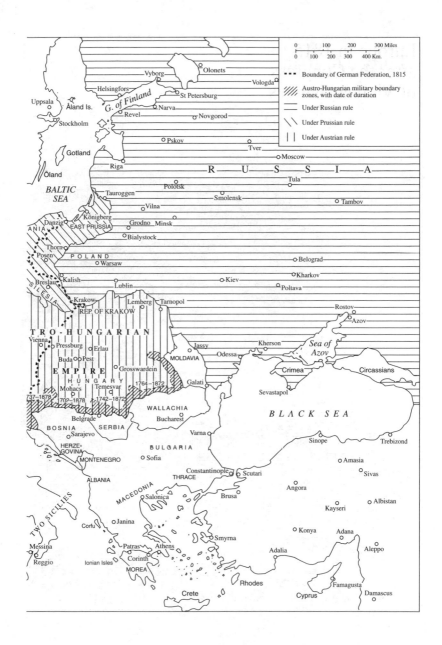

0	100	200	300 Miles
0	100 200	300	400 Km.

- - - Boundary of German Federation, 1815

/// Austro-Hungarian military boundary zones, with date of duration

— Under Russian rule

\\ Under Prussian rule

| | Under Austrian rule

Uppsala

Åland Is.

G. of Finland

Vyborg

Olonets

Vologda

Helsingfors

St Petersburg

Stockholm

Revel

Narva

Novgorod

Gotland

Pskov

Tver

Moscow

Öland

Riga

R — U — S — S — I — A

Tula

BALTIC SEA

Tauroggen

Polotsk

Smolensk

Tambov

Vilna

Danzig

Königberg

EAST PRUSSIA

Grodno

Minsk

ANIA

Bialystock

Thorn

Posen

POLAND

Warsaw

Belograd

Breslau

Kalish

SILESIA

Krakow

Lublin

Kiev

Kharkov

REP. OF KRAKOW

Lemberg

Tarnopol

Poltava

Rostov

TRO-HUNGARIAN

Azov

Vienna

Pressburg

Erlau

Jassy

Kherson

Sea of Azov

Buda

Pest

MOLDAVIA

Odessa

EMPIRE

Grosswardein

Crimea

Circassians

H U N G A R Y

1764–1872

Galati

Mohacs

Temesvar

Sevastopol

37–1878

702–1878

1742–1872

WALLACHIA

BLACK SEA

Belgrade

Bucharest

BOSNIA

SERBIA

Sarajevo

Varna

Sinope

Trebizond

HERZE-GOVINA

BULGARIA

MONTENEGRO

Sofia

Amasia

ALBANIA

THRACE

Constantinople

Scutari

Sivas

Angora

MACEDONIA

Salonica

Brusa

TWO SICILIES

Janina

Kayseri

Albistan

Corfu

Konya

Adana

Messina

Patras

Athens

Smyrna

Aleppo

Reggio

Corinth

Adalia

MOREA

Ionian Isles

Rhodes

Famagusta

Damascus

Crete

Cyprus

Europe in 1648

Faroe Is.

Shetland Is.

Orkney Is.

SCOTLAND

Edinburgh

IRELAND

Dublin

Durham

York

ENGLAND

WALES

Oxford Cambridge

Bristol

London

Amsterdam

English Channel

Calais

Channel Is.

BRITANNY

Paris

Orleans

Nantes Tours

FRANCE

Bordeaux

NAVARRE

Pamplona

ANDORRA

Toulouse

Marseilles

Oporto

Valladolid

Saragossa

SPAIN

Madrid

Barcelona

Lisbon

Toledo

PORTUGAL

CASTILE

Valencia

Seville

Granada

GRANADA

Tangier Cuerta

Gibraltar

Melilla

Oran

MOROCCO

ALGIERS

NORTH SEA

Heligoland

DENMARK–NORWAY

Bergen

Christiania

Särna

Göteborg

Aalborg

Copenhagen Malmö

Lübeck

Hamburg

Bremen

Stettin

BRANDENBURG

Brunswick

Berlin

Brussels

Cologne

SAXONY

Dresden

Mainz

Frankfurt

BOHEMIA

Prague

Verdun

Trier

Nuremberg

LORRAINE

Strassburg

BAVARIA

FRANCHE COMTE

Basle

Munich

AUST

Salzburg

STY

Charolais

Berne

TYROL

Geneva

SWITZERLAND

CARINTHIA

Lyons

SAVOY

Turin Milan

Venice

Trieste

Genoa

Ferrara

SAN MARINO

Avignon to the Papacy

Florence

PAPAL STATES

Corsica

Rome

Sardinia

Naples

Cagliari

MEDITERRANEAN SEA

Balearic Is.

Bugia Bona

Biserta

Palermo

Sicily

Algiers

Tunis

Malta

TUNIS

S W

Chapter 1

Introduction

The study of international relations has evolved from an essentially narrow nineteenth-century view, that concentrated on diplomatic activity and diplomatic archives, into the more complex subject it is today at the beginning of the twenty-first century. There is greater interest now in the mental world within which international relations were considered and conducted, and a stronger and more sophisticated concern with the domestic causes and consequences of foreign policy. The study of the copious diplomatic archives of the period has to be set in the context of an awareness both of the limitations of these sources and of the role of domestic pressures. The archives contain the carefully preserved records of a quasi-professional insider group, diplomats and the ministers to whom they were answerable, concerned with the minutiae of their trade, and especially alert to the details of intelligence, marriage proposals and treaty clauses. The wider contexts of diplomatic activity have to be appreciated, as does the extent to which both change and continuity can be discerned in diplomatic activity and in the nature of international relations.

This study rejects structural and 'deterministic' explanations in favour of emphasizing contingency and the generally unpredictable nature of international relations in the period covered by this book. Whereas other interpretations stress factors such as geography, or economic or social structures, here there is an emphasis on the significance of personalities and the detailed shifting web of war and diplomacy. This rejection of other theoretical models is not simply a return to nineteenth-century empiricism (fact-focused history), but also a theoretical position. By stressing elements like agency and contingency, there is a move away from structural or 'macro' features such as those advanced in theories that employ the concept of the balance of power or probe relations between global economic trends and power politics,[1] or indeed in the Marxist approach to international relations.

Instead, there is a focus on the unpredictability of developments in this period and the volatility of international relations. This volatility could not be successfully disguised by terms such as balance of power and natural interests, which implied that a hypothetical international system operated according to certain rules. The modern equivalent – the systemic approach – suffers from the same drawbacks. In practice, the nature of monarchical authority and power ensured that the often changing and always unpredictable personal views of rulers were extremely important. Chance factors of birth and death played a major role in creating and affecting a diplomatic agenda in which dynastic considerations were often paramount. Aside from the logical problem of arguing from a general theory, such as that of an international system operating in accordance with particular rules, whether of the balance of power or not, to individual government policies, it is apparent that these policies arose from particular and, therefore, changeable views and interests.

These changes accentuated the uncertainty faced by other powers. Monarchs, ministers, diplomats and generals faced a hazardous and difficult international and domestic prospect. Information was difficult to obtain, and often unreliable. Rulers were short of money, generals of trained men. Social historians have emphasized the generally precarious nature of life in this period. The relative inflexibility of the agrarian economy and its susceptibility to climatic change heightened general feelings of uncertainty. Activities, whether military operations or the journeys of couriers, were dependent on climate and weather, the condition of the roads, the crops and the countryside. These limitations have to be borne in mind when considering how international relations operated and changed, and their role in altering power relationships and affecting state development.

Setting the scene

It is first necessary for a reader to consult a historical atlas for, although most of the 'states' of the period can be given names that are the same as modern states, their territorial extent was very different.

As far as European possessions were concerned, Portugal has essentially remained unchanged, but there were considerable differences in such cases as France and the United Provinces (modern Netherlands), both of which have since made gains, while Poland, Russia, Spain, Denmark and Sweden were fundamentally different.

In 1648, the King of Denmark ruled Norway, while his Swedish rival ruled Ingria, Estonia and Livonia (the Baltic provinces) and Finland, making a sizeable block of territory along the eastern Baltic, reaching down as far as Riga, with territories in northern Germany as well. Poland was a large state that included the western Ukraine, much of White Russia (Belarus), Lithuania and Courland. Russia lacked not only a Baltic frontier but also one on the Black Sea, though the Caspian had been reached. The King of Spain ruled half of Italy (Sicily, Sardinia, the Kingdom of Naples, the Duchy of Milan, Finale and the Tuscan coastal *presidios* – garrisons), the Spanish Netherlands (essentially modern Belgium and Luxemburg), and the largest overseas empire, including most of Central America, all of South America (except Portuguese-owned Brazil, and the Guianas) and the Philippines.

Geographically, Germany, Italy and south-eastern Europe were most different to the situation today. The Balkans were ruled by the Turkish or Ottoman empire, an Islamic monarchy based at Constantinople, that also ruled Egypt, the Near East and the northern shores of the Black Sea, where the Khanate of the Crimea was a dependent state. This empire had two principal rivals, the Islamic Persian empire (modern Iran) with which it competed from the Caucasus to the Persian Gulf, and the Christian powers of Eastern Europe: Russia, Poland and, especially, the Austrian Habsburgs. This dynasty, closely related to the Spanish Habsburgs, ruled a collection of territories that are collectively, though somewhat inaccurately, referred to as Austria. They included most of modern Austria, Silesia in modern south-west Poland, Bohemia and Moravia (modern Czech Republic), what is now Slovenia, and what they had been able to preserve of the Kingdom of Hungary (the western part of modern Hungary, Croatia, and Slovakia) from the Turks. For over two centuries, the Austrian Habsburg ruler had been elected Holy Roman Emperor, which provided him with a measure of authority, although less power, in the Empire, an area roughly coterminous with Germany, Austria and northern Italy. In these areas, sovereignty was divided and a large number of territorial princes, mostly lay but some ecclesiastical, as well as Imperial Free Cities exercised effective power, within the loose bounds of an Imperial constitution.

In the seventeenth century, most of Europe was ruled by hereditary monarchs. The most important dynasty was the Habsburgs, who had interrelated Austrian and Spanish branches. Emperor Leopold I (1658–1705) was a brother-in-law of Charles II of Spain (1665–1700). Another brother-in-law of Charles was Louis XIV of France (1643–1715), the head of the Bourbon dynasty. The Stuarts ruled England, Ireland and Scotland in the person of Charles II (1660–85), the Vasas Sweden under Charles XI (1660–97) and the Romanovs Russia under Tsar Alexis (1645–76). The United Provinces (modern Netherlands), Venice and Genoa were the leading republics, dominated in practice by groups of wealthy oligarchs, while the Papacy, Poland, Hungary and the Empire were elective monarchies. Other than in the cities, wealth and prestige were based on the ownership of land, most of which was owned by a hereditary nobility, whose most powerful members constituted an aristocracy. Armies and central and local government were dominated by aristocrats, who were also extremely influential in the churches. Government worked best where the social elite could be persuaded to govern in accordance with the views of the monarch, and the most politically effective states were those where a consensus based on shared interests and views had developed. This consensus characterized states such as France which have been misleadingly described simply as absolutisms.

Chapter 2

What Was at Stake?

The conceptualization of international relations

It would be surprising if the question above were to be given a single answer when we are considering the multiplicity of 'players' in European international relations at any moment, let alone over 160 years. A focus on an international system, with the system treated as something that existed in the real world, rather than as an analytical category, might suggest that a single answer is possible. However, in practice, it was the individual states that were crucial, with the term 'states' understood as shorthand for the variety of independent players in international relations. These varied greatly in constitutional form: from, for example, the United Provinces (modern Netherlands), a mercantile, federal republic, to the autocratic monarchy of Russia. In the seventeenth and eighteenth centuries, the concept of the international system was expressed through terms which denoted alliances and other formal agreements between states. Thus the system was the relations between states and the latter were the essential element.

New words coming into use in the early nineteenth century reveal a concept of the international system that differed from that of the previous century. But it did so as a concept, rather than as an accurate description. Among the new phrases were 'community of states', 'general concert', 'cultural family' and 'society of nations'. The new concept, or system, was presented as a mediating agent which constrained the activities of its member units and controlled the interactions between them and the system's environment. The system had to be flexible and dynamic in order to be able to respond to the changes of its members. This concept was drawn from the model of a living body and can be termed organic or biological. The system was presented as an entity in its own right, not as the derivative of its members. Conversely, units – the states – appeared as dependants of the system. The system had to be sufficiently flexible to respond to the dynamism of individual states, and the biological assumptions and vocabulary of nineteenth-century systems theory addressed themselves to this dynamism. Since then, it has informed international relations theory in Europe and the New World.

The value of this approach for the nineteenth century is open to debate. For earlier periods, the situation is more problematic, as the approach supports anachronisms in the description of *ancien régime* international relations (those of the late seventeenth and eighteenth centuries), leads to teleological interpretations, and hinders the understanding of change. Eighteenth-century thought and practice were mechanistic rather than biological. States were seen as sovereign but linked as if within a machine. This system was seen as self-contained, and part of a static and well-ordered world. The concept was based on the model of the machine which, in turn, was regarded as well-ordered and enabling its parts to conduct activities only in accordance with its own construction. The mechanistic concept of the system of states was well-suited to the wider currents of thought in the period: Cartesian rationalism, as well as its successors in the early eighteenth century.

These currents of thought have to be heeded because they provided not only an analytical framework but also a moral context for international relations. This can be seen by considering the balance of power, a concept and process that has taken a central position in much subsequent treatment of the period. It has often been taken to serve as central to a notion of international relations as involving the drive for the self-preservation of the sovereign states and the maintenance of the status quo, in the context of a struggle of all against all. Thus, balance-of-power politics, as generally presented, appear as selfishly pragmatic, bereft of any overarching rules and lacking theoretical foundations.

In practice, the situation was somewhat different. There was a widely expressed theory of the balance of power, and rules for its politics, outlined in tracts, pamphlets, doctoral dissertations and explanations of the reasons for the resort to war. The relationship between such theoretization and rules on the one hand and decision-making processes on the other is obscure, and clearly varied by ruler and minister, but, rather than assuming simple neglect, if not contempt, by the latter, it is worth considering the role of such discussion in setting normative standards that shaped policies and responses. Thus, rulers who broke the rules, for example Frederick II, 'the Great', of Prussia (1740–86), affected their capacity for negotiating alliances and for winning lasting recognition of their gains; while those who were perceived as defending norms, such as the Grand Alliance against Louis XIV of France (1643–1715) in the 1700s obtained benefits. The aggression of the Seven Years' War (1756–63) and the Partitions of Poland (1772, 1793, 1795) can be seen as exemplifying *ancien régime* international relations, but were just as much contrary to its precepts and practice.[1]

As an example of a different process, it is worth noting the settlement of the 'Western Question', with the Bourbons dominant in Western Europe, but no longer expanding in the Continent; and the consequent decades of peace in the Low Countries, along France's eastern borders, and in Italy that followed 1748. By 1740, French control of Alsace, Lorraine, Franche-Comté, Artois and French Flanders was generally accepted. A moderation in French policy was crucial to this acceptance. After the War of the Spanish Succession (1701–14, but not officially declared until 1702), further gains in the Low Countries, on the Rhine and in Italy were not pursued by the French, and there were no attempts to reconquer what had been lost in the war. Furthermore, having spent much of the sixteenth and seventeenth centuries not only at war but also exacerbating disputes elsewhere in Western Europe and destabilizing rivals, France and Spain did not fight each other between 1720 and 1793. The settlement of differences between Spain and Austria in 1752 was crucial to the stability of Italy. This search for a peaceful settlement can be seen as more typical than the Seven Years' War and the Partitions.

This issue is part of the more general problem of judging the *ancien régime* and its international relations. It is widely believed that they were characterized by a cynical lack of concern for stability and peace, but this draws as much on the subsequent critique of the period as on any understanding of seventeenth- and eighteenth-century thought and values, a frequent problem in much scholarly discussion of the period. There is need for care in the subsequent interpretation of the contemporary conceptualization of international relations. The balance of power can be presented in terms of obtaining equivalent gains, in other words as a device that served and encouraged aggression, but it is also appropriate to see it as a way to bring order to chaos, a characteristic feature of seventeenth- and eighteenth-century attitudes. Rulers, ministers, diplomats and politicians, far from recognizing clearly their position in an international system, from assessing clearly the interests of others and, therefore, from discerning structural tensions and rivalries, instead operated in a context of opacity and controversy. There was also a lack of clarity and agreement about 'national interests', about the views of others and about resulting relationships. Contemporary conceptualization, classically in terms of the balance of power, or of related or similar terminology, served to disguise this confusion and division, frequently for political or polemical purposes. The concept of the balance reflected concern for stability and, in general, the conduct of politics as a zero-sum game.

In analytical terms, the balance of power and the related concept of natural interests can be criticized as ambiguous and misleading, but, in practice, their very flexibility ensured their value, both because they could be applied widely and because they could readily serve differing political views. To a certain extent, systemic theory is the modern counterpart, and descendant, of the balance of power. It has a similar apparent – a critic would say spurious – precision, and a similar openness to quantification and consequent analysis. Indeed, the extensive use of the balance of power in the eighteenth century reflected in part the fascination with Newtonian physics and its mechanistic structures and forces, and, more generally, with reason or rationality. Understood in terms of secular cause and effect, the latter characterized the age.

There was an awareness of change and of the role of the vicissitudes of dynastic arrangements, the hazards of war and all sorts of contingent factors. These all made international relations less calculable. Theorists tried to reduce those factors to the extent that such relations could be perceived as calculable. Power was to be understood as conserved, not driven or changed by forces outside the system, such as providence. Similarly, modern systemic theory can be traced to the determination to try to make rational, analysable and readily comprehensible the inchoate nature of the world – a laudable goal, but one that can lead to misplaced precision in the analysis of interests, structures, changes, and processes of causality. Both sets of theories suffer from a propensity to emphasize a conception of reason, at the expense of passion, greed and inertia. In other words, they reflect a sense of comprehension and manageability (that competed with any emphasis on the uncertainty of human affairs), and thus a search for order and peace.

The relation between such ideas and the attitudes that influenced the formulation and execution of policy is unclear. Even if a systemic analysis is to be adopted and, for example, certain conflicts are seen as resulting from attempts to change position in the international system, or to resist such change, then it is necessary to consider the contemporary perception of such attempts, and of the system itself, and the confusions and complexities of intentionality. Here again, we move from the apparent clarity and precision of systemic theory, and from its openness to quantification, into a world that is more tentative, problematic and opaque.

Caution arises because of the difficulty of establishing how a system was supposed to work. If a system and its development are defined, then it is all too easy to assume that events that corresponded to the system are explained by and prove it, and that those that did not are due to deviations from the model. They can be explained in terms of the idiosyncrasies of individual statesmen. Such an interpretation was employed in *ancien régime* Europe when accounting for the descriptive and proscriptive (what ought to happen) limitations of the theory of a balance of power and the concept of natural interests. This theory appeared to establish an equilibrium model in which balance worked to reconcile the pursuit of these interests. Specific interpretations in terms of idiosyncrasies were sometimes accurate, and they had, and have, the merit of leaving a major role for contingencies and individuals. They also suffer from the assumption that there was a core policy that was necessary and should have been obvious. This sense of natural interest neglects the uncertainties of the past, the role of choice and the difficulties of choosing. It is necessary to ascertain what attitudes and ideas meant to specific individuals or groups at particular moments. Such specificity subverts long-term models and is difficult to incorporate into them.

Diplomatic sources tend to rationalize decisions, but can be a misleading guide, not least because foreign policies were not the products of discrete semi-autonomous bureaucratic institutions, nor were they largely unrelated to domestic affairs. Instead, the relevant institutions tended to be small, unspecialized and lacking in independence, and foreign policy was not an autonomous activity. Policy in most states was the product of court politics; and the personal views of monarchs, and those who could influence them, were crucial. Monarchs only had to be responsive to a limited extent, if at all, to the views of others, and foreign policy was the field of government activity where royal power and authority tended to be greatest, precisely because there was little need for the cooperation between crowns and elites that was a characteristic feature of government. This personal concentration of authority led to a pronounced tendency towards volatility that was a common theme of diplomatic correspondence.

Dynasticism

Dynasticism was central to monarchical interests, and one of the reasons why it is not always helpful to classify interests as international or domestic. At the same time, it would be misleading to simplify the position of monarchs and to neglect limitations on dynasticism. In particular, the elective crowns of Poland and the Holy Roman Empire were very different to hereditary monarchies, although the chief elective monarchies were also bound within the wider web of European dynasties.

Monarchs in the late seventeenth century operated in a different context to that of their successors a century later. The suggestion that rulers should be, as Frederick II put it, 'first servants of the state', clashed with conventional assessments, not least in assuming a clear concept of state identity and interest that could serve as a guide. Instead, the customary view stressed the patrimonial nature of royal authority. Diplomatic documents referred to sovereignty as property. Most monarchies were hereditary, not elective. Rulers were conscious of their position as part of a family, and of their responsibility to it. This encouraged a stress not only on dynastic and personal honour, but also on the specific rights that were held to be the family's inheritance.

These were a repeated theme not only of royal remarks, but also of the diplomacy of the period. Dynastic claims were pushed by powerful rulers, such as Louis XIV, but also by their weaker colleagues and the nature of these claims discouraged rulers from compromising them by concessions. For example, the Hohenzollerns of Brandenburg-Prussia (from 1701 usually called Prussia for short) maintained their claim to the Silesian duchy of Jägerndorf, confiscated from a Hohenzollern who had opposed the Habsburgs in the early 1620s, and they went on doing so for over a century. A sense of responsibility to descendants was captured by the Duke of Holstein-Gottorp when he told a French diplomat in 1725 that he preferred to rely on providence and wait for helpful international developments, rather than to take any step that would render him contemptible to his posterity.

Dynastic issues ranged in size from the Spanish succession, which spanned the world, and played a major role in international relations in the first seventy years of the period, to the frequently as bitterly contested minor disputes that were so prominent in Germany and northern Italy, both areas of divided sovereignty. These disputes were heavily legalistic in character, and it is difficult to apply the notion of rulers as servants of their states to them.

Many disputes reflected the problems of defining and defending rights in a situation of overlapping authority and multiple sovereignty. Thus, rulers sought to resist the claims of overlords. This opposed territorial princes in Germany and Italy to the/pretensions of the Holy Roman Emperor, the elected sovereign ruler over Germany and much of Italy, whose authority and power were both very limited. With one exception, the Emperors of the period were members of the Austrian Habsburg dynasty. The enforcement of Imperial jurisdiction reflected power politics, but there was also a concern with the laws of the Empire:[2] the interaction of both is an aspect of this book's theme that it is necessary to understand values alongside power. In 1715, Victor Amadeus II of Savoy-Piedmont sought to prevent Imperial officials from heeding claims for immediate dependence on the Emperor from those who he claimed were his vassals in the Langhes. Similarly, in the 1720s, the Duke of Parma appealed for Anglo-French support against what he saw as Imperial backing for disobedient vassals.

Such disputes commonly lasted for a long time with scant impact on broader diplomatic questions, and they could be referred to the lengthy processes of generally Imperial jurisdiction. When, in 1716, the French envoy pressed Prince Eugène, a leading Austrian minister, on a number of largely Italian issues in which the Emperor had used his power in French eyes to dispossess others, including the successions to Mantua, Mirandola and Castiglione, and the interests of a large number of individuals, Eugène retorted that the litigants should use judicial remedies. Often such issues were of limited wider significance, but, in contrast, complex disputes between Austria and the Elector Palatine over feudal rights to fiefs helped to block the Imperial Election Scheme in 1752–3.

Dynastic interests, especially succession claims, were an important means of aggrandizing both powerful and minor families, and thus played a large role in the diplomacy of the period. The great disappointment for Frederick I of Prussia (1688–1713) was that he failed to obtain the bulk of the Orange inheritance, while his great triumph was

11

the exaltation of himself and his dynasty by the acquisition of a royal title (King in Prussia) and its recognition, so that the family ceased to be simply Electors (of Brandenburg). His son, Frederick William I (1713–40), was unwilling to renounce the family's claim to the Orange inheritance for nearly two decades, while, in 1732, he demonstrated his claim to the succession to East Friesland by adding it to his coat of arms. This was an important step in an age when titles were maintained, even if ridiculous, such as those of the Kings of Britain to France, and of the rulers of Savoy-Piedmont, from 1720 Kings of Sardinia, to Cyprus and Jerusalem. At a more modest level, the Dukes of Baden-Durlach devoted their efforts in the mid-eighteenth century to gaining the succession to the Duchy of Baden-Baden, whose male line was dying out, and in 1771 negotiated an acceptable agreement.

Marital links were pushed in order to influence policy, as well as to further dynastic interests and pretensions, and, also, to deal with the practical problem of securing successions. The French minister Choiseul sought the marriage of the future Louis XVI and an Austrian archduchess in order to strengthen the Austro-French alliance. His scheme succeeded in 1770, finally defeating proposals for a Saxon marriage for Louis. However, hostility towards this marriage provides a good example of how criticism of particular dynastic strategies could interact with opposition to ministers, their policies and their legacy.[3]

The extent to which dynastic issues were not only pursued by monarchs but also by leading ministers, such as Mazarin, underlines the difficulty of distinguishing national from personal interests. This leads to a questioning of the emphasis in much scholarship on consciously pursued state-building, because ministers cannot be seen as embodiments of impersonal states that can be contrasted to the interests of the dynasties. More generally, it has been suggested 'that the ideology of hierarchy and lineage ... exerted ... pressure' on seventeenth-century individuals.[4]

Far from being an anachronistic goal and policy, dynastic advantage was actively pursued at the close of the period by a ruler who prided himself on his modernity, Napoleon, crowned as Emperor in December 1804 and blessed by Pope Pius VII. Dynastic prestige played a major role in his creation of kingdoms and principalities for his family. Napoleon made himself both Emperor of France and King of Italy, and appointed his stepson Eugène de Beauharnais as his viceroy in Italy. One of Napoleon's brothers, Louis, became King of

Holland (1806), another, Joseph, King of the Two Sicilies (1806) and then King of Spain (1808), and another, Jerome, King of Westphalia, while Joachim Murat, Napoleon's brother-in-law, became Grand Duke of Berg and then King of the Two Sicilies.

If rulers sought dynastic aggrandizement, this did not prevent a more general interest in territorial gains, although a number of rulers and ruling groups were content with the extent of their territories. This was either because they believed them satisfactory, as did the Swedes in the last four decades of the seventeenth century, or because it was imprudent to take the risk of offending others. Republics, which had no dynastic pretensions, tended simply to retain what they possessed. The United Provinces (the Dutch state) did not pursue territorial gains in Europe after 1648, although, for security reasons, Dutch garrisons were established in neighbouring territories. Reports that the Dutch might try to annex East Friesland proved inaccurate. The Swiss Confederation, which also became an independent state as part of the Westphalia peace settlement in 1648, also did not pursue territorial gains. The situation was very different for the new republics created in the late eighteenth century, first the United States and then republican France. Both actively sought territorial gains, a response not only to opportunity but also to a clear sense of superiority over their neighbours. This serves as a warning against the notion that territorial aggrandizement was anachronistic or 'unmodern'; indeed, the contrary could be argued.

Retaining what was already possessed was always the first priority for all rulers. Personal preferences and circumstances ensured that the views of many went no further. Defensive treaties were more common than offensive clauses, although a desire to regain lost territories could give an offensive direction to diplomacy, as with the Austrian quest to recapture Silesia after its loss to Frederick II in 1740–2. If Maria Theresa of Austria (1740–80) strove to defend her inheritance rather than to acquire additional territories, the effect of the loss of Silesia was to make Austria a dissatisfied state and to lead to coalitions against Prussia.

Rulers achieved much through diplomacy and war. In the eighteenth century, Spain regained an Italian empire, Russia obtained a 'window' on the Baltic, and Prussia became a major power. Rulers were willing to consider significant changes. This was made most brutally apparent with the Partitions of Poland, but similar schemes had been considered on a number of earlier occasions. The partition of the Spanish succession was extensively discussed in the late seventeenth century, while that of the Austrian Habsburg inheritance was planned in 1741. More generally war plans, if successful, would have entailed fundamental alterations in European relations. The most ambitious plans related to the Balkans where, on a number of occasions, the Austrians and Russians planned major conquests. Elsewhere in Europe, ambitious plans for territorial redistribution were advanced, as in the Baltic during the Great Northern War (1700–21), or in 1784 when Gustavus III of Sweden was forced to drop his aggressive plans against Danish-ruled Norway. During the Wars of the Spanish (1701–14) and Austrian (1740–8) Successions, the reversal of Louis XIV's gains along France's eastern frontier was a goal of his opponents, while, during the War of the Austrian Succession and the Seven Years' War (1756–63), the partition of Prussia was proposed. Although difficult to execute, these schemes were not obviously beyond the military capabilities of the powers of the period. However, there is a contrast between peacetime plans, many of which were cautious, and the more ambitious and opportunistic character of war goals.

Aggressive plans were particularly serious for minor states. Frequently occupied by other powers or forced to provide supplies in wartime, they could suffer in subsequent peace treaties. The minor Italian powers were vulnerable. Genoa feared the rulers of Savoy-Piedmont, and Venice the Austrians. The seizure of the inheritance of the Gonzaga Dukes of Mantua by the Austrians, when the last duke died in 1708, revealed the ability of the powerful to determine inheritances. In the same year, Austrian forces occupied the papal town of Comacchio and easily defeated Pope Clement XI in the subsequent war.

If minor Italian states suffered most from Austria, their German counterparts had more varied persecutors. Joseph Clément, Archbishop-Elector of Cologne and Prince-Bishop of Liège, found that the Dutch, having occupied his fortresses of Bonn, Huy and Liège during the War of the Spanish Succession, could only be removed with considerable difficulties. Louis XIV was a very frightening neighbour for the rulers in the west of the Empire, but his successors were less troublesome neighbours until the French Revolution radically altered the situation. In the meantime, Austria and Prussia were seen as threats. Prussia bullied the surrounding princes, in particular by forcible recruiting for her army, from which neighbouring Mecklenburg suffered greatly. Prussian treatment of her neighbours illustrated the degree to which strength bred strength, and this increased the gap in relative power between states. In the north of the Empire, Sweden played a progressively more minor role, but the Danes gained control of ducal Schleswig.

Most lesser German princes were not prepared to surrender the initiative to their more powerful neighbours and the conditions of the Empire after the Peace of Westphalia made it imperative that they continue to play an active role if they sought to maintain their status and autonomy. Although the Empire did provide a protective framework for its weaker components, it did not allow them to retreat into passivity because the rights and privileges defining a territory's position had to be protected from the ambitions of neighbours.[5]

In Eastern Europe, weaker political units also suffered. Hungary, the Ukraine and Moldavia all failed in the first eleven years of the eighteenth century to break free from the embrace of Austria, Russia and Turkey respectively. Russia exercised an effective protectorate over Poland for most of the period from the 1710s to the final Partition in 1795, and also controlled the Duchy of Courland whose eighteenth-century dukes were appointed in response to Russian wishes.

For several powers, dynastic pretensions did not provide a framework for territorial expansion. This was especially true in Eastern Europe and for Britain. Britain, for example, had no claim to Gibraltar and Minorca, both of which she was ceded in the Peace of Utrecht of 1713, other than her conquest of them during the War of the Spanish Succession, in 1704 and 1708 respectively. The major division however was between Western and Eastern Europe. In the former, the essential unit of diplomatic exchange and strife was jurisdictional-territorial, not geographical-territorial. This was reflected in the dominance of succession disputes.

In Eastern Europe, by contrast, geographical-territorial issues played a larger role. The major states lacked good historic claims to the areas in dispute, the texture of sovereign polities was less dense than in Western Europe, and dynastic succession was not the major diplomatic idiom, nor generally a means by which large areas of territory changed hands and through which relative power could be assessed. This owed much to the impact of the Turkish advance, while the fact that Poland-Lithuania became a clearly elective monarchy in 1572 was also important. The Habsburgs gained the throne of Hungary by dynastic means, but had to fight the Turks in order to achieve their claims. Succession disputes were not the issue at stake between Russia and its rivals. Instead, the idiom of disputes was geographical-territorial, and there has been a stress on the inherently competitive nature of geopolitics in discussing international relations in this area. At the same time, issues of prestige, as well as traditional Russian claims in the eastern Baltic and the role of Peter the Great's marital diplomacy in Courland, Mecklenburg and Holstein-Gottorp, have also been emphasized.[6]

In Western Europe, the pursuit and acquisition of territories without benefit of legitimate claims was scarcely novel but it could cause outrage. However, the legitimist principle of basing pretensions on dynastic and other legal claims was also tempered by a more general stress on considerations of *raison d'état* (reason of state). This entailed an emphasis not on the patrimonial imperatives of competing dynasties, but on interests such as defensible frontiers, contiguous territories, and military and economic strength. Dynastic objectives or at least claims could be advanced to forward these aims, and Frederick II was unusual in his willingness to admit that such claims were merely a matter of form. Such ideas could serve to accentuate the willingness to negotiate and the importance of compromise, especially by exchanges and equivalents, but it is difficult to demonstrate that *raison d'état* helped to defuse crises whereas dynasticism accentuated them.

More generally, it is not clear that it is always helpful to distinguish between the two categories; to which it is anyway difficult to allocate particular rulers or countries. The objectives and views summarized by the term *raison d'état* were scarcely novel, and it was quite possible for rulers such as Louis XIV to pursue such views, not least in colonial expansion, while, at the same time, defending dynastic pretensions. The greater territorial stability of Mediterranean and Western Europe in 1749–91 has led to an underestimation of the continued importance of dynastic themes in these regions. If the dissection of Poland in accordance with cold-blooded notions of *raison d'état* might appear to exemplify a different diplomatic idiom and rationale, it is difficult to see it as removed in effect from the Russian gains of the eastern Ukraine and the Baltic provinces in 1667 and 1721 respectively.

Exchange plans paid as little attention to the views of the inhabitants concerned as dynastic schemes did. Some exchange plans were far-ranging, for example, the proposal in 1669, revived in 1688, for France to gain the Spanish Netherlands in return for Roussillon and acceptance of a Spanish conquest of Portugal. The possible exchange by the Dukes of Bavaria and Lorraine of their territories for gains elsewhere, principally in Italy, was a persistent theme in the diplomacy of the period 1698–1713. So also was the idea that the ruler of Savoy-Piedmont should yield Savoy to France in return for Italian gains, an idea that recurred during the first half of the century, for example in 1725 and in the 1740s, and that was to be realized in 1860. Another long-standing proposal was that of the exchange of Bavaria for the Austrian Netherlands, which was actively pressed by Joseph II in the 1770s and 1780s.

Many exchange schemes were smaller in scale. Frederick William of Brandenburg-Prussia (1640–88), the 'Great Elector', sought, as part of the price for providing troops against the Turks in 1683, the satisfaction of Hohenzollern claims in Silesia, but he was willing to accept as an equivalent the acquisition of Stettin. In 1698, Augustus II of Saxony-Poland proposed an exchange of territory in order to obtain a direct territorial link between Saxony and Poland through Silesia. In 1744, the Elector Palatine pressed for the cession of the distant Duchy of Neuburg, in order to obtain an equivalent in the Austrian Netherlands that would be contiguous with his territory of Jülich. None of these took place, any more than the proposal of 1774 for an exchange between Mecklenburg, which was a neighbour of Prussia, and the central German territories of Ansbach and Bayreuth, which were held by another branch of the Hohenzollerns to which those of Berlin hoped to succeed. The exchange, in 1773, by the King of Denmark of the non-contiguous German Duchies of Oldenburg and Delmenhorst for the continuous ducal parts of Holstein, as well as Russian recognition of his position in Schleswig, was secured only after years of negotiation.

The difficulties that exchange schemes encountered suggest that there was considerable reluctance to surrender dynastic claims and to envisage new arrangements. A related aspect of the grip of traditional ideas was the continued importance of diplomatic ceremonial as an expression of monarchical glory and reputation, and the reluctance to accept compromises and new suggestions in this sphere. For rulers to lose either lands or honours that had been theirs or their predecessors' was to some extent to lose face.

Considerations of *gloire* and honour appear less frequently in the correspondence of the 'Enlightened Despots', Catherine II of Russia (1762–96), Frederick II and Joseph II, than earlier in the eighteenth century. This was to lead on to what was a more pronounced shift after 1815 from personal monarchical honour to notions of national honour as a motive and justification for action. However, the extent and nature of the shift has not been systematically studied, and it is by no means clear what significance should be attached to what may be shifts in style as much as substance. *Gloire* and honour did not disappear from correspondence, while benefits were believed to flow from the diplomatic eminence that was fostered and defended by a stress on precedence and magnificence. Such concerns, as well as the weight placed upon royal marriages as symbols and supports of alliances, were indicative of attitudes that were certainly conservative. Furthermore, the entire structure of diplomatic representation followed similarly conservative and hierarchical lines, with the rank of accredited diplomat and degree of ceremonial appropriate to each capital carefully graded and jealously watched.

At the same time, it is important not to adopt too static an assessment of dynasticism. It had different meanings in particular contexts, and was affected by the character of individual monarchs. There was also a tension between, on the one hand, the role of a ruler or dynasty and, on the other, the more formalized nature of dynastic government, which could indeed limit rulers.[7]

Religious factors

The role of religious considerations was another aspect of international relations that can be seen as conservative. The role of religious considerations from the beginning of the Reformation in 1517 to the Peace of Westphalia (1648) is much debated, but less attention has been devoted to the topic for the succeeding 150 years. In fact, religion was not only an important source of moral views, but also a powerful ideological force that could play a major role in creating tensions between and within states. Furthermore, in the absence of strong nationalist traditions, religious loyalties served to articulate political loyalties, and thus provided an additional reason for hostility to, or from, religious minorities. The most important religious divide, that between Christendom and Islam, is considered in Chapter 5.

Within Christendom, international tension arising from religious differences was common, although it did not dictate the diplomatic agenda. Religion was most important as a cause and subject of dispute in the Empire, Poland and Hungary, but in the last two it was essentially a domestic matter. Protestants were seen as a potential fifth column. Thus, the Sardinian envoy reported from Vienna on 11 March 1733 that Silesian and Bohemian Protestants would support any challenge to the Pragmatic Sanction.[8]

Ideas of state sovereignty did not prevent Protestant diplomatic pressure on behalf of co-religionists, such as the Dutch rescue of Hungarian clergy from the galleys in the 1670s, Anglo-Dutch intervention on behalf of Hungarian Protestants during the Rákóczi rising of 1703–11, Anglo-Prussian complaints after the so-called Thorn Massacre in Poland in 1724, and Prussian pressure over the treatment of Bohemian Protestants in 1735. Pages of diplomatic correspondence were taken up with the case of girls supposedly inveigled into nunneries and the burial and inheritance problems of merchants dying abroad. Catholic powers similarly interceded over the treatment of co-religionists, for example in Ireland and Minorca.

The effectiveness of such action varied. Episodic impact could not compensate for the general political and social pressure that had by 1717 led to a ban on the construction of Protestant churches in Poland. It is unclear how far such tensions influenced governmental policies, although their reiteration contributed to perceptions of other states. Episodes that were of limited importance in themselves, for example, British intercession on behalf of the Piedmontese Waldensians, Swedish pressure in 1686 on behalf of Alsatian Lutherans, whose religious rights were guaranteed by the Peace of Westphalia, and papal complaints about treatment of priests in the United Provinces in 1687, also raised the level of tension.

There were no shortages of talk of religious leagues. This could serve as a diplomatic tool, as when Louis XIV unsuccessfully sought Bavarian and Spanish support against William III in late 1688, and thus tried to win Catholic support for essentially French goals. In early 1689, court preachers told Pedro II of Portugal to attack the Dutch in the Indian Ocean in order to retake ancient losses to the Protestants at the same time that the Dutch envoy was citing the Austrian and Bavarian support for William III as proof that his policy was not confessional. Pedro did nothing. The Bavarians criticized the Austrians during the War of the Spanish Succession for allying with Protestants and destroying Catholic solidarity, but that had no more effect than Protestant pressure on behalf of Hungarian co-religionists. There was talk of Protestant leagues in 1719–22, the late 1730s, and during the Seven Years' War, but there is little sign that shared religion created a strong disposition to negotiate such leagues.

Just as monarchs and ministers might seek to benefit from shared sympathies, they could also be worried, as Louis XIV was in late

1714, that their apparent policies might serve to create a contrary league. Once wars began they were often conceived of as, in part, religious struggles, and this was certainly the case in Britain and the United Provinces during the conflicts with Louis XIV, and in Britain, France and Prussia during the Seven Years' War.[9] However, that did not prevent active wartime peace negotiations with opponents, alliances with powers of a different confession, and interwar diplomacy in which religion played a much smaller role.

There is a tendency to treat religion as a diminishing factor, receding steadily from Westphalia, but in fact it became more important in the French Revolutionary and Napoleonic Wars as religion helped to inspire opposition to revolution and to France. This was particularly true at the popular level.

Religion also affected international relations through the role of church issues in negotiations. This was especially true of Catholic powers at Rome and in the Empire, as the choice of popes and of ecclesiastical rulers could be of great importance. Individual candidates for the Papacy were often seen as Austrian, French or Spanish. Candidates and elections thus provided a way to test influence and demonstrate power.

In the Empire, where there was a number of ecclesiastical principalities or church states, the influence of the Bavarian branch of the Wittelsbach family owed much to ecclesiastical pluralism. Before he was elected at Cologne and a number of other sees, Joseph Clément, born in 1671, had already become Prince-Bishop of Freising in 1684 and of Regensburg in 1685, both principalities that increased the power of Bavaria. The Wettins of Saxony and the Habsburgs were generally less successful, but Clément of Saxony was Prince-Bishop of Freising before becoming Archbishop-Elector of Trier in 1769, while Frederick II failed to prevent the succession of Joseph II's brother, Maximilian, in Cologne and Münster. Such elections led to a considerable amount of activity on the part of Catholic and, to a far lesser extent, Protestant powers, as rulers competed to use and increase their influence. In general, the major sees went to men chosen by the powerful rulers, and the dominance of the major dynasties increased the gap between their influence and that of minor rulers. The latter were generally forced into the role of interceders for favour, Duke Leopold of Lorraine, for example, seeking Imperial aid for his brother in 1711.

Another issue that involved much activity on the part of the envoys of Catholic powers was the support of religious foundations patronized by their rulers. The kings of France protected the Carthusian order and the Order of Malta,[10] and this led to action against apparent injustices. This posed greater problems in the second half of the eighteenth century, as, in a partial 'nationalization' of the Catholic Church, rulers showed more determination to control the ecclesiastical system in their own territories, and often considerable hostility to those owing extraterritorial loyalties. The order which suffered most was the Society of Jesus (the Jesuits), which had few protectors. Their suppression represented the culmination of intensive diplomatic activity by many Catholic powers, including France, Portugal and Spain, in the 1760s and early 1770s. Conversely, France had to help the Carthusians, for example in Naples, where the envoy, the Marquis de Clermont d'Amboise, devoted much time to the subject in the late 1770s.

The treatment of the Church by the so-called Enlightened Despots and other late-eighteenth century rulers was scant preparation for the vicious and comprehensive anti-clericalism of the armies and agents of Revolutionary France. These made a particular impact in the Austrian Netherlands, the Rhineland, Italy, and France itself. In command of the Army of Italy, Napoleon defeated the weak army of Pius VI in 1797, and in 1798 his successor oversaw the proclamation of the Roman Republic. The French assumed they had brought the Papacy to an end.[11]

Nationalism

The importance of religious factors for international relations varied, but it would be unwise to underrate them, not least by adopting a teleological perspective that looks towards more recent times when they played a smaller role in Europe. Conversely, it would be misleading to exaggerate the extent and impact of nationalist feeling. Such feeling was strongest in countries with clearly defined territorial borders, representative institutions and a sense of common history, such as Britain and Sweden. In these countries, policies, such as British opposition to France and Swedish to Russia, evoked a popular resonance within the political nation – the groups accustomed to discuss politics – that could influence policy, and that certainly affected the debate over it.

In territories lacking such unifying and distinguishing features, the situation was more complex. In much of Europe, monarchs ruled what were often legally distinct territories, and their possessions lacked either a shared sense of the past or often one of present interests. Many territories were divided ethnically, linguistically and over religion. Within the Empire, the political system opposed an overarching constitutional and cultural sense of common German identity to a reality of conflicting territorial policies. When stressing the need for good relations to an Austrian envoy in November 1768, Frederick II might say 'we are Germans', but he also encouraged his nobles and his army to think and talk of a Prussian 'fatherland'. More generally, the sense of common German identity was more important in arousing and sustaining a degree of popular animosity against outsiders, for example Louis XIV from the 1670s, than in influencing policy. In addition, animosities could be strongly developed within the German and Italian 'nations', for example between Bavaria and the Habsburg-ruled Tyrol.

Contrasts between governmental policies and more widely diffused popular views were frequent. They indicate the limited role of the ordinary people in foreign policy, which was essentially an aspect of sovereign authority and therefore non-consultative. Popular views were more important at times of war when the ability to mobilize resources, and thus to win public support, was of great consequence. Popular views could be sharply divided in wartime, as was often the case in the United Provinces.

Even if 'nationalist' sentiment could define a common threat, it was often the case that there were significant differences over the policies that should as a result be adopted, especially in the context of alliance politics. In the second half of the eighteenth century, the voice of political opinion became more clearly defined and heard over much of Europe. However, although it was generally agreed that the Austro-French alliance of 1756–91 was unpopular in France, this had scant impact on policy.

Nationalist opinion only became really important with the French Revolutionary and Napoleonic Wars. Then politicized groups responded to developments along national as well as ideological lines. The wars also encouraged a language of national sentiment, as in 1814 when there were calls for the Italians to fight for their freedom against France. Nationalist pressure had little impact on the deliberations at the Congress of Vienna in 1814–15 – Norway's fight for independence in 1814, for example, not winning support – but it was to play a major role in setting the agenda for international relations over the following century.

Commercial issues

Trade was a cause of disputes in which non-governmental and some-times widely popular views played a major role. Commercial issues were a common topic of diplomatic activity. European states followed protectionist rather than free-trade policies, establishing tariffs on manufactured imports in order to encourage domestic production and sponsoring trading companies. Their policies, described as mer-cantilist, reflected a sense that there was only a finite amount of demand, and thus that domestic production and foreign trade could only be boosted at the expense of those of other states. This led to a belief in the need for, and efficacy of, regulation.

As the economy was seen as a source of political and, especially, military strength, a competitive commercial policy was regarded as necessary. It was extended to the transoceanic world as a result of the belief that the mercantilist analysis was equally, indeed particularly, valid for transoceanic trade and colonial activity. The prevalence of regulation ensured that a major topic of diplomatic activity was the attempts to win favourable terms and to prevent the deterioration in those already enjoyed by a state's merchants. Although collaborative initiatives were occasionally made, for example, as a hostile response to Britain's wartime treatment of neutral trade, most commercial diplomacy took place in a competitive atmosphere. Thus, even during the Anglo-French alliance of 1716–31, both powers anxiously watched the position of the other in the important trade with Spain and the Spanish empire.

The idea that for every gain there must somewhere be a loss led to concern about the position of rivals. Thus, in 1724, the Duchy of Lorraine pressed for the same duties on its salt imports into the Duchy of Luxembourg as the salt from the United Provinces enjoyed. There was also concern over the effects of new trade routes. The Genoese were anxious about the development of Sardinian and Modenese ports on the Mediterranean; the Dutch were opposed to Prussian attempts to develop the trade of Emden, including plans to improve the naviga-tion of the river Lippe; while, in 1763, the Austrians feared that the trade of the Austrian Netherlands would be harmed by a possible road between Liège and the United Provinces.

Trade regulations could serve as weapons of political and com-mercial policy. Louis XIV stopped the Liège customs from charging French goods in 1688, and there was a trade war between France and Avignon in 1730–4. In the 1760s, Frederick II employed hostile tariff policies towards Austria and Poland, and thwarted Austrian attempts to divert Saxon trade from Silesia. Baden competed with neighbouring Württemberg in wine and cloth production and tariffs were set accordingly. In 1783, the ruler of Baden interceded personally to have some restrictions abolished. In 1788–9, the alleged mistreatment of Bavarian merchants by the Imperial Free City of Augsburg led to a partial embargo.

Trade played a relatively substantial diplomatic role in relations between countries that had only modest political links, such as Denmark and Spain, or France and Naples. Clermont d'Amboise, the French envoy in Naples, devoted many pages of his dispatches to the subject. In July 1776, he complained that, whereas the British were allowed to sell prohibited goods, the French were not, and that their ships were searched despite their privilege to the contrary. He added that French vice-consuls alone were threatened with the loss of the privilege of putting up their ruler's arms. The following month, he complained about the more favourable treatment of the Genoese in the Calabrian oil trade, while, in September, the Neapolitans protested that a French ship had given a murderer refuge: episodes which reflected the degree to which commerce and national rights and sensibilities were never truly separate. The year 1777 brought renewed disputes over the customs, the respect not paid to the French flag, and the debts owed to Marseilles grain merchants. The French were concerned about the willingness of Neapolitan consuls to allow Genoese and Tuscan smugglers to use their flag, while Clermont d'Amboise suggested that if the orders to visit Neapolitan ships in Marseilles were revoked this would help French traders in Naples. In 1778, he pressed the Neapolitan government to allow grain exports to France and to stop the imprisonment of French sailors seized for smuggling.[12]

Such complaints could be mirrored elsewhere, but, although they could be a considerable diplomatic irritant, they were generally ineffective. The major trading powers were faced by the determination of other states to improve their economy and to derive greater benefit from foreign trade. Thus, Austria, Denmark, Portugal, Prussia, Russia, Sardinia and Sweden developed policies that the major trading countries of the late seventeenth century, England, France and the United Provinces, regarded as hostile.

The political consequences of these policies varied. It is easily possible to find examples of the personal commitment of rulers to commercial projects in the face of international hostility. The Emperor Charles VI (1711–40) founded and fostered long-distance trading companies based at Ostend and Trieste despite marked Anglo-Dutch hostility to the former. Between its foundation in 1722 and its suspension in 1727, the Ostend Company was generally the major contentious item in Austro-Dutch relations. However, it was also the case that the enthusiasm of most monarchs for commercial projects did not extend to the point of compromising diplomatic relations, and one must not exaggerate the influence of commercial lobbies or governmental determination to foster trade. Economic advantage played only a modest role in the competing currents of alliance diplomacy.

Trade, for example, played only a minor role in French foreign policy, despite the strong interest in commerce, particularly that of Spain and her colonies. The French attack on the Dutch in 1672 was presented by the famous economist Adam Smith, over a century later, as an economic war; but any stress on economic considerations exaggerates the influence of the finance minister, Colbert, underrates the personal direction of Louis XIV and the infrequency of economic considerations in his correspondence, and fails to appreciate the extent to which Louis regarded mercenary considerations as incompatible with his *gloire*. When, in 1745, the Swedish envoy tried to convince the French finance minister of the advantages of purchasing iron from Sweden, he was told that Louis XV was not an iron merchant. In 1749, denying charges of Franco-Spanish contraband trade, the French envoy in Spain stated that Louis was no merchant.

In Britain and the United Provinces, trade was more important, domestic pressure from mercantile lobbies stronger, and governmental determination to support commerce greater. In the United Provinces, however, the political influence and goals of the stadtholders from the House of Orange clashed with those of the major towns. In the latter, republicanism was strongest and commercial interests played a large role in affecting views on foreign policy. However, these varied. In the War of the Spanish Succession (1702–13 for the Dutch), Amsterdam, with its strong interests in the East Indies trade, was readier to come to a compromise peace with France than the province of Zeeland, where privateering was important and the role of trade to the Caribbean ensured greater concern over French influence in the Spanish empire.

Trade was clearly a force in Anglo-French and Anglo-Spanish enmity and British ministers frequently referred to the domestic pressures they were under in trade disputes with foreign powers. Nevertheless, the political context was crucial, because a united and powerful ministry in Britain could be as insensitive to domestic criticisms as any Continental counterpart. More generally, the relationship between international and domestic developments was far from fixed. The role of commercial factors in policy climaxed during the Napoleonic period. Napoleon's attempt to pressure Britain by blocking her trade with the Continent, the Continental Blockade, was an aspect of wartime policy that also had a major effect on France's relations with other Continental powers as he sought to push them into line with the blockade.

Conclusions

Assessing the impact of different factors is made more difficult by the nature of foreign policy. As studies increasingly stress the wider political context of diplomacy, in particular the character of court politics, so the misleading nature of the abstraction, foreign policy, becomes clearer, and the substantial diplomatic records that remain seem more satisfactory as evidence of the attempted execution of policy than as a guide to its formation. For many countries, it is not possible to follow what happened in conciliar discussions, let alone those outside the council. Diplomats did not always enjoy the confidence of rulers and ministers by whom they were appointed, let alone those to whom they were accredited. In writing their reports, diplomats sought, consciously or unconsciously, to please their masters, to enhance their own importance, and to save face. Diplomatic exchanges and correspondence were as much intended to persuade as to explain. Sometimes, the relative precision of negotiating by the exchange of memoranda, rather than verbally, was preferred. Frederick II instructed his envoy in Paris to follow this method in 1752, in order to obtain more precise responses. However, this was not a method suited to the characteristic ambiguities of diplomatic exchange.

There is also the problem of assessing the impact of the expression of the expected: in seeking to create a good impression, diplomats stressed the friendly intentions of their masters and presented their moves as defensive. Chavigny, French envoy at the Imperial Diet, argued in January 1727 that France should stress the disinterestedness and innocence of her views and her concern for the public good, but his views of the possibility of reestablishing 'good order' in the world and of a French policy based on Louis XV's *gloire* and prosperity were not readily compatible with those of others who proclaimed their concern for the public order. 'General unmeaning answers', such as those the British envoy in Paris promised his Swedish counterpart in January 1773, can be found throughout the diplomatic correspondence, but they are not always easy to pick out, and the question of the importance of the language used as a guide to the thinking of contemporaries is complicated by the role of deceit and dissimulation.

The unstable nature of international affairs probably encouraged an attempt to retain fixed points of reference and thus accentuated the weight of the past. Urging an Austro-French alliance, the Jacobite agent in Vienna wrote in June 1727, 'there was no sort of obstacle, but mere shadows, ancient impressions, and groundless prejudices which ought to vanish before the eyes of sound statesmen'.[13] In 1781, Frederick II complained that the Dutch acted as though Europe had not changed since 1688. Continuity was important in a political culture that stressed hereditary rights and was heavily influenced by legalistic conceptions and dynastic interests.

Nevertheless, there was both change in the international system and a widespread willingness to negotiate new alignments and to develop bold schemes. Thus, as an example of change, the United Provinces suffered relative economic decline in the eighteenth century and, increasingly, took a more quiescent role in international relations.[14] Bold schemes were frequently unsuccessful, and Frederick II reassured himself in August 1748 that hostile Austrian plans were likely to fail; 'grand projects are easier to conceive than to execute because the vaster they are, the less the different interests of those who participate will allow them to succeed'. In 1763, the Russian Vice-Chancellor attributed the failure of Austria's anti-Prussian strategy to 'unexpected misfortunes, particularly the death of the Tsarina Elizabeth' the previous year and the change of policy under her successor.[15]

The uncertainty of events and the instability of alliances seems to have encouraged rulers to negotiate more widely and to develop several plans, often contradictory, at once. This, in turn, helped to sustain a sense of instability and fluidity, and of the unexpected becoming plausible, that is such a feature of the diplomatic correspondence of the period. Thus the relatively fixed nature of the language employed in diplomacy did not betoken a rigid approach to international relations. Aspirations changed little, but there was a continued willingness to manoeuvre diplomatically in order to further them.

Chapter 3

How Did International Relations Operate?

In peacetime, diplomacy served a variety of goals, including dynastic objectives, commercial objectives, and the interests of the courtiers and corporate bodies whom the monarch chose to favour. Principal goals were furthered by negotiations either through diplomats at foreign courts or between ministers and foreign diplomats. In wartime, military might and strategy were of central importance, but so, also, were negotiations that sought to influence the conduct of allies, enemies and neutrals. Access to power and influence at court or in government was widely enjoyed by aristocrats, and their factions could play a major role in influencing policy.

Diplomacy

By the second half of the seventeenth century, most important states reciprocally maintained permanent embassies in peacetime and, together, these constituted the diplomatic corps and an increasingly defined world with particular privileges and modes of operation. The three major exceptions were Russia, which only established its first permanent embassy, in Poland, in 1688, the Turkish empire, which did not decide to establish permanent embassies in Christian Europe until 1793, and the Papacy, whose representation was restricted to Catholic courts.[1] Papal diplomatic relations with Protestant courts were only established slowly, and, in the case of Britain, the papal acknowledgement from 1689 of the claim to the throne by the male Stuart line (the Jacobite pretender) blocked relations.

The major Christian states maintained embassies in Constantinople, but the Turks preferred to send individual missions for particular negotiations. Other powers, even when they maintained permanent embassies, often used the same method to deal with important negotiations and to fulfil ceremonial functions, such as congratulations on accessions, marriages and births, or installations with chivalric orders. The majority of rulers did not, however, maintain permanent embassies in more than a few capitals, if that. This was because of the cost, the difficulty of finding suitable diplomats and the absence of matters requiring negotiations. The idea of an integrated diplomatic network ignores the many rulers who had no, or very few, permanent embassies. Instead, they might use their courtiers for special missions, share an agent, or rely on confidential newsletters. Thus, Ernst-August, Prince-Bishop of Osnabrück (1716–28), received confidential newsletters from a number of capitals.

Minor powers tended to maintain envoys, if at all, at Vienna, whose Imperial position and law court attracted German and north Italian envoys; Paris; The Hague; Rome, if they were Catholic; Madrid, for the Italians; and London, increasingly after 1688. These courts, especially Paris, were important not only as political centres, but also as production and marketing centres for luxury industries that provided opulent and high-quality goods that were sought by rulers, such as mirrors, furniture, watches, clothes, paintings, mathematical instruments and books. The Bavarian envoy in Paris sent substantial quantities of furniture and clothes to Munich in the 1720s and 1730s. This emphasizes the extent to which the personal concerns of rulers dominated diplomacy.

The capitals to which minor powers sent envoys became the general places of negotiation with them, as, however widely spread their embassies might be, major states generally did not retain permanent envoys to these powers and lacked business sufficient to justify special embassies. The French, for example, maintained permanent embassies at only a few German courts. Such a system did not encourage the clear transmission of opinions, although it did enhance the diplomatic importance of particular capitals, especially Paris. The Hague was termed 'the whispering gallery of Europe' for its ability to register and repeat reports from throughout Europe. At the second-rank level, in terms of accredited diplomats, St Petersburg, Berlin and

Turin became more important in the early eighteenth century, although Turin's importance diminished as Italy became more stable from 1748. The ending of Dutch representation led Charles Emmanuel III to threaten to withdraw his envoy from The Hague, because notions of reciprocity were important in determining the maintenance or not of diplomatic links.

As diplomats represented their sovereigns, who were themselves conscious both of their own rank within a monarchical hierarchy and of the need to grade representation carefully, the senior diplomatic ranks were dominated by aristocrats and reflected this hierarchy. The most senior grade, ambassador, was allocated only to a small number of courts, generally Paris, Madrid, Vienna and Rome, although the situation was far from rigid. The rest of the diplomatic hierarchy, from Envoys Extraordinary, through a series of grades, including Ministers Resident, down to Secretaries of Embassy and unaccredited agents and secretaries, provided a large number of ranks, that allowed distinctions in relations to be made and reciprocated. Similarly, monarchs devoted great care to the forms of address with which they honoured other rulers and to those they expected to receive.

Senior diplomatic ranks were expensive, in large part because of the importance of lavish hospitality and court ceremonial in the establishment of royal *gloire*. As the cost was not generally fully paid by the monarch, there was a further reason to appoint aristocrats. Many aristocratic envoys held military posts in wartime and were thus in fairly continual service to their monarchs. Others took one or two missions, and then returned to less onerous honorific service, often in ceremonial court posts, or left direct royal service. A few were permanent or semi-permanent diplomats, although that was much more common at the more junior ranks. The employment of clerics, very rare in Protestant Europe, was increasingly uncommon among Catholic states, with the prominent exception of the papal nuncios. Consular posts were dominated by merchants, and they were crucial to the protection of commercial interests and privileges.

The calibre of diplomats is difficult to assess. Social skills were an important requirement. Frederick II complained in June 1753 that a French diplomat lacked 'politesse', and that was a quality much in demand. Influence often reflected the ability to make the right impression at court, whether hunting or taking part in the evening smoking and drinking sessions of Frederick William I of Prussia (1713–40), or paying court to the Queen's chamber woman whom Clermont d'Amboise believed was influential at Naples in 1777. The following year, both he and the Austrian envoy sought to have compatriots appointed to teach the heir to the throne.

Thus, training in skills such as riding, as well as their general demeanour, made aristocrats the most suitable choices as senior diplomats. Some disgraced themselves, the Duke of Richelieu having to leave Vienna in 1728 for his supposed involvement in black magic rites, but most represented their monarchs in the manner that they were supposed to do. Their ability in negotiation was tested less continually than their court skills and could be compensated for in part by accentuating the role of the respective ministers to whom they reported and by treating the diplomats more as gilded messengers.

The ability and experience of ministers responsible for negotiations varied. Many, including Bestuzhev, Choiseul, Kaunitz, Lionne, Pombal, Vergennes[2] and Wall, were experienced former diplomats. Between 1688 and 1713, both Portuguese Secretaries of State had been diplomats. Some diplomats complained about the courts to which they were accredited, but, in general, diplomats complained not about the competence of the ministers they had to deal with abroad, but about these ministers' lack of power or consistency in the face of court politics and monarchical views. Certain monarchs, such as Philip V of Spain (1700–46)[3] and Frederick William I of Prussia, acquired justified reputations for being difficult to deal with, and, in those circumstances, it was not sufficient to reach an understanding with their ministers. In states with powerful representative institutions, there was the additional hazard that policies might be overturned or qualified in light of unexpected domestic pressures.

Rulers and ministers frequently complained that envoys exceeded instructions, but it was difficult to provide orders that would cover all eventualities, and impossible, in light of the available communications, readily to respond to developments by sending new instructions; so much responsibility lay in the hands of the diplomats. Communications were uncertain, as well as slow. Couriers could travel from The Hague or Paris to London in three days, but adverse winds would prevent the packet-boats from sailing, and persistent westerlies could leave the ministry in London waiting for several posts from each of the capitals of northern Europe. The ordinary post from St Petersburg to Hamburg took seventeen days in 1745, but floods and bad roads made the posts very irregular. Rainfall affected the roads particularly badly in the Empire, Poland and Russia, and there were often insufficient posthorses. Many rivers were crossed, as in northern Italy, by ferries, rather than bridges, and heavy rains could make passage impossible. Rivers were affected by drought, freezing and weirs, mountain crossings by ice and snow, and sea routes by ice, heavy winds and, in the case of the Baltic, poor charts. Diplomats as well as messengers were delayed. It is not surprising that details of the movements of letters and couriers and their mishaps occurred frequently in the diplomatic correspondence, nor that diplomats posted at any distance often felt forced to respond to developments without obtaining fresh orders. This situation did not change greatly during the period, although there was a general improvement in road links in the second half of the eighteenth century. However, there was no equivalent to the transformation that the combination of the telegraph, steamships and railways was to bring to communications later in the nineteenth century.

Moves towards training diplomats were episodic, in keeping with the nature of administrative reform in this period. The Académie Politique, founded in 1712 by the French foreign minister Torcy to train diplomats, was affected by his fall in 1715 and disappeared in 1720. Regius Chairs of Modern History were founded at Cambridge and Oxford in 1724 to help in the training of possible recruits, but few British diplomats were obtained this way. Peter I sent Russian nobles abroad to increase their knowledge, especially of foreign languages, but the composition of the Russian diplomatic service was eclectic and included a number of foreigners.

This was a common, though decreasing, feature of many diplomatic services. It reflected the ability of rulers to pick whom they wished, which also manifested itself in the large number of foreign military officers. Many Italians and Germans found employment in the service of major rulers. Italians were employed by, among others, Augustus II of Saxony-Poland, while La Chétardie and Saint-Séverin both served Louis XV. Émigrés could be appointed. The Jacobite Lord Marshal of Scotland was appointed envoy in Paris by Frederick II, while the Earl of Tyrconnel was his opposite number in Berlin, both choices that angered George II. The Duke of Liria, son of a bastard of James II, was appointed Spanish envoy to Russia in 1727; the following year, his cousin, Lord Waldegrave, arrived at Vienna as British envoy. Hiring foreigners, some of whom had already obtained relevant experience, was one way to acquire talent. Like the use of military officers, it was employed more persistently than training establishments, all of which, with the exception of the Pontifical Ecclesiastical Academy, founded in Rome in 1701, were short-lived.

Aristocrats were disinclined to accept formal training, and the prevalence of French as a diplomatic language helped to reduce the need for linguistic training. In the seventeenth century, French had only been one of the leading diplomatic languages, and German, Italian, Latin and Spanish had all been important. However, French went on to become the closest to an international diplomatic language before the modern ascendancy of English. This owed much to developments in the period 1660–1715. The weakness of Spain, followed by the accession of a Bourbon in 1700, the prestige that Louis XIV brought France, the greater role of Paris as a diplomatic centre, the decline in papal prestige and the importance within the Empire of German dialects helped to ensure that, by the time of the negotiations for the Peace of Utrecht (1713), French was the leading diplomatic language in Western Europe. The Franco-Spanish Treaty of Nijmegen (1678) was drawn up in French and Spanish, and the Austro-French treaty was in Latin, but at Utrecht the Austrians used French. In Eastern Europe, German and Latin, and in Constantinople Italian, remained important, but, in Europe as a whole, French became the first language of most diplomats, used in international negotiations and treaties, between diplomats, and sometimes as the language of diplomatic correspondence between rulers and ministers and their envoys. It was thus generally used in Sardinian, Saxon and Wittelsbach diplomatic correspondence. Austria under Charles VI (1711–40) largely used German and Italian, although some French was also employed in confidential correspondence. With the accession of Frederick II in 1740, French largely replaced German for Prussian diplomacy and, under Maria Theresa (1740–80), it became more commonly used by Austrian diplomats.

The prominence of French reflected the international character of diplomacy and its interrelationship with monarchical and aristocratic society. The development of accepted conventions of diplomatic immunity, and the increased ability to overcome confessional and precedence barriers, further helped to create a united diplomatic world. This had an uneasy relationship with the growth in specialized national departments for the conduct of foreign affairs. In many countries, these became more distinct and sophisticated, with greater care being taken to ensure that there were permanent specialized staff, translators, maps and archives. In 1719, the old Russian Department of Embassies was replaced by the College of Foreign Affairs; and in France a more systematic organization was created. In Portugal, a separate office for foreign affairs was created only in 1736, although it had been considered desirable earlier.

Increasingly, the institutional conduct of foreign affairs was segregated. In 1698, the authority of the French Secretary of State for the Marine over diplomats was defined and limited. In Britain, the office of Foreign Secretary was founded in 1782, replacing the earlier system by which two, sometimes competing, Secretaries of State had been responsible not only for foreign affairs but also for a host of domestic matters, including public order.

Nevertheless, it would be misleading to exaggerate the scope or extent of these administrative changes. Many polities lacked specialized institutions and, where they existed, their staff was generally small and only trained on the job. Furthermore, the influence of such institutions was limited by the continued direct intervention of monarchs and other ministers. The comment, in the instructions drawn up in 1725 for a Savoy envoy to Spain that, without an appreciation of the internal state of a court, it was impossible to understand its foreign policy,[4] was equally true throughout the period. The frequency of correspondence with many diplomats was low and, especially in distant postings, such as Constantinople, they were often left essentially to their own devices. It would be inappropriate to think of an administrative revolution in diplomacy or its oversight in this period.[5]

Frontiers and maps

One area in which the mechanics of diplomacy improved was mapping. This was linked to what has been seen as a more defined notion of frontiers, a move away from the idea of a frontier as a zone to the idea of a distinct border that could be reproduced and charted on a map as a line. This change reflected a greater stress on undivided sovereignty that made ambiguous relationships, such as that between France and ten Alsatian cities established by the Peace of Westphalia, unacceptable to some rulers. However, traditional ideas proved to be very persistent and mapping often served simply to clarify the existence of incompatible notions and disputed territories.

The pursuit of sovereign power could cause particular difficulties when relatively coherent states expanded into or acquired territories whose control was divided, which was particularly the case in Germany and northern Italy. The situation can be appreciated if it is stressed that abstractions such as France in fact described the patrimonies of ruling dynasties whose possessions and pretensions extended as a result of, and in the context of, feudal overlordships, rather than one of 'natural' linear frontiers, such as rivers. This was to be less the case in the second half of the eighteenth century.

In wartime, control was asserted by powerful rulers, but, with peace, the process of legal and diplomatic definition and contention was revived, especially as general peace settlements commonly ignored such specific minor points. In the conferences held at The Hague in December 1734, to try to settle the War of the Polish Succession, it was agreed that the limits of French royal authority in Alsace and Flanders were hard to adjust but would be part of the general peace ending the war. In fact, the issues continued to be agitated for decades.

Typical of the points in dispute were those described in a memorandum to the Imperial Diet presented by the Palatine envoy on 4 July 1715 complaining of contraventions of the Peace of Baden of 1714, which had on the Upper Rhine substantially confirmed the Peace of Rijswijk of 1697. The first complaint was that on 13 January 1715, the French had forcibly dislodged Palatine troops and taken possession of Seltz, an under-baillage of Germersheim, on the pretence that it formerly belonged to the district of Hagenau and was situated in Alsace, the sovereignty of which had been yielded to France by the Emperor and the Empire. That was the old basis of Louis XIV's forcible *réunions* policy of the years from 1679, and the Palatine envoy claimed that Seltz was held by the Elector Palatine until 1680, when it had been thus seized, but that Rijswijk had determined that it should be restored to Germersheim.

The second complaint arose from a provostship at Seltz which Louis XIV had given as part of the foundation to the Jesuit college at Strasbourg. The French argued that the college should keep it as the Peace of Rijswijk had stated that ecclesiastical benefices collated during the Nine Years' War (1688–97) were to remain with their present possessors. The Elector Palatine countered that collation was only personal, that it was to fall to its rightful owner on the death of an incumbent, that the French incorporation would defraud the owner of his right for ever, and that the provostship had been secularized at the time of the Reformation and then incorporated by the Elector into his territories.

Third, the memorandum charged that the *intendant* of Alsace had forbidden French ships to pay tolls on the Rhine by Seltz, though that right had been confirmed to the Elector Palatine at Rijswijk and the tolls had been paid by the French until the start of the War of the

Spanish Succession (1701–14). In addition, it was claimed that the French had seized two castles on the pretence of their being located within the sovereignty of Alsace, by virtue of a sentence of the Sovereign Council of Alsace to the princes of Birkenfeld and Sülzbach, who were disputing the succession with the Elector Palatine, whereas the Elector had been put in possession by the Emperor in accordance with a decision of the Aulic Council, an Imperial court that met in Vienna, where the case was still in process. Such localized disputes, small though they were, enmeshed diplomats, sometimes for decades, and also touched the interests of greater powers.

In 1715, the Archbishop-Electors of Cologne, Mainz and Trier, the Prince-Bishop of Speyer and the Duke of Württemberg–Montbéliard had grievances of the same nature with respect to fiefs and benefices in Alsace, all of which would have been as difficult to represent on a map. In 1721, the Prince of Öttingen complained to the sovereign court of Colmar about the overlordship of eleven villages in Lower Alsace that his family had possessed for over three centuries, which the Prince of Rohan had disputed with him, and which the French court had allocated to Rohan.

Greater clarification was brought both to borders and to competing rights in frontier zones as a result of the rationalism associated with the Enlightenment intellectual tendency of the second half of the eighteenth century and, subsequently, as a consequence of the willingness of French Revolutionary governments and then Napoleon to recast boundaries and to insist on undivided sovereignty. Enlightenment rationalism was seen in attempts to use knowledge in order to delimit boundaries and thus solve frontier disputes. For example, the Treaty of Turin of 1760 between France and Sardinia settled the Alpine boundary of Savoy-Piedmont on the basis of the watershed. The treaty incorporated eight maps.

Maps were increasingly referred to in negotiations and diplomacy. Rivers were used to delimit frontiers at the peace negotiations at Nijmegen, and the practice was continued at Rijswijk. In 1712, Torcy told his British counterpart to look at a map in order to assess the strategic threat posed by Victor Amadeus's Alpine demands. In 1718, a map formed part of a treaty delimiting the frontier between the Austrian Netherlands and the United Provinces. In 1750, Puysieulx, the French foreign minister, claimed that a simple examination of a map would show that it was in the interest of the Elector Palatine to be united with France. Maps brought a new territorial precision to frontiers, replacing what became seen as anachronistic criteria. In the extensive negotiations between France and the Prince-Bishop of Liège over Bouillon, which France had annexed in 1678, between 1697 and the mid-eighteenth century, references were made as far back as the eleventh century, and fantastic genealogies, legendary medieval tales and ancient authors who based their comments on hearsay played a major role.

The replacement of such criteria was part of a self-conscious rationalization of the spatial dimension of diplomacy and, increasingly, of international relations. In 1699–1701, Austrian and Turkish commissioners were forced to deal with the ambiguous and contradictory wording of the Peace of Karlowitz (1699) on such matters as the 'ancient' frontiers of Transylvania, the status of islands where the rivers Sava and Maros formed the new border, and the course of the frontier where it was defined as a straight line. The treaty stipulated that the commissioners were to survey and agree on the new frontier and the Austrian commissioner was instructed by his government to produce a definitive map.

Maps were not without their problems. They could make conflicting territorial views more readily apparent and thus accentuate them. In addition, the devices of printed linear boundaries, different coloration and textual specification were only introduced slowly and were sometimes of limited applicability. Nevertheless, as part of a widespread long-term advance in the collection, classification, display and analysis of information in more systematic ways,[6] surveying and mapping provided more precise geographical information than hitherto, and embryonic foreign offices began to collect and store them on a systematic basis. In the 1770s, the French foreign office created its own geographical section and acquired a large collection of maps. However, only in the Revolutionary and Napoleonic period were there to be the wholesale reorganizations of European frontiers, the sweeping aside of overlapping sovereignties, the reduction in the number of royal and princely rulers, and the qualification of traditional territorial rights which brought widespread dramatic changes in the nature of European frontiers, territoriality and political cartography.[7]

A changing system

The extent to which the French Revolution changed the European system can be debated, and is discussed in Chapter 10. What was clear was that the Revolutionaries thought of themselves as acting in a new fashion. This was particularly important given the reverence of, and reference to, the past, so significant in contemporary culture, and also given the reluctance to embrace change in discussion of *ancien régime* international relations. The Revolutionary argument that treaties entered into by rulers could not bind people was subversive. In addition, the subordination of foreign policy and the foreign minister to control by a committee of the popular assembly was new for a major state: control passed from the executive to the legislature.

Particular episodes over the previous century prefigured some of the experience of the Revolutionary period. This is true of the xenophobic popular pressure in Britain in 1738–9 for war with Spain that played a role in limiting the options of the Walpole ministry and thus helped to cause the War of Jenkins' Ear, and of the outburst of popular action that drove occupying Austrian forces from Genoa in 1746 and then sustained the city against Austrian attack, even if that was largely a response to Austrian financial and other demands. The Revolution was still different because it affected France, the most populous state in Western Europe, the paradigm of European monarchy, and the most important Western European participant in Continental international relations, because the radicalization of the Revolution was unprecedented, and because the French Revolutionary Wars, which began in 1792, involved and affected all of Europe.

Although oppressive, widely unpopular and eventually defeated, French expansion in 1792–1814 was of great importance, not least for its energizing of nationalism in response, and for its role in provoking governmental change in a number of states, most obviously Prussia, an echo of the impact of mid-eighteenth-century defeats on the Austrian state.

These issues indicate the extent to which it is not appropriate to present states as static throughout the period, or as acting within a static context. This was true both of major powers and of more minor counterparts. Any attempt to offer a graduated account of state power and a classification of states faces difficulties, not least the important issue of how best to evaluate strength. The respective weight of territory, resources, population, army size and state finances is unclear (and some indeed are difficult to quantify), while issues such as the weighting for colonial possessions, alliance structures and political stability are even more tricky. Allowing for this, in 1648, the major powers would be Austria, France, Russia, Spain, Turkey and the

United Provinces, accepting that such countries are employed as short-hand for dynastic conglomerations and interests.

During the period covered by this book, Britain and Prussia entered the category of major powers and the United Provinces left it. However, the timing of such shifts is less clear. Should Britain be seen as a great power in the 1650s, when Oliver Cromwell's army forcibly united the British Isles, and Britain played an active role in international relations, or is it more appropriate to wait until this achievement was repeated by William III in the 1690s? Should Prussia be seen as a great power after Frederick II conquered Silesia in 1740-1, or is it more appropriate to wait until after he defeated Austrian attempts to reconquer the province in 1744-5 and 1756-63?

As a related issue, major powers hit low ebbs when much of their territory was invaded and occupied, and their fate was in part controlled by outsiders. This was true of Spain in the 1700s and again in 1808-13, and of Austria in 1741. Turkey was clearly a great power in the late seventeenth century, but, over the following century, although her territorial extent was vast, not least in Europe, she was increasingly seen as a victim because of her failure to introduce governmental and military reforms.

The leading powers did not have a Continent-wide range. Russia was a major force in Eastern Europe from the outset, but did not appear obviously such to the Western European countries until after the defeat of Charles XII of Sweden in 1709 and the consequent Russian conquest of Sweden's eastern Baltic provinces. Spain was the largest colonial power in the world throughout the period, and a considerable European territorial power until 1700, but her role and influence in Eastern and Northern European diplomacy were minor. The same was true for the Mediterranean of Prussia and, until the late 1760s, Russia.

The second-rank powers varied considerably in consequence whatever criteria are adopted. Within the category, there were major differences in power and independent initiative: it is necessary to consider the specific political context. Whatever their respective strengths, Sardinia and Naples could play an independent role in Italy that was different from that of the Palatinate or Lorraine in the Empire. Until the rise of Russia, the Baltic was dominated by second-rank powers – Denmark and Sweden – and each was therefore of considerable consequence, but that situation was transformed by Peter the Great. The second-rank category encompasses, at the outset, Portugal, Savoy-Piedmont (Sardinia), Naples, Lorraine, the Palatinate, Bavaria, Hanover, Saxony, Prussia, Poland, Denmark and Sweden.

Prussia rose from this group in the eighteenth century, the United Provinces fell into it, and Poland and Lorraine were removed from it, both victims of more powerful neighbours.[8]

There is no clear divide between second-rank and minor powers, but the latter included all the German Imperial Free Cities and ecclesiastical principalities and the vast majority of German and Italian territories. Minor powers were militarily weak, diplomatically insignificant, and not generally capable of initiating political moves that would substantially affect the second-rank and great powers. Although it was stronger, the Swiss Confederation may be included as it played little role in international relations.

In Eastern Europe, it is possible to point to Polish aristocratic families who were more powerful, not least in the size of their military forces, than many minor princes elsewhere. They followed policies accordingly, pursuing independent diplomatic negotiations with foreign powers, and using diplomatic methods in their political activities within Poland. Their feuds were like wars and when the houses of Tarlo and Poniatowski made peace they were solemnly reconciled in a convention of agreement. Nevertheless, although great houses, such as Radzivill and Sapieha, might follow independent policies, they were not sovereign.

The diplomatic status of a number of autonomous territories within the Eastern European empires was unclear. This was true of the Khanate of the Crimea, the Danubian principalities (Moldavia and Wallachia), Transylvania, and, though to a lesser extent, as their independent actions were more clearly the result of rebellion, Hungary and the Ukraine. In 1750, the British envoy resolved to ignore the efforts of the Prussian government to treat a Crimean envoy as an accredited diplomat of equivalent rank on the grounds that he was not the representative of a sovereign body.

With the exception of the Khanate of the Crimea, the autonomous principalities of Eastern Europe were subdued by 1715, more particularly in 1700–15; but in Western Europe in this period the picture was more diverse. Some second-rank powers, such as Bavaria and Lorraine, had their aspirations quashed, were overrun, and only regained independence as the result of the intercession of the great powers with which they were allied. Other second-rank powers, such as Savoy-Piedmont, Hanover and Prussia, made important gains in the treaties of 1713–21 that ended the Spanish Succession and Great Northern Wars.

Although these gains were considerable for the powers concerned, and influenced the regional relationship among powers, and thus more general European relations, they did not involve large areas of land. Only Austria and Russia gained substantial territories, as a result of the Spanish Succession and Great Northern Wars respectively. The Austrian gains were the result of dynastic claims, military success, an equivalence for the acceptance that a cadet Bourbon would succeed in Spain, and the death without sons of the Emperor Joseph I (1705–11), so that the Habsburg claimant to the Spanish territories succeeded to Austria. These were the sole substantial territorial gains in the western half of Europe between 1679 and 1721; although there were several major dynastic gains, principally the Orangist (1689) and Hanoverian (1714) successions in Britain and the Bourbon (1700) in Spain.

Between 1721 and 1791, there were no comparable gains in Western Europe. Naples (1735), Sicily (1735) and Parma (1748) were acquired for the cadets of the Spanish Bourbons, the most substantial territorial changes of the period, Tuscany by a cadet branch of the Habsburgs (1737) and Lorraine by France (1766), while the extinction of several branches of the family united the Wittelsbach territories. However, none of these changes were comparable, in their scale or effect, to the Austrian and Russian gains in Eastern Europe after 1683. The Prussian conquest of Silesia was important not only because of the wealth and size of the province but also because the repeated Austrian failure to defeat Prussia indicated a major shift in the power relationships in the Empire and in Eastern Europe. The Prussian gain also indicated the importance of the relationship between domestic changes and foreign policy, for Silesia was not such a major gain as to lead automatically to Prussia acquiring the role that she did achieve under Frederick II. Instead, the successful knitting of elite and dynasty in the service of the Prussian state, not least through the expansion of the army, played a major role in the growth of Prussian power.

Nevertheless, Prussia was the most problematic of the great powers, as indicated by the enormous costs, over half a century, of Prussian military preparedness, and by Frederick's anxieties about Austrian and, in particular, Russian intentions. The problems he encountered suggest how difficult it was for a ruler to enlarge his holdings by war and aggression, as opposed to dynastic succession.

Second-rank and minor powers

This arguably affected all the second-rank powers. The majority of states were 'small' in terms of relative power, but they were also unwilling to abandon their ability to take independent initiatives and simply become dependent on the major states. The pertinacity with which second-rank states, for example Savoy-Piedmont (Sardinia), pursued their policies was a marked feature in the international relations of the period and helped to circumscribe the options of the major powers. Geopolitical approaches that focus on a state system present international relations in this period in terms of the major powers, but detailed attention to the diplomacy reveals repeatedly the role of the initiatives of second-rank states.

The contexts within which such states operated varied, as did the quality of their leadership. In their diplomatic schemes and military activity, second-rank powers were greatly affected by the views of the major powers, although they could hope to influence these. There were examples of major powers that were in effect led into diplomatic initiatives as a consequence of the suggestions of weaker counterparts. The Saxons considerably influenced Austrian and British policies in the 1740s and 1750s. In addition, many rulers could become so committed to their allies, while at the same time lacking control over them, that the weaker allies affected their policies. Arguably, this happened in Franco-Bavarian relations during the Wars of the Spanish and Austrian Successions. This pattern of dependence, yet still some influence, was repeated in the relationship between the second-rank and minor powers.

In both cases, the situation was made more complex by the number of powers involved, which commonly allowed weaker rulers to seek or receive assistance. In 1679, for example, Louis XIV and the Dukes of Brunswick blocked a Dano-Prussian attempt to coerce Hamburg. The failure to obtain a Spanish answer over the Tuscan succession led the Grand Duke to seek the intercession of the Emperor Charles VI and George I in 1722. In 1748, the French offered Genoa support against possible Sardinian aggressive steps. In 1752, Frederick II could not believe that the Danes would attack Holstein because that would offend Russia. Three years later, the ministers of the Prince-Archbishop of Salzburg, then in dispute with the Elector of Bavaria over the profitable salt trade, boasted of Austrian support.

The room for manoeuvre of small states was increased by tension between more powerful rulers. In 1715, Victor Amadeus II of

Savoy-Piedmont stressed the nature of the Austrian threat to France and called for the creation of an anti-Austrian league which would make him less vulnerable to Austrian power in Italy. In 1733, the Swedish envoy in London feared that any Anglo-French reconciliation would be unfortunate, as their mutual security would lead them to have less concern for other powers such as Sweden.

However, as well as creating opportunities, differences between major powers could create problems for their lesser counterparts, by leading the major powers to press for assistance and commitment. This could result both in hostile steps from other powers and in neglect from allies once the commitment had been made. The Wittelsbach agent in The Hague warned in 1726 that Charles VI would show less care for the Wittelsbachs if they joined either him or the opposing Alliance of Hanover, and he therefore urged a policy of neutrality. When French troops were let into Münster in 1757, the Duke of Cumberland, who was in command of an opposing army, took possession of Paderborn which was ruled by the same prince-bishop.

It was not, therefore, surprising that some rulers did not wish to commit themselves militarily or diplomatically. Portugal was not involved in the Devolution, Dutch or Nine Years' conflicts in the late seventeenth century, and Denmark stayed out of eighteenth-century warfare after the Great Northern War, until foolishly tempted to attack Sweden in 1788. Both Denmark and Sweden kept their involvement in the Nine Years' War as minimal as possible. Denmark was no longer in a position to refuse passage through the Sound into the Baltic to a Western maritime power. Her consistent reluctance in the latter half of the eighteenth century to work with other Baltic powers to close the Straits and treat the Baltic as a *mare clausum* (closed sea) arose from a recognition that such a policy would no longer be politically or militarily realistic, an assessment confirmed by British victories in 1801 and 1807.[9]

A past sufferer from war, whose allies could not provide sufficient to compensate for his losses,[10] Victor Amadeus II resisted pressure to commit himself during the confrontation between the Alliances of Hanover and Vienna in 1725–7. The United Provinces negotiated with France a neutrality agreement for the Austrian Netherlands for the War of the Polish Succession, refused to become involved in the War of Jenkins' Ear and the Seven Years' War, and delayed formal hostilities with France during the War of the Austrian Succession until 1747. The British envoy in Lisbon described Portuguese policy in 1773: 'we have here so little connection with quarrelsome powers, that we are contented with the events, and do not trouble ourselves much with speculation: Jesuits and trade are the only objects of politics in this corner'. Eight years later, the Bavarian foreign minister described his Elector's system, 'to observe an exact neutrality whatever happens, in order to give ourselves time to breathe and for improvements that would put the Elector in a respectable state, not that he would ever abuse that, as he prefers with justice the description of pacific to that of warrior or conquering'.[11]

It was certainly prudent not to offend major rulers, as Frederick II's forcible recruiting and intervention in lawsuits between Prussian and Saxon subjects indicated. These pacific hesitations could be repeated at the level of the minor rulers. Suspecting the Duke of Modena of an anti-Bourbon understanding with Charles Emmanuel III of Sardinia, the French foreign minister, nevertheless, reflected in 1742, that 'to some extent this is excusable, because he thinks the Sardinian party the strongest. Small princes are often in the situation of not knowing which side to turn to'.[12]

That did not, however, prevent minor powers from disputing with each other. Disputes often arose over frontier and overlordship differences. In 1670–1, for example, the Duke of Brunswick-Wolfenbüttel and the Prince-Bishop of Münster differed over the suzerainty of a Westphalian town, while the Imperial Free City of Cologne and the Archbishop-Elector of Cologne, whose territories did not include the city, clashed. Economic issues could be involved. In the early 1750s, the Archbishop-Elector of Trier had a dispute with a local count over a boat bridge, while, in the mid-1750s, the small Italian city republic of Lucca complained of floods caused by river alterations in Tuscany.

The minor rulers tended to suffer more seriously at the hands of their powerful colleagues, especially in wartime. Forcible billeting, contributions and recruiting were then a general problem. Louis XIV broke his promises over the neutrality of Liège and seized the citadel there in 1675, declaring that he had only done it to better maintain the territory's neutrality. This was not uniquely cynical, as Louis's Dutch opponent behaved in much the same way. Hesse-Darmstadt was burdened with French winter quarters in 1744–5, and the Electorate of Mainz troubled by their exactions the following spring. In March 1748, the Landgrave of Hesse-Cassel informed George II, who had sought permission for his Russian allies to cross Hesse, that his territories had been affected by the nearly continual march of troops. Ignoring the complaints of the Princes of Anhalt, Frederick II sent in troops to obtain recruits, leading the Bavarian foreign minister to reflect in January 1773: 'it seems that the right of the strongest now determines all the moves of the great'.[13]

Bullying and oppression were not restricted to military matters. They frequently characterized economic issues and they could be seen in ecclesiastical matters, such as the Habsburg attempt to dominate the appointment of prince-bishops in the early 1780s. The strength of the major rulers did not relegate all their weaker counterparts to diplomatic and military nullity, but it cannot be said that most enjoyed the power of peace and war to any extent.

Nevertheless, the manipulative policies of major rulers were often unsuccessful, not least because of their rivalry. Major powers frequently bewailed the self-interest and perverseness of weaker states. Subsidies, for example, were generally used to further the policies of these states: they were not bought. Any detailed study of particular regions or years can only qualify any notion of the international relations of this period as being controlled by the great powers.

Domestic politics and foreign policy

The interrelationship of domestic circumstances with foreign policy and international success was a common theme in the diplomatic correspondence. Considerable attention was devoted to these circumstances, although it was generally not systematic and concentrated on court politics and military matters to the detriment of a fuller assessment of the domestic situation. Thus, the coverage of economic developments and social trends was generally superficial. This is scarcely surprising as governments commonly were little better informed. In an age without, or at least with few, statistics, information was sparse or unreliable and ministers were aware of the situation outside the capital to only a limited extent.

If foreign policy was influenced by the subtle interplay of internal processes, this was not simply a matter of the functioning of a domestic political system and the international configuration of which the domestic system was a part. The strength of a state's finances and military forces and their government's ability to mobilize resources were both crucial and seen to be so. This ability was most important in wartime. The greater financial strength of Britain played a major role in her wars with France, not least in enabling her during the War of

American Independence (1775–83) to fight both a war in America and an alliance of European enemies.

In addition, the foreign perception of national strength was a constant factor of diplomatic importance. The role of 'reputation' was stressed by many diplomats. Just as it was necessary for rulers to have a reputation for honourable behaviour, firmness, justice and bravery, so their territories had to be regarded as prosperous and militarily strong. A failure to be thus regarded could compromise a state's actual and potential value as an ally. In 1716, Victor Amadeus II's envoy in Paris reported that governmental and financial weakness would ensure that if France under the regency that followed Louis XIV's death was ever obliged to fulfil the guarantees in the Peace of Utrecht, she would do so slowly, feebly and with difficulty. Victor Amadeus was discouraged in his opposition to Austria by his envoy's reports that France was not only unwilling but also unable to provide clear diplomatic support. Conversely, in 1726, the French envoy in Turin reported that French military preparations against the Alliance of Vienna had changed the Sardinian opinion of the state of France's finances. If second-rank powers could view the major states as potential patrons and allies with reference to their resources as well as their intentions, the process worked both ways. In March 1744, the French foreign minister instructed the envoy to Charles Albert of Bavaria, the Emperor VII, to press him to create a more efficient administration, so that he would be able to use French assistance more effectively.

The relationship between domestic circumstances and foreign policy was complex. It was possible to blame what appeared to be misconceived views or weak government on the part of other states for policies that were disliked when in fact it is more likely that they reflected a different assessment of interests and needs. Frederick II was particularly fond of ascribing the failure of powers to act as he believed they should to weakness and court intrigue. In the early 1750s, he was scathing about what he saw as the consequence of France's failure to compete effectively with the Anglo-Austrian defensive system by gaining new allies and better supporting her current ones, such as him. He attributed this to ministerial instability and governmental weakness. In March 1752, Frederick predicted problems from the frequent changes of French ministers and instructed the Lord Marshal, his envoy in Paris, to press the French to follow the example of Louis XIV and his concern for foreign policy. That December, the Lord Marshal reported that the French ministers sought tranquillity, because they were disunited, the finances in a poor state, the populace irritated by the price of grain, and their betters dissatisfied. In November 1753, Frederick complained that the Danes were being wooed from the Franco-Prussian system by reports of the poor state of the French army and finances, the weakness of her government, and the political problems with the Parlement of Paris. The Lord Marshal also gave some weight to policy, attributing French passivity in part to the influence of Madame de Pompadour, Louis XV's mistress. Her ascendancy, he argued, depended on the continuance of peace. The Prussians failed to consider the extent to which Louis XV and his ministers did not see themselves as obliged to commit themselves to further Frederick's interests and views to the degree he expected.

Louis XVI's policy was also misunderstood. In March 1777, Frederick attributed the French failure to act against the ambitious projects of Austria to the supposed role of Louis's wife, Marie Antoinette, the sister of Joseph II (an accusation frequently made by French critics),[14] and the total weakness of French finances, which led him to describe France as a power only in title. Frederick argued that, unless her finances were improved, France would never be able to occupy the rank she had hitherto enjoyed. He also asked whether it would be possible to encourage Louis to develop an interest in mistresses in order to limit the influence of the Queen,[15] only to be informed that Louis was not interested in mistresses. In fact, financial problems did not prevent France from opposing Britain, and Marie Antoinette did not lead Louis XVI to support Joseph II over the Bavarian succession, the Bavarian Exchange scheme, or the opening of the Scheldt, issues that mattered greatly to Joseph in 1777–85. Foreign observers might rightly assess domestic circumstances, but these were not necessarily directly linked to policy decisions.

This was also true of Britain, the constitution of which was very different from that of France. Contemporaries overestimated British ministerial weakness and its effects on foreign policy. With their experience of the more controlled societies of the Continent, envoys exaggerated the unpredictability of British politics and found it difficult to accept that monarchical power could be as great in Britain where it was sharply limited in constitutional terms as it could be in states where the theoretical and institutional restraints on it were less.

More generally, as foreign policies were at least influenced by domestic circumstances (while it is similarly inappropriate to separate the military from politics),[16] it was considered worthwhile for diplomats to intervene in domestic politics, in both peace and war. In 1719,

Philip V of Spain supported the opposition to the Duke of Orléans, and sought to replace him as Regent of Louis XV by a more sympathetic minister.

Conclusions

Intervention in the domestic politics of other states helped to increase the volatility of politics and policy. Rulers, ministers and diplomats sought to limit this volatility in order both to understand/explain developments and to control them, or make it appear that they could be controlled. The small groups that determined policy were not oblivious of wider domestic circumstances, any more than they only concerned themselves with the views of similar small groups abroad. Just as rulers and ministers were concerned with the military and financial strength and political stability of foreign powers, so they were aware of the importance of their own.

These issues, which were most important in periods of brinkmanship and war, did not mean that diplomacy was a simple measure of power, with success going to the strongest. First, power and authority were difficult to assess, and, second, the effect of multistate diplomacy was to enhance the options for, and role of, foreign policy. Power aroused opposition as much as compliance. In addition, contemporaries had to consider the impact of domestic circumstances on strength and resolution without having any sure guides as to how to assess them or to gauge their likely effect.

Talk of systems and mutual interests appeared to provide little guidance to the future. Frederick II and Puyzieulx both commented on the shared nature of French and Prussian interests in 1749, Frederick telling his envoy in London that these reciprocal interests were so solid, natural and durable that neither power could leave the other unless the European system changed. It did, and, eight years later, at Rossbach, Frederick destroyed France's military reputation and the prestige of her monarch. Many ministers and diplomats complained of the disjointed nature of international relations and of a lack of system; although they commonly presented their own policies as consistent. Kaunitz criticized Frederick II for lacking a system, in other words a coherent plan implemented in a consistent fashion, but his own theorizing methods did not prevent him from following an indefinite and, at times, confused policy during the period 1768–74, when the number of independent variables he had to contend with, not least Maria Theresa and Joseph II, defied any predictive analysis. The French Revolutionary and Napoleonic period confirmed what was already apparent, the interrelationship of political developments in different countries and the centrality and unpredictability of international developments.

Chapter 4

Wars and the Military

Wars were and are one of the major subjects in the conduct and study of international relations. This can, however, present several serious problems. First, there is a danger of a disjuncture between specialists on international relations and military historians. Their different concerns can extend to a focus by the latter on the operational dimension of war – campaigns, battles and weapons – rather than on its political cause, context, course and consequence; while specialists on international relations may have an incomplete understanding of military developments and capability. In fact, both of these were necessarily important to the effectiveness of particular states in both war and peace, not least because a belief in the threat posed by a specific power could help it to gain an edge in negotiation. This chapter tackles two different, but related, topics: first, the extent to which the causes of war throw light on the character of international relations, and, second, the nature of warfare and its impact on these relations.

In so far as the causes of war are concerned, the period is commonly divided into two at 1792, with the outbreak of the French Revolutionary Wars signifying a move towards ideological and unlimited warfare. In the earlier period, states were, and are, presented as being motivated by non-ideological objectives, principally dynastic and territorial advantage, and as seeking limited wars. This analysis was developed in the eighteenth century by critics of the 'secret diplomacy' of the period and, later, by exponents of the policies of Revolutionary France. It was subsequently advanced in the late nineteenth century when states appeared to operate their foreign policies in a cool and dispassionate fashion, unaffected by ideology. However, this view was an inaccurate assessment of the international relations both of the late nineteenth century and of the period before the Revolution. Because all the European great powers of the nineteenth century were already major states in the earlier period, it is understandable that the diplomatic relations of the earlier age should be treated in terms of the analyses and attitudes that appeared to be most appropriate for later analysts. The general stress was on policy and long-term planning, carried out rationally and in accordance with an unemotional *raison d'état* by monarchs and ministers without illusions, preeminently Frederick II and his leading opponent, the Austrian Chancellor, Count Kaunitz.

Thus, historians of the foreign policy of Louis XIV, the principal late seventeenth-century topic that engaged the interest of diplomatic historians two centuries later, searched for some policy, such as the quest for 'natural frontiers' or for the Spanish succession, that would reduce the varied themes and episodes of their subject to some order by which his moves could be explained, judged and linked to subsequent episodes in French foreign policy. Similarly, the response of other rulers was seen in terms of a coherent counterpointing of French moves, to be understood and assessed in terms of the reply to the intentionality and systematic planning of Louis's policy. An inherent competitiveness was stressed and presented as both product and motor of international relations.

In such an analysis, the so-called 'realist' paradigm was adopted, and war tended to be regarded as a device of deliberate policy, the decision to resort to it based either on a rational consideration of national advantage, or, in the case of rulers or ministers who were to be condemned for folly, on a failure to make such an assessment. Ideological demands for war were seen as limited, and domestic pressures for conflict were generally ignored, with the exception of states possessing powerful representative assemblies, such as Britain and the United Provinces.

The *mentalités* that affected the conduct of foreign policy in Europe were rarely discussed, but, when they were, they were judged to be – what was implicit in the vast bulk of the scholarship – a matter of *raison d'état*, a prudential, at times machiavellian, assessment of opportunities and interests. This was illustrated by the publication of documentary series, most prominently Frederick the Great's *Politische Correspondenz* from 1879 and the *Recueil des Instructions données aux Ambassadeurs et Ministres de France depuis les Traités de Westphalie jusqu'à la Révolution Française* from 1884. This approach,

1 11 1164376 4

however, had serious limitations, not least because it presented an account of the political culture of the period that is a less than rounded treatment of the attitudes and aspirations of the rulers.

For the period prior to the French Revolutionary Wars, it is possible to emphasize both the willingness to pursue interests short of conflict and the readiness to resort to war. Inevitably a section on the causes of war would suggest the latter, but it is also necessary to stress the large number of disputes that did not lead to conflict. In 1679–81, for example, in the *réunions*, Louis XIV occupied much of the Spanish Netherlands, as well as neighbouring parts of Germany, advancing often fanciful claims to the dependencies of territories earlier ceded to him. Despite the construction of an opposing alliance system in 1681–2, the unwillingness of the powers to fight France ensured there was no major European war. Similarly, the Baltic crisis of 1683 did not lead to war; nor did the crisis between Denmark and its neighbours in 1686–9.

More generally, Europe could be divided into hostile camps and forces could be prepared, but war would be avoided. This was true, for example, of the confrontations between the Austro-Spanish alliance system and its Anglo-French rival in 1725–9, between Austria and the league of Britain, France and Spain in 1730, between Britain and France in 1731, Austria and Spain in 1732, Prussia and Britain-Hanover in 1729 and 1753, and France and Russia in 1773. Diplomatic Europe was full of speculation in 1732 that Spain would attack Italy, particularly the island of Sardinia, and the Spanish armament was described by the Sardinian ambassador as holding all Europe in suspense,[1] but, in the event, the Spaniards restricted themselves to an assault on Oran in North Africa. Thus brinkmanship did not have to lead to war and, of course, most disputes were pursued without such tactics.

Nevertheless, the fact that some crises did not develop into war, as threats and other moves were handled without a serious breakdown, does not mean that such threats and moves could not be crucial in leading to war. Equally, the pressure for action made it difficult to avoid moves that would serve to provoke others or vindicate claims about the malevolence of a state's intentions. Brinkmanship did lead to an inherent instability that made war possible. Once threats were uttered or moves were made, it was difficult both to retract them, lest that was seen as a sign of weakness, and to control their consequences. The attempt to obtain benefits by military preparations and the threat of force led both to hostile responses and to the pressure to deliver on threats.

This was especially true of contested successions. A vacant succession lasted only for a certain period before being filled by a coronation and, in some cases, the election of a new monarch. This event forced interested parties, such as Austria in 1701, Russia in 1733 and Bavaria in 1741, in the case of the Wars of the Spanish, Polish and Austrian Successions, to act speedily. It was necessary to threaten more obviously and to intervene, if intervention was judged necessary, before a certain date. The need for speed accentuated the habitual difficulties of brinkmanship, such as rumour and the obligation to begin military preparations early if they were to have any impact. The advance in 1701 of an Austrian force, sent to seize Milan, led to the beginning of hostilities in the War of the Spanish Succession. In 1733, the Russians could not delay moving their troops for long if they were to reach Warsaw by the date of the royal election and thus block the election of a hostile candidate. In 1740, Frederick II felt it necessary to force concessions from Maria Theresa while her position seemed vulnerable, and therefore invaded Silesia. The following summer, the French had to move troops into the Empire and secure allies for action against Austria, in enough time for them to be able to contribute to what was planned as the destruction of Habsburg power.

Whether or not disputes involved a succession, many rulers were willing to resort to force to secure their interests. This was not simply the case with rulers who were notoriously aggressive (whether or not this was justified), such as Louis XIV. For example, Danish conduct towards weaker neighbours, such as Hamburg, Holstein-Gottorp and Lübeck, was characterized by violence and the threat of violence, including blockades of Hamburg. This particular issue indicated how the clarification of rights and authority led to disputes. The Danes had a legal claim to Hamburg which had not been an Imperial Free City in the sixteenth century. A situation which then was open and, in legal terms, poorly defined, with the absence of a clear notion of sovereignty – Hamburg claimed to be a Free City when the King of Denmark demanded taxes and a *Landstadt* (subject town) when the Emperor did so – gave rise to conflict, once the need was felt by both sides to clarify the position.

It was not only strong monarchies which were aggressive. The Dutch proved unwilling to withdraw their garrisons from a number of nearby towns, such as Wesel, occupied in the first half of the seventeenth century. In addition, immediately after the death of the childless William III in 1702, the Dutch seized the Orange counties of Moers and Lingen, in north-west Germany, ostensibly on behalf of a claimant, the Prince of Nassau-Dietz, but in reality to prevent the claims of Frederick I of Prussia, who was seen as an unwelcome neighbour. Despite protests by Frederick and the Westphalian Circle, and a judgment by the Imperial Court, the Dutch refused to withdraw. During the Swedish 'Age of Liberty', when the monarch was constrained by a powerful representative assembly and political parties, the Swedes attacked Russia in 1741 and Prussia in 1757.

In considering these and other steps, it is necessary to take note of the extent to which the uncertainties of the past led to war and, also, of the causes advanced by contemporaries when explaining the decision for conflict: glory, honour and opportunity. France, for example, went to war in 1733 more to support royal honour – one candidate for the Polish throne was Louis XV's father-in-law – and to prevent humiliation and isolation, than from a wish to establish her power in Eastern Europe.

It is necessary to discard the notion that glory, honour and prestige were somehow 'irrational' pursuits, and that opportunism and the absence of consistent policies were somehow less intelligent than long-term plans. Even if glory and honour are to be seen as pretexts – a reductionist approach that has to be handled with care – it is still necessary to assess the way in which *gloire* or national dignity could serve the emotional impetus that might lead to war being risked.

Prestige and glory were the basis of the power of early-modern monarchs, both domestically and in international relations. They conferred a mantle of success and magnificence that was the most effective lubricant of obedience in societies that had poorly developed systems of administration and that essentially rested on willed obedience. Failure undermined stability. Although an elaborate 'cover-up' campaign of receptions, prayers, rewards and eulogies greeted the return of Prince Golitsyn, lover and leading minister of the Russian regent Sophia from the Crimea in 1689, the court factions that opposed Sophia were encouraged by this failure, and it helped to ease Peter the Great's path to power.[2]

Most monarchs had only a limited personal interest in domestic 'reforms' or administrative change, and that which took place is frequently correctly linked to important ministers. Far from being a diversion from intractable domestic problems, or a means of solving these problems, war was regarded as the natural activity, indeed 'sport', of monarchs. Their upbringing conditioned them to accept such a notion, and most male monarchs spent their years of peace in activities that were substitutes for war and which served to keep their minds on military matters: manoeuvres, reviews, and the royal cavalry exercises for the court aristocracy known as hunts. Peter the Great's war games were matched by those of other young princes.

At times of war, most monarchs took seriously their role as warriors, leading their armies towards, if not always into, battle. Jan Sobieski, King of Poland, led his army to the relief of Vienna in 1683; Peter the Great led his army to the sieges of Azov in 1695 and 1696, at the battle of Poltava in 1709, on the Pruth expedition in 1711 and on the advance down the western shore of the Caspian Sea in 1722; Augustus II of Saxony-Poland commanded the invasion of Livonia in 1700, and Frederick IV that of Holstein-Gottorp the same year; Charles XII led the Swedes throughout the Great Northern War (1700–21) until his defeat at Poltava; and Joseph II commanded the Austrians during the War of the Bavarian Succession (1778–9). In peacetime, eighteenth-century European monarchs dressed increasingly in military uniform.

The iconography of kingship, the theatre of display and ceremonial, within which monarchs lived and through which they sought to have their role perceived, stressed martial achievements, as it had done from the outset. Louis XIV had his new palace of Versailles, where 'new techniques were used to enforce old values', decorated with frescoes and paintings of his triumphs, such as the crossing of the Rhine in 1672. In the *Allegory of the Peace of Aix-la-Chapelle* by Jacques Dumont 'Le Romain', exhibited in the Paris Salon of 1761, Louis XV, portrayed as the peace-giver, was dressed in armour as Alexander the Great, who was seen as an appropriate model of kingship.[3] In the War of the Austrian Succession, Louis, who was not an obvious candidate for warrior-kingship, had indeed been present at the battles of Fontenoy (1745) and Lawfeldt (1747) and at the siege of Freiburg (1744).

In the culture of the age, it was necessary to be a warrior to bring peace: peace was caused by war. The glory of waging war was thus also the glory of imposing peace: it was victory, not negotiation, that was glorious. On tapestries and in equestrian statues, monarchs were depicted in military poses.

A rethinking of political culture in terms of such issues, rather than more bureaucratic themes, helps explain both the general character of policy and more specific decisions. Louis XIV helped to set the tone of monarchical conduct both for his contemporaries in Western Europe and subsequently. Seeing victory as a crucial source of *gloire*, at once an attitude and a policy that joined him to Napoleon, Louis favoured war in his early years. His decision to attack the Dutch in 1672 serves as an important opportunity to throw light on the causes of war by discussing an individual conflict; although clearly there was a distinct group of factors in the case of each war. Fluctuations in French policy in the build-up to the conflict can be attributed to Louis and to particular ministers. While clearly favouring conflict with the Dutch, Louis was also willing to heed ministerial arguments for delay, although these arguments had to be couched in terms he found acceptable: in short, they had to accept the value of war. The finance minister, Colbert, who attempted to subject warfare (both the decision to go to war and its conduct) to economic and fiscal criteria, was outmanoeuvred by Louvois, the army minister, and forced to find the funds for the war in order to avoid dismissal. Louvois's reiterated pressure for action appealed to Louis who disliked passivity. Turenne, the general closest to Louis, offered the prospect of easy alliances and quick victories and although, in 1669–70, he was initially thwarted by other advisers, his ideas gained currency, especially because they appealed to Louis and were known to do so.

As with most conflicts in this period, there was scant sense of how any war would develop in diplomatic and military terms. Louis hoped that Spain would come to the aid of the Dutch and that he could, therefore, resume the conquest of the Spanish Netherlands, broken off when peace had been negotiated in 1668. The actual outbreak of war was delayed until the diplomatic situation was favourable, with the Dutch isolated and Louis certain of the support or neutrality of most of Western Europe.[4] As with other wars, that might appear an argument in favour of a prudent assessment of the decision to fight and of relative risks, but such an assessment was made within a context overwhelmingly shaped by the desire of Louis and Louvois for a series of gratifying acts of valour. Thus, reason was in the service of passion, if such a questionable dichotomy can be advanced. Once war had broken out, Louis failed to use the opportunity of early successes to negotiate peace, and he lost control of the international situation.[5]

War brought gains and *gloire*, personal and dynastic honour, to aristocrats as well as monarchs. Aristocrats were often eager for war, for a variety of reasons that included personal profit and prestige, a hope for advancement, and a sense that conflict was their proper role in a society in which derogation of rank for participating in a range of economic activities epitomized aristocratic notions of behaviour.

Thus, the French court nobility pressed for military glory, not least in 1667 and 1741 when decisions were made for war.

Throughout Europe, there was a marked preference for aristo-crats in command positions, particularly senior positions. This was true of the appointment and promotion policies of rulers, whether Louis XIV or Frederick II. In Russia, the duty of the nobility to serve the ruler was stated and employed to rank society in Peter the Great's Table of Ranks of 1722. The prestige of military service in Europe was not undermined by the fact that many aristocrats did not serve.

An emphasis on the views of individual rulers, rather than on 'systemic' interpretations, generally of a geopolitical type, can be criticized as entailing a return to the traditions of the historiography of the period when great events were commonly ascribed to the often trivial views of individuals, or to their passions. In the late seventeenth and first half of the eighteenth century, passions had been regarded as momenta for action that could be standardized as classifiable and predictable attributes of general behaviour, and it was believed that passions were something that could be subjected to standard norms and rules. By contrast, towards the end of the century, passions began to be conceived as something that related only to the individual, were unpredictable, and could not be calculated at all.

For modern commentators to stress the role of the court, of concepts of kingship and of the atmosphere in which decisions were taken is not simply to rely on explanations that focus on the personal predilections of particular rulers. Instead, it is to suggest that the prevalent ideas and cultural norms of the period played a crucial role in the context within which decisions were taken. These ideas have to be understood to appreciate the views of individuals and groups who sought war, and to realize that that was not, necessarily, the product of diplomatic failure but, rather, something sought be-cause it produced what were seen as benefits.

An emphasis on the views of rulers, on the expectation that monarchs should and would wage war, and on the role of *gloire*, helps to explain why differences led to disputes and why unresolved disputes led to wars, but does not explain why particular wars broke out on specific occasions. This was a matter of the interaction of dispute and opportunity, an interaction in which perceptions of domestic and international circumstances by both parties played a crucial role in the attitudes and politics of brinkmanship and confrontation from which wars emerged.

Alongside the theme of continuity, it is also appropriate to stress elements of change, as can be seen by contrasting Louis XIV and Frederick II. Both sought to gain glory in and through war and were not too scrupulous in the pursuit of their interests. However, Louis based his claims to German and Spanish territories, and eventually the Spanish crown, on feudal or dynastic claims. Some of these were spurious, but Louis went a long way to make them seem as plausible as possible.

In contrast, Frederick did not really trouble to establish any legal claims to Silesia which were even remotely plausible. This reflected not only differences in personality, but also changes in circumstances. In the eighteenth century, it had become natural to seek to trade off claims and titles against each other: Sicily could be exchanged for Sardinia and Naples for Parma. It proved impossible to exchange Bavaria for the Spanish, later Austrian, Netherlands (Belgium), but it was conceivable to seek to do so. Thus, Frederick could believe he could trade off his support for Maria Theresa for one of her provinces. Frederick's attitudes and policies prefigured those of Napoleon, although there was a crucial difference. Whereas Napoleon was determined to remould Europe and to destroy any sense of balance, Frederick acted to adjust the balance in Prussia's favour. This reflected not only a consciousness of relative strength, but also the extent to which the mechanistic notions of balance that prevailed in international relations entailed correlating ends and means, aspirations and opportunities.[6]

Territorial bartering had always existed, as the fate of Charlemagne's inheritance in the ninth century displayed, but, in the eighteenth century, it became less limited by considerations of prestige and historic titles than hitherto. This shift made it easier to reach peace settlements after a conflict, but they also made it simpler to begin a war when it seemed appropriate. However, this convenience and the more general issue of intentionality have to be understood within the context of a bellicose political culture and belligerent political practices. Thanks to this bellicosity, it is misleading to think in terms of modern criteria of the rationality of causes of conflict. The timing of individual wars might be unfortunate for particular combatants, but conflict itself was not irrational: it reflected an important strand in the political dynamics of the age. Ideology, understood in modern terms, came to play a major role in the causes of war first with the War of American Independence (1775–83) and then with the French Revolutionary Wars, which broke out in 1792.

The general trend in military developments is also relevant to any discussion of international relations in this period. The most important aspect of the situation was that organized force remained for most of the period under the control of states. There were important rebellions that led to irregular forces battling their regular counterparts, but the Rákóczi rising (1703–11) in Hungary was overcome, as were the Jacobite uprisings in Britain (1715–16, 1745–6) and the Irish rebellion (1798). In Russia, risings led by Stenka Razin (1669–71), Bulavin (1707–8) and Pugachev (1773–4) were all suppressed, as was the Bohemian rising in 1775 and that in Transylvania in 1784. The latter two were the most prominent of a whole series of peasant insurrections in Eastern Europe. Rebellions and irregular forces received a fresh impulse from the experience of French occupation and oppression during the French Revolutionary and Napoleonic Wars. The majority were suppressed, although French forces were unable to crush the rebellion in Spain in 1808–13, despite major efforts.

Thus, the history of organized large-scale force in this period is essentially that of regular forces. Whereas, for example, the fortifications of individual towns and castles had been able to defy royal forces in earlier centuries, the new-style fortifications that became increasingly prominent in the sixteenth and seventeenth centuries and the siege armies that could take them were both developed by sovereign rulers, and then only by those who could afford the cost.[7] The same was true of land and sea forces.

Furthermore, regular forces were under greater state direction than in previous centuries as a result of the more effective implicit social contract between rulers and nobilities, and the extension of central governmental control over recruitment, supply and command. Military entrepreneurs increasingly operated under governmental direction.

This extension of control was related to an expansion in the size and effectiveness of armies. In terms of the size and permanence of armed forces, and of changes in tactics and weaponry, the period 1660–1720 was one of major developments. In place of converted merchantmen, navies came to rely almost exclusively on specialized vessels. On land, the spread of the use of bayonets, whether plug, ring or socket in type, was of greater tactical significance. In place of a division between pikemen and musketeers, all infantrymen could be armed with the same weapon, and infantry firepower increased. Pikemen were phased out. Heavy and often unreliable matchlock guns were replaced by lighter and more rapid-firing flintlocks.

Increasingly effective military forces were important in aggregate terms, and also as they affected relations between individual states. Not all states increased their military at the same rate or to the same extent. For some rulers, the creation of a larger army provided an encouragement and/or opportunity to take a more assertive, even aggressive, line in international relations. This was particularly true of the French, Russians and Prussians on land, and of the British at sea. The Prussian army, 40,000 men strong in 1713, and 81,000 men strong in 1740, had, according to Frederick II, increased to 188,000 troops by the peacetime year of 1781, having been 260,000 men strong in 1760 at the height of the Seven Years' War. In addition, the armies of some second-rank powers significantly increased. Savoy-Piedmont's army grew from 8700 in 1690 to over 24,000 in 1730 and to 48,000 in 1748, although its peacetime level was lower – 24,000 in 1778. This difference between wartime and peacetime numbers could also be found elsewhere: military growth was not always sustained. Nevertheless, the transition to permanent forces was such that peacetime numbers were higher than in the sixteenth century.

These forces represented a considerable financial burden. In 1689, the army accounted for about one-third of the total government expenditure of Savoy-Piedmont. By 1731, a year of peace, it accounted for close to one-half of a budget twice as big. In the early 1780s, a period of peace, 75–80 per cent of Prussian revenues were spent on the army, and the French budget of 1781, when France was at war with Britain, envisaged 25 per cent of their more substantial revenues being spent on the army, at a time of major naval expenditure. Naval races pushed up the cost of maritime power. The ability to meet the costs of naval strength reflected the power of the sponsoring interest groups.[8] However, financial crises hit military power. For example, financial problems have been linked directly to the administrative deficiencies of the mid-eighteenth-century French navy. A lack of money hit naval recruitment, and was the crucial obstacle to French naval construction after 1758. Conversely, a sudden influx of funds had allowed a reform and renewal of naval organization and a rebuilding of the fleet from 1749.[9]

The substantial military growth of a number of powers, and the absence of any marked technological or organizational edge, except increasingly between the Turks and their Christian neighbours, made military predominance on the Continental, as opposed to the regional, scale impossible to achieve, although the British managed to achieve naval dominance in successive wars, in 1747 and 1759, 1782 and

1805. This helped ensure that they were best placed to benefit from the growing global reach of European power.

Rapid victory on land was not impossible, as the Swedish attack on Denmark in 1700 or the Prussian invasion of the United Provinces in 1787 indicated. However, prior to Napoleon's success in the mid-1800s, it was elusive in land wars between major powers. Austria appeared near to collapse in 1703–4 and 1741, but it survived because of domestic resilience and foreign assistance. On the other hand, rulers could be driven by defeat to abandon their objectives. Philip V of Spain abandoned his Italian plans and dropped his chief minister, Alberoni, in 1720, as a result of failure in the War of the Quadruple Alliance. Defeat could also lead rulers to be willing to surrender what had seemed vital interests, as Louis XIV was willing to do during the War of the Spanish Succession. However, by then, he was without undefeated allies, as was also true of Sweden when forced to surrender its eastern Baltic provinces in 1721 at the close of the Great Northern War. In contrast, when monarchs fought as members of alliances, it was difficult to translate victory over them, however stunning, into an equally clear political settlement. To translate military advantage into total victory was also difficult.

Difficult, but not impossible. In 1805–7, Napoleon was able to achieve stunning victories over powers linked in a system against him and then to drive them to a political settlement that acknowledged his primacy in Western and Central Europe. This achievement was cemented by fresh success against Austria in 1809. Napoleon's system was rejected however by Britain, the Spanish population from 1808, Russia from 1812, and both Austria and Prussia from 1813. This rejection was not inevitable, but it ensured that, despite the new possibilities for sweeping political changes stemming from the military and other developments of Revolutionary and Napoleonic France, the end result was a return to the multipolar (many states) system of the *ancien régime*.

Chapter 5

Europe and the Outer World

Any account of European international relations has to take note of the wider world for a number of reasons. First, relations between European powers were, in part, pursued outside Europe and, at times, were greatly affected by clashes between them in the colonies. Second, this was an age of colonial expansion, less so than in the remainder of the nineteenth century, but still significant. This was important to the history of Europe, including its international relations, as well as to non-European peoples. Last, it is valuable to consider parallels and contrasts between European international relations and those in other parts of the world.

There is not the space to provide a detailed narrative of European colonial conflict or expansion, but the main points have to be recounted, not least because it is all too easy to treat these as much less consequential than a central narrative of European international relations from Louis XIV to Napoleon. The presentation of relations in terms of such a narrative is problematic, not only because it presumes a central organizing issue in an international system but also because, whether such a system is credited or not, it puts an emphasis on a particular part of Europe and not, by extension, on other areas. A reminder of the role of colonial expansion and of conflict between European powers outside Europe serves as a further illustration of the drawbacks of this approach. It pushes further against the notion that Europe had a central system. Instead, in so far as a systemic approach is advanced, it becomes more pertinent to think in terms of several systems, one of which was an Atlantic system that spanned the European Atlantic powers and their Atlantic colonies. The Balkans provide another system, though one that links not only Christian powers but also the Turks.

In so far as Europe and the world is to be considered, there is an implicit assumption that the Atlantic system was more important than relations along the long frontier between Europe and the Islamic world, particularly the Turkish empire. This was true for the later development of much of the world: oceanic range enabled the Western European maritime powers to impose, or seek to impose, on areas at a considerable distance, not only in the Atlantic world, both the 'New World' and the coasts of Africa, but also in India and more generally in coastal regions in Asia.

Nevertheless, for much of Europe, the crucial relationship was not across the oceans but far closer, along the fault-line between Christendom and Islam. From the modern perspective, this might appear anachronistic as, by 1913, the Turkish presence in Europe was restricted to a small area around Constantinople (Istanbul). By 1815, the empire, while still in control of much of the Balkans, was no longer able to threaten the rest of Europe. Instead, the partition of the empire had been actively debated for decades.

However, for much of the period covered by this book, the issue of Islamic, more particularly Turkish, power was more pressing. This was not simply a matter of the role of the past, although it is true that the Turks made very few acquisitions after 1660, and no medium-term gains after they annexed Podolia (part of the western Ukraine) from Poland in 1676. Nevertheless, the Turks had, within Europe, already made greater gains over the previous three centuries than any other power.

This failure to make fresh conquests conceals considerable vitality on the part of the Turks and an ability to thwart Christian European plans for their overthrow. In 1380–1500, they had gained control over Bulgaria, Wallachia (southern Romania), Constantinople, the Morea (the Peloponnese), Serbia, Bosnia, Albania and the Crimea. In the sixteenth century, Belgrade, Rhodes, Croatia, Hungary, Cyprus and overlordship over Moldavia and Transylvania followed. Vienna had been besieged, albeit unsuccessfully, in 1529. If the Turkish advance had essentially stopped in Europe in the mid-sixteenth century it had not been reversed, and it was not surprising that Christian Europe was in awe of the Turks.

The narrative chapters will consider the course of relations between Europe and Islamic neighbours and will do so without suggesting that they were a subsidiary adjunct to relations within Europe.

Instead, causal links were more complex and 'two-way' in character. The decision to include relations with Islamic neighbours within the narrative, rather than to deal with them separately, reflects an assessment not only that they cannot be helpfully segregated, but also that these relations form a central theme in international relations. This is more apparent since the end of the Cold War, which has encouraged a conception of Europe in which Eastern Europe does not play the secondary role it has generally been hitherto allocated. This ensures that European history has to be rethought.

At this point, a brief introductory overview would focus on the need to avoid determinism and teleology in the account of the Turks, and would draw attention to the implications of the contrast between Islamic and Christian state power in the zone of contact. Neither culture had a hegemonic power, for, within Islam, the position of the Ottoman Turkish empire was contested by that of Persia which, until the 1720s, was controlled by the Safavid dynasty. In addition, there was a series of other independent Islamic states, most prominently the Mughal empire in the Indian subcontinent and the empire of Morocco. However, although relations between Persia and Russia were important in the 1720s and 1730s and then again from the 1800s, the zone of contact on Europe's land frontiers was overwhelmingly with one empire, that of Turkey. The Europeans also lacked a hegemonic power, but, in contrast, had no single dominant power in the zone of contact.

In north-west Africa, Portugal and Spain both had coastal enclaves, and there was episodic conflict as Morocco and Algiers sought to take them. However, the situation was essentially static. The bold attempts at conquest in the late fifteenth and sixteenth centuries had been thwarted and were not revived. The situation did not change until the French seized Algiers in 1830. In the central Mediterranean, the Christian enclaves on the coasts of what are now Tunisia and Libya had been lost in the sixteenth century. The local Christian powers – the Kingdom of Naples and, more particularly, the Knights of Malta – sought to protect European trade but there was no programme of territorial conquest and, as in the western Mediterranean, no need to resist one.

The situation was very different in south-eastern Europe, but there the Turks were opposed by a number of Christian powers, at the outset, Venice, Austria, Poland and Russia. By 1720, it was a case of Austria and Russia, although from the 1780s and, more particularly, 1790s, greater French and British interest in the eastern Mediterranean led to a growing concern about the fate of the Turkish empire.

The role of a number of European powers ensured that developments in the Balkans interacted with shifts within European power politics. More particularly, territorial gains were not simply all made by one power. Had that been the case (and, even more, had this been true of expansion outside Europe), then Europe might well have been threatened by a hegemonic power. Indeed, part of the concern, from the 1770s and, even more, 1790s, about what was to be termed an Eastern Question stemmed from an anxiety that Russia would so dominate gains at the expense of the Turks that it would become too strong within Europe.

Similar concerns can also be seen in the case of expansion outside Europe. This is generally seen in terms of maritime activity, but that neglects Russia's position in North Asia. Although the dramatic period of expansion into and across Siberia had occurred in the last quarter of the sixteenth and the first half of the seventeenth centuries, thereafter the Russians consolidated and sought to expand their territories. This brought them into conflict in north-east Siberia, where the Itelmen and Koryaks were crushed but the Chukchi successfully resisted attack; and along the southern fringes of their possessions east of the Urals. Significant gains were made, but not to compare with the century before or after our period. The Khanates of Central Asia remained outside Russian control, and further east the Russians were bested by the Chinese. Attempts to hold the Amur valley were thwarted by Chinese advances in the 1680s and, by the Treaty of Nerchinsk of 1689, the Russians accepted the Chinese position. The situation was not to be reversed until 1859–60. Chinese regional predominance was further shown in 1695–1760 when, in a series of campaigns, the Chinese gained control of Mongolia, Xinjiang, Tibet and parts of Turkestan. Chinese ability to make and sustain such expansion is an interesting contrast to landward expansion by European powers within Europe: Austrian expansion at the expense of the Turks was more small-scale and was, in part, reversed.

Chinese expansion brought their sphere of control close to that of Russia, and represented a major success, for the Chinese, not the Russians, defeated the Dsungars of Xinjiang, while treaties between Russia and China deprived the Dsungars of the possibility of Russian support. The next powerful Central Asian people to the west, the Kazakhs, accepted tributary status and remained under Chinese influence until the mid-nineteenth century, when it was supplanted by Russian control.

In the eighteenth century, the Russians were also unsuccessful in gaining lasting benefit from the collapse of the Safavids in Persia. Peter the Great hoped to benefit from the disintegration of Persia at Afghan hands to gain control of the silk routes, annex territory and preempt Turkish expansion. Derbent fell to Peter in 1722, and Baku and Rasht to his subordinates the following year, and the Russians sought to create a permanent military imprint, for example, by the construction or improvement of forts and roads, so as to anchor and sustain their presence.

This proved a campaign too far. The Russians found that their gains to the west and south of the Caspian were of little use. Large numbers of garrison troops, possibly as many as 130,000 men, were lost through disease and, at a time of Persian revival under Nadir Shah, the lands to the south of the Caspian were ceded by the Russians in 1732. Although, in the nineteenth and twentieth centuries, the Russians would occupy parts of northern Persia on occasion, their best opportunity for creating a territorial presence there had been lost. Russia was not to benefit from the collapse of the Safavid empire – as Britain did from the collapse of Mughal power in India – and would face more resilient Persian governments thereafter.

A consideration of Russian policy in Asia underlines the degree to which the European powers were not the only expansive states in the world. In East and South Asia in particular, although also to a certain extent in Africa, the Europeans were not stronger or more successful than other powers on land, other than in a few areas; while in North America in the late seventeenth century the Iroquois confederation can be seen as just as dynamic as European powers. However, the extent to which it is helpful to read from successes or failures in particular areas in order to produce a general account of European relative capability is unclear. Any aggregate measure of achievement fails to address the multifaceted nature of European activity. In particular, it is probably mistaken to compare wars along Europe's land frontiers with those waged across the oceans. The latter in Asia and Africa, but not North America, had an episodic character that reflected both the role of decisions whether or not to attempt landward expansion or control from coastal enclaves, and the dominance of essentially commercial roles.

The central role of trade in the European presence in Africa and South and East Asia ensured that a set of values and relationships that did not focus on control or defence came into play; unlike along the land frontiers of Europe and European America. In both cases there was also a major contrast between the response to densely inhabited lands and that to those that were more sparsely populated. The establishment of an intensive structure and practice of control over the former involved serious problems. In India, it proved easier, more profitable and more necessary to create a European presence short of conquest than was the case in North America, Cape Colony and Australia. In the latter, the conquest of extensive, relatively lightly populated territories inhabited by people labelled as primitive was a long-term project, largely achieved by emigration of a large number of Europeans. Across much of the world, this process was more pronounced in the nineteenth century than earlier, although it can be seen in operation in the Russian steppe lands and near the east coast of North America in the seventeenth and eighteenth centuries.

These settlements are a reminder of the extent to which the most significant aspect of Europe's international relations was the conquest and, sometimes, settlement of large tracts of territory outside Europe that were eventually to give power, first to European states and second to European peoples. As a prelude to the narrative chapters, it is necessary to note briefly the extent of the European imprint at the outset of our period.

The first great European transoceanic imperial power was Portugal. In Asia, by 1600, there were Portuguese bases in Malacca, Macao, coastal parts of the East Indies (Indonesia), Ceylon (Sri Lanka) and India, and in the Persian Gulf at Bahrain, Hormuz and Muscat. Many of these bases were subsequently lost, however, especially to the Dutch who, by 1680, had seized the Portuguese positions in Sri Lanka and Malacca, and had established themselves in the East Indies, especially on Java. Although the Dutch, like the Portuguese, were a major trading power, the political impact of the Europeans on the major Asian territories was limited in the seventeenth century. The Spaniards had gained control of much of Luzon and had become the dominant power in the Philippines, while the English had established bases in India. The East India Company, the mercantile body that directed English interests there, had bases at Madras, Bombay and Calcutta by the end of the century. However, the European presence in Japan, coastal East Asia and South-East Asia was limited, while in India it was restricted to coastal enclaves that were vulnerable to local powers.

The European presence in Africa was mostly restricted to coastal bases, from many of which slaves were exported to the New World. Knowledge of the interior was slight. The Portuguese ruled coastal areas in Angola and Mozambique and, on the route to India, the French had settled the island of Réunion in 1642 and the Dutch Cape Town a decade later. Ambitious Portuguese schemes for penetration up the Zambezi into the area of modern Zimbabwe failed. In 1698, the Portuguese base of Fort Jesus at Mombasa fell to an Omani siege.

In the New World, Central America and the Caribbean were mostly under Spanish rule, although at Belize and on the Mosquito Coast (the Caribbean coast of modern Nicaragua) the English had a mainland presence. Furthermore, a number of islands belonged to other European powers, including England (Barbados, Jamaica, the Bahamas), France (Guadeloupe, Martinique, and St Domingue – modern Haiti), the United Provinces and Denmark. Most of coastal South America belonged to Spain or to the Portuguese colony of Brazil, although Patagonia, southern Chile and most of Uruguay were unsettled, and the last was becoming an area of conflict between the two powers. Large areas of the interior of South America, especially Amazonia, were under only nominal Portuguese or Spanish control. After the Dutch had been driven out of Brazil in the 1650s, the English, Dutch and French presence in South America was restricted to the Guiana coast.

In North America, most of the eastern seaboard was settled by the English, but the St Lawrence valley of modern Canada was controlled by the French and Florida was a Spanish colony, although most of Canada and Florida were under Native control. The Delaware Valley colony of New Sweden had been acquired by the Dutch colony of New Netherland in 1655 and that, in turn, had been seized by the English, New Amsterdam becoming New York. This was one of the results of the Anglo-Dutch Wars (1652–4, 1665–7, 1672–4). Although primarily motivated by European disputes, they had the important consequence of helping ensure the passing of Dutch maritime primacy.[1] Earlier French exploration in, and territorial claims to, the Mississippi Valley were followed in 1699 by a major expedition to Louisiana, the name, like those of some other colonies and settlements, an assertion of the dynastic presence.

All these developments were of great importance for the future, but it is necessary not to exaggerate the role of transoceanic concerns in European diplomacy. In the seventeenth century, struggles between

European powers were essentially neither wars of overseas expansion nor wars of trade, although both elements were crucial in the conflicts between the United Provinces and first Portugal and later England. As will be seen, colonies and transoceanic trade played a more major role in international relations in the second half of the eighteenth century and, as a consequence, naval strength became more significant.[2] However, it is inappropriate to push this point too far, as the transoceanic imperial powers remained greatly concerned about European power politics.[3]

As with the discussion in Chapter 2 of the role of aggression and territorial aggrandizement in relations within Europe, it is possible in Europe's relations with non-European powers to focus on a drive for European expansion; or, alternatively, to suggest that this was only one aspect of a more complex situation and one in which there was often a search for adjustment and mutual benefit. Parallels and contrasts between European international relations and those in other parts of the world focus on the contrast between the hegemonic position of China and, to a lesser extent, the Mughal empire as far as their neighbours were concerned, and the multipolar nature of Europe; although not by 1810, when Britain dominated the oceans, of the transoceanic European world. It can be argued, in Darwinian terms, that competitiveness within the European multipolar system led to a process of governmental efficiency by emulation that made European states more effective in global terms, with consequences for the expansion of their power in the age of nineteenth-century imperialism. For example, an action–reaction sequence can be seen in Prussia and Austria in the mid-eighteenth century with Austria improving its army and seeking to enhance its governmental modernity and effectiveness in response to Prussian successes. Similarly, Prussia responded to defeat by Napoleon with reform programmes, which encompassed military, governmental, economic and political change. However, the applicability of this model to Europe's relations with the remainder of the world is unclear, and it is also uncertain how far it is helpful to focus simply on the multipolar–unipolar contrast when assessing international systems and their consequences.

Chapter 6

The Late Seventeenth Century 1648–99

Before 1648

Although there is often reference to turning points, no period in history can be discussed without reference to what had come earlier, and this is also the case with supposed turning points which only take on meaning in the context of change. The rulers, ministers and others who considered international relations from 1648 were affected by earlier experiences and perceptions. Furthermore, what happened from 1648 onward in part derives its meaning as well as cause from previous developments.

In the sixteenth century, a series of transformations had major impacts on political relations. These included the Protestant Reformation, the advance of the Turks, the impact of the creation of European empires in the New World, especially the flow of bullion to Spain, and a profound socioeconomic shift characterized by a major rise in population after nearly two centuries of decline or stagnation, and by inflation. The resulting strains affected social and political relations within states, helping to make them more volatile, and also interacted with developments in international relations. However, the distinction between the two is less than clear-cut, particularly in the Empire, but also in states that won independence through rebellion (the United Provinces) and in those that failed (Ireland). The quasi-hegemonic position of the Habsburgs in Western and Central Europe created by the Emperor Charles V in the 1520s–40s fell victim in the 1550s to an alliance of Henry II of France with some of the German Protestant princes. Charles's son, Philip II of Spain, benefited from French weakness during the French Wars of Religion (1562–98) and overran Portugal after the king died, but was unable to suppress rebellion in the Low Countries or to overcome the opposition of Elizabeth I of England.

In Northern Europe, the Union of Kalmar, which had bound Denmark, Norway, Sweden and Finland together under one crown since 1397, finally collapsed in 1523 and in its place two opposing states, Denmark–Norway and Sweden–Finland, competed for hegemony. The expansion of Muscovite power towards the Baltic interacted with the question of the fate of the extensive lands of the crusading orders, the Teutonic Knights and the Livonian Order, as a result of the Reformation. Extensive warfare left the Swedes with Estonia, and the Poles with Livonia. Poland, Lithuania and the Ukraine had formed a union in 1569, and appeared the strongest power in Eastern Europe after the Turks. In 1611, the Poles captured Smolensk when they intervened in Russia during the Time of Troubles (1604–13) caused by a disputed succession. The struggle for domination in the Baltic was to remain unresolved into the eighteenth century.

In the first half of the seventeenth century, much of Europe was convulsed in the Thirty Years' War (1618–48), which was in fact a combination of a number of different but related struggles. The most important was the attempt by the Austrian Habsburgs to resist the challenge to their authority in their lands, particularly Austria and Bohemia, and to gain greater control within the Empire. The war initially began as a reaction against Habsburg authority in Bohemia. The Protestants there turned to Frederick V, Elector Palatine, a leading Protestant prince of the Empire, and elected him king. In 1620, Bohemia was invaded by larger forces and its army crushed at the battle of the White Mountain. Habsburg authority was then reimposed and Bohemia was Catholicized. At the same time, Spanish troops from the Army of Flanders overran Frederick's Rhineland territories in order to protect the communication routes between the Spanish bases in north Italy and the Spanish Netherlands known as the 'Spanish Road'. These were crucial because in 1621 the Twelve Years' Truce between Spain and the Dutch came to an end and war resumed. The Dutch encouraged opposition to the Habsburgs in Germany, but it was defeated, in 1626, as was intervention on the Protestant side by Christian IV of Denmark who sought Catholic prince bishoprics in north-west Germany. The Danes were forced out of the war in 1629.

The Habsburg Emperor, Ferdinand II, then dominated the Empire, but he failed to use this period to win support and consolidate his position and was challenged by Gustavus Adolphus of Sweden (1611–32). This warrior monarch had spent his early years fighting Denmark (1611–13), Russia (1611–17) and Poland (1617–18, 1621–9), but, in the late 1620s, he became increasingly concerned about growing Habsburg power on the German shores of the Baltic.

Gustavus was encouraged to act by France. Poor relations between France and Spain were not inevitable. The two powers had maintained passable relations in the 1610s, and the French had done nothing to help the Bohemian rebellion. After 1624, however, when the anti-Habsburg Cardinal Richelieu became the leading minister of Louis XIII (1610–43), relations deteriorated. Although French Protestantism was destroyed as a politico-military force in 1627–9, abroad Richelieu was eager to ally with Protestant powers in order to cripple the Habsburgs. France and Spain fought the War of the Mantuan Succession (1628–31) over control of northern Italy.

To undermine Habsburg dominance of the Empire, Richelieu encouraged Gustavus to invade in 1630. He did so, reversing the Habsburg success of recent years, but was killed at the battle of Lützen in 1632. The initiative then passed to the Habsburgs. At Nördlingen in 1634, a joint Austro-Spanish army defeated the Swedes, leading to the Peace of Prague of 1635 by which Saxony, which had allied with Sweden in 1631, now abandoned her. Most of the German Protestant princes were now reconciled to the Emperor, and the war was increasingly one in which foreign powers contended with each other on the soil of Germany.

Worried about Habsburg success, France entered the war in 1635, and began a gruelling struggle in which it was not possible to win a decisive victory. Louis XIII and Richelieu had hoped to achieve this over Spain in one campaign. Like Philip IV of Spain (1621–65) and his first minister, the Count-Duke of Olivares, they did not seek a lengthy or attritional war. However, it proved impossible to create the large armies required to achieve the bold strategic plans that were devised. Armies were badly affected by supply problems and desertion. In 1636, the Spaniards invaded France, advancing as far as Amiens and Corbie. This invasion showed the vulnerability of France to attack from the Spanish Netherlands and caused great anxiety there, but it failed to overthrow Richelieu. After Corbie, the French launched attacks into the Spanish Netherlands, conquering Artois with the fall of Arras in 1640. Breisach was captured in 1638: its fall cut the 'Spanish Road' and opened the way into Germany. Perpignan, the capital of Roussillon, fell in 1642. The French were helped by rebellions in the Spanish empire, particularly in Catalonia (1640) and Portugal (1640), as the financial burdens of the war interacted with strong regional antipathy to rule from Madrid and to its attempts to share the cost of the conflict.

The period 1638–48 is commonly presented in terms of French triumphs, especially the victory at Rocroi over the Spaniards in 1643; but these victories were offset by defeats and logistical problems. Furthermore, the consequences of Rocroi have usually been exaggerated: the Spaniards speedily regrouped. After the mid-1640s, it was not so much that the French suffered defeats, but rather that they failed to make much progress: certainly they made insufficient headway to defeat Spain before France's heavily indebted finances collapsed. Despite major efforts in the mid-1640s, the Spaniards resisted French attacks and the French were unable to exploit anti-Spanish rebellions in Palermo and Naples in 1647.

The conflict in Germany was meanwhile drawing to a close. The second half of the Thirty Years' War has never seemed as dramatic and important as the first, but this is misleading. In 1636, the Swedes were nearly driven back to the Baltic, but in 1639 they advanced as far as Prague. In 1643–5, Sweden overwhelmed Denmark in a conflict that showed how decisive warfare could sometimes be. Joint Franco-Swedish operations succeeded in 1645–8 in defeating the Austrians and Bavarians in southern Germany, and, as the war ended, the Swedes were besieging Prague. The French had fought on against the Emperor until the Swedes had achieved their goals.

The Peace of Westphalia 1648

The treaties that ended the war were signed at Münster and Osnabrück, and are collectively known as the Peace of Westphalia. The Austrian Habsburgs were left in secure control of their hereditary lands, and they were not to lose Bohemia until their empire collapsed in 1918. The Swedes gained much of Pomerania, as well as the ecclesiastical principalities of Bremen and Verden; these gains brought control over the estuaries of the Elbe, Oder and Weser, and consolidated

Sweden's position as the leading Baltic power. Brandenburg-Prussia also gained much territory, and emerged ahead of Saxony as the leading north German Protestant state. France gained control over much of Alsace. Calvinism was accepted as a permitted religion in the Holy Roman Empire. France and Sweden were made guarantors of the peace, and thus given opportunities to intervene in German politics. The war had caused terrible devastation in Germany, but the religious and political compromise it brought helped to lessen conflict within Germany for nearly a century.[1] The major efforts made by German rulers to fight France and the Turks in this period suggest that it is wrong to claim that the war had exhausted Germany.

The Westphalian settlement is frequently seen as the beginning of the modern state system and of modern international relations. This owes much to the acceptance in the treaty that German princes were free to pursue their own foreign policy, which marked an effective end to the pretensions of unity provided by the Holy Roman Empire. The decline of the Imperial ideal has been seen as a transition from medievalism to modernity. The Westphalian state system and the Westphalian notion of sovereignty are terms that have been extensively used since the early 1990s. They hinge on the idea that the individual state is a sovereign body answerable to none, and are thus contrasted to supranational institutions and theories, such as those propounded by liberal universalists in the 1990s and those supposedly advanced by exponents of Imperial ideas prior to 1648.[2]

This analysis places too much weight on the changes brought by Westphalia. First, effective autonomy had long existed within the Empire, second, the process of Imperial disunity and the effective sovereignty of individual princes had been greatly advanced as a result of the Reformation, and, third, the changes should be seen as an adaptation of a weak federal system, rather than as a turning point. Many of the German states were too small to pursue seriously an independent foreign policy, and this, in part, explained the continued role and importance of the Emperor and the Empire. In addition, the treaty allowed princes to ally amongst themselves and with foreign powers to ensure their preservation and security, in other words, not for offensive purposes and only on condition that the alliances were not directed against the Emperor, the Empire or the terms of the treaty. In theory, this was an important limitation that ensured that the princes did not gain sovereignty as understood in the nineteenth century.

Franco-Spanish conflict 1648–59

The Franco-Spanish struggle was not ended by the Peace of Westphalia. The French lost much ground when Spain took advantage of the Fronde, the French civil wars of 1648–53. These arose from the unpopularity of the ministry of Richelieu's successor, Cardinal Mazarin, an unpopularity that owed much to the taxation and other burdens produced by the war. Allied with the Prince of Condé, one of the leaders of the Fronde, the Spaniards were able to retake French gains, such as Dunkirk, Gravelines and Ypres. In Italy, the fortresses of Porto Longone and Piombino were regained in 1650 and Casale in 1652. The Spaniards also regained Catalonia, with Barcelona falling in 1652, after a fourteen-month blockade had reduced the population to starvation. However, Spain's attempt to intervene directly in the Fronde, by invading Gascony in order to help Mazarin's opponents in Bordeaux, was a failure.

The end of the Fronde brought little improvement in French prospects, although a Spanish attempt to regain Arras in 1654 was unsuccessful. The Spaniards captured Rocroi that year. Defeats at Pavia in 1655 and Valenciennes in 1656 led France to offer reasonable peace terms, only for Philip IV to reject them. The French demand that the peace include the marriage of Louis XIV with Philip IV's daughter, Maria Teresa, then first in line in the succession, was unacceptable. Valenciennes was a spectacular victory in which the French baggage train and supplies were captured, but it does not enjoy the fame of Rocroi in 1643 because it does not fit in with the conventional view of the inevitable decline of Spain and rise of France. In northern Italy, Pavia was followed by the overrunning of the Duchy of Modena whose Duke had abandoned Spain and encouraged Mazarin to invade Lombardy. In 1657, Spain had more successes in Lombardy.[3]

The war ended only after the intervention of fresh English forces on the side of France, under an alliance signed in 1657, had tipped the balance in Flanders. Oliver Cromwell's Ironsides helped Turenne to defeat the Army of Flanders at the Battle of the Dunes. Turenne went on to capture Dunkirk, Gravelines, Menin and Ypres, and to threaten an advance on Brussels.

This led to the Peace of the Pyrenees of 7 November (1659), signed at the Isle of Pheasants at the western end of the mountain chain. France made valuable gains, principally Artois and Roussillon, but the peace was more of a compromise than is usually appreciated: the French had failed to drive the Spaniards from the Low Countries or Italy as had been planned. The Spanish empire remained the largest in Western Europe. The marriage of Louis XIV and Maria Teresa was now acceptable as Philip had had a son, a reminder of the role of dynastic fortune. As an indication of the extent to which policy was debated and thus of the danger of treating states as unproblematic building blocks, there was opposition to the negotiations by the Queen of Spain, who wanted Maria Teresa to marry Emperor Leopold I, and by courtiers concerned to secure better terms for Condé.[4] Dunkirk was ceded to England, only for the recently restored Charles II to sell it to Louis XIV in 1662.

Conflict from the Ukraine to the Baltic

Further east, the 1650s saw a revival of the struggle to dominate the Baltic that had last been intense in the eastern Baltic in the 1620s and between Denmark and Sweden in the 1640s. These rivalries were of more wide-ranging importance because the Baltic was the principal source of 'naval stores' – flax, hemp, pitch, tar and timber – for Western Europe, and also a major supplier of copper, grain and iron. England and the Dutch had major commercial interests in the Baltic, and both generally sought to maintain the peace there, and to prevent either of the two regional maritime powers – Denmark and Sweden – from dominating the sea.

Baltic developments were also closely linked to those in Poland, and thus to the expanding crisis that had begun when the Cossacks of the Ukraine, part of the Polish state, rebelled in the winter of 1647–8. In 1654, at Perejaslaw, Tsar Alexis took the Dnieper Cossacks under his protection, and moved his troops into the Ukraine. He also set out to conquer Belarus, but victory led him to expand his objectives. Having captured Smolensk in 1654, Alexis set out to seize Lithuania in 1655: Vilna and Grodno fell and Alexis offered protection to Danzig (Gdańsk). Another army invaded Galicia and threatened Lvov. There was a strong religious element in the conflict. Russian troops were sprinkled with holy water and fought under holy banners, officers were ordered to take communion, and Orthodox churches were built in captured towns.

In 1655, Charles X of Sweden (1654–60) attacked Poland in order to make gains, particularly on her Baltic coast, from a state that appeared to be collapsing before the advancing Russian armies.

Warsaw and Cracow fell to the Swedes in 1655. However, Livonia, gained by the Swedes from Poland in 1629, tempted Alexis, who attacked Sweden in 1656. He besieged the great Livonian port of Riga, one of the major centres of Baltic trade, but without success. In 1658, faced with Polish and Tatar attacks and trouble in the Ukraine, where the Cossacks, concerned about Russian policy, sought to rejoin Poland, Alexis abandoned his hopes of a Baltic seaport and signed a truce with Sweden. It also became clear that the Polish throne would elude him. By the Treaty of Kardis of 1661, Alexis was obliged to accept the Swedish position. Livonia was restored to Sweden.

The previous year, by the Peace of Oliva, Sweden had had to abandon Charles X's Polish adventure, while the Duchy of Prussia was confirmed to Brandenburg as a sovereign possession. Charles had faced not simply the intractability of campaigning in Poland but also the enmity of Denmark and the determination of England and the Dutch to prevent Sweden's domination of the Baltic; although Swedish victory over Denmark led, under the Treaty of Roskilde of 1658, to the permanent gain of the Danish territories on the eastern side of the Sound in what is now southern Sweden. Conflict in the Baltic would revive in the 1670s, but, although important, the Baltic was over-shadowed for the remainder of the century by developments in the Balkans.[5]

The Peace of Oliva enabled the Poles to concentrate their efforts against Russia, which they did successfully in the early 1660s. However, Poland was affected by fiscal exhaustion and political discontent, culminating in a civil war in 1665–6. This led in 1667 to a thirteen-year truce with Russia agreed at Andrusovo: Alexis kept Smolensk and took the eastern Ukraine, while the Poles were to retain the western Ukraine.

The Turkish Question

In the first half of the seventeenth century, the Turks had been heavily engaged in war with Persia (modern Iran), but the end of this conflict enabled Mohammed IV (1649–87), and the energetic grand viziers of the Köprülü family whom he appointed, to direct their attention to their Christian neighbours. The long war with Venice begun in 1646 was brought to a successful conclusion with the fall of Crete in 1669. Furthermore, Turkish authority in Transylvania (in modern north-west

Romania) was made more effective as a result of a war in 1658–61. Austrian intervention in Transylvania in 1661 was unsuccessful and led to war with the Turks in 1663. A Turkish attack that year was repelled. The following year, the Grand Vizier, Fazil Ahmet, advanced into Austria, but was met near St Gotthard by an Austrian force under Montecuccoli, supported by German contingents, and by French troops sent by Louis XIV. The Turkish forces, prevented from advancing across the river Raab, lost their cannon, but avoided a rout. The war was terminated swiftly by the Peace of Vasvar (1664), with an Austrian agreement to respect the Turkish position in Transylvania and to pay a tribute. This reflected the Emperor Leopold I's lack of confidence about any forward policy in Hungary. The Austrian army was clearly capable of defensive operations, but there was doubt about the ability of both Austria and its army to sustain a major war.

Had conflict rapidly resumed, then Leopold would have found it difficult to resist Louis XIV in Western Europe, for Austrian commitments across Europe brought an important measure of interconnectedness. Instead, in 1671, the Turks attacked Poland. As a result, Montecuccoli was able to devote his energies in 1673 to outmanoeuvring French forces in the Rhineland.

The Ukrainian rebellion, and the consequent increase of Russian influence, had destroyed the regional balance of power and created in the Ukraine a vortex that drew in the great powers. Initially very successful, the Turks, under Mohammed IV, captured the major fortress of Kamieniec Podolski on the Dniester in 1672. Its cathedral was turned into a mosque. By the Peace of Buczacz (1672), King Michael of Poland (1669–74) recognized Turkish suzerainty over the western Ukraine and promised a large annual tribute. However, Polish resistance stiffened when John Sobieski, who had rejected the treaty, defeated the Turks and became king in 1674. The Peace of Zuravno of 1676 still saw the Turks emerge with the gain of Podolia, a large territory stretching from the Dniester to the Dnieper that increased their ability to intervene in Poland and the Ukraine.

The disturbed state of the Ukraine and Turkish opposition to the Russian control of Kiev and Left Bank Ukraine (east of the Dnieper) encouraged the Turks and their Crimean allies to invade the eastern Ukraine and attack the Russians in 1677. The major Dnieper fortress of Chigirin was besieged, but resisted long enough to permit the arrival of a relieving army. The following year, the Turks advanced again, and this time the Russians were forced to evacuate Chigirin, blowing up the fortress during their retreat.

Traditional Russian musketeer units, the *streltsy*, fared badly in these campaigns, and the artillery, though numerous, was ill-equipped and mismanaged. But the Russians fought hard and limited the Turkish advance. At the price of an annual tribute to the Khan of the Crimean Tatars, a Turkish vassal, Russia retained Kiev and Left Bank Ukraine in the Treaty of Kakhchisarai (1681).

The Turks were already planning to concentrate their resources against Austria. A revolt in those parts of Western Hungary ruled by the Habsburgs encouraged the Grand Vizier, Kara Mustafa, to begin aiding the rebels and to recognize their leader, Count Imre Thököly, as Prince of Middle Hungary; he, in turn, agreed to become a vassal of the Sultan and thus to extend a system of Turkish buffer states. Worried about the prospect of French attack on the Rhine, the Habsburgs were reluctant to fight the Turks, but French agents encouraged Kara Mustafa to march on Vienna by promising that France would not aid Austria, as it had done in 1664.

The Turks used the winter of 1682–3 to assemble their forces and the main contingent left Adrianople on 31 March, advancing rapidly through occupied Hungary in June. Kara Mustafa, at the head of about 100,000 troops, appeared before Raab (Györ), the key to the Austrian military frontier, on 2 July, but, instead of besieging it and other fortresses near the frontier, determined, without the approval of the Sultan, to march directly on Vienna. As panic mounted, Leopold and his court left Vienna on 7 July, retreating to Passau, while Turkish raiders devastated the surrounding countryside. The Austrians had intended to defend the line of the river Leitha, but were thwarted by the rapid Turkish advance.

The defence of Vienna was left to Count Ernst Rüdiger von Starhemberg, who had the suburbs burnt to deny the Turkish troops cover. The army surrounded the city on 16 July and began building siegeworks. They also launched a series of increasingly successful assaults. The garrison suffered heavy casualties, as well as losses from dysentery. The Turks suffered similarly, but, during August, the city's outer defences steadily succumbed, although, lacking heavy-calibre cannon, the Turks were outgunned and forced to rely on undermining the defences. There was bitter fighting in the breaches and, on 4 September, Starhemberg fired distress rockets to urge the relief army to action.

This army had built up as Leopold I sought general support and Pope Innocent XI (1676–89) pressed all Catholics to unite in a crusade. John Sobieski of Poland brought a large contingent, assumed overall command and advanced through the Vienna woods. Kara Mustafa was aware of this deployment, but made scant preparation for an attack.

On 12 September, the relieving army descended from the hills and defeated the Turks. By the end of the day, Kara Mustafa was in retreat towards Györ. He was punished for his failure by strangulation, while Christian Europe celebrated the relief of its most prominent bulwark.

There will not be space in this book to give more than brief mention to most campaigns and battles, although they were as important as negotiations and treaties in determining the course of international relations. Nevertheless, the Vienna campaign is worthy of note, because it makes clear how inevitability is inappropriate in the discussion of military success. Rather than seeing one military system as necessarily superior to another, it is important to focus on how forces were used and to note the range of factors that affected success. In the case of 1683, divisions among the Turkish commanders, that reflected an absence of common purpose and reliable command structures, played a major role. Murat Giray, the Khan of the Crimean Tatars, distrusted the Grand Vizier and deliberately did nothing to prevent the Christian forces from crossing the Danube. The Turkish right flank abandoned the subsequent battle.[6]

Suleiman the Magnificent's failure when he besieged Vienna in 1529 had been a check, but not a disaster. Kara Mustafa's, in contrast, led to the loss of Hungary and a major change in power relations within Europe. In 1683, it was followed up by an advance by Christian forces along the Danube and their capture of Gran. The following March, Leopold, Sobieski, Innocent XI and Venice formed a Holy League, which Russia joined in 1686. Those who urged Leopold to concentrate on the challenge from Louis XIV were overruled. The creation of this major offensive alliance was an important achievement, which had eluded many earlier opponents of the Turks, such as Tsar Alexis in the 1670s. Further assistance was contributed by German rulers, especially Max Emmanuel of Bavaria and John George of Saxony. The cooperation that had led to the relief of Vienna was sustained, while the Turkish war enabled Leopold to fortify the Habsburg role as the defender of Christendom and the Empire, and increased Imperial loyalty in Germany.

The conquest of Hungary is sometimes presented as the creation of a Danubian monarchy and a turning away from the Imperial role. However, at least initially, it represented and sustained traditional notions of Imperial action. The general support the Habsburgs received in the Empire in 1685–1740, a marked contrast to the early seventeenth century, reflected not only the decline in religious rivalry, so that Protestant rulers were willing to lead forces to help the Emperor, and the opposition to Louis XIV, but also the bonding of Emperor and Empire in the Turkish wars.

In 1684, Austrian forces under Charles of Lorraine besieged Buda, the key to Hungary, but the fortress was strong, and disease and supply difficulties hampered the four-month siege which was eventually abandoned. In 1685, however, Thököly's position in Upper Hungary was undermined. The Turks sued for peace, but would not accept the Austrian terms which required a withdrawal from Hungary.

In 1686, Buda was again attacked. A shell landed on the main powder magazine, blowing open a breach in the walls. Repeated assaults then led to the fall of the city after a brave defence. In 1689, Charles of Lorraine defeated the Grand Vizier, Suleiman Pasha, at Berg Harsan (Harkány). Esseg then fell, while the cumulative pressure of defeat led to a rebellion which drove Mohammed IV from his throne. Charles advanced into Transylvania and took control of its major forts. The Transylvanian Diet designated Leopold I 'hereditary King of Hungary', and, in September 1688, the Imperial Army, under the control of Max Emmanuel, captured Belgrade, which had been held by the Turks since 1521. The collapse of the Ottoman position in the Balkans and an Austrian advance into the Greek Orthodox world appeared imminent. The Turks began peace talks, but the Austrian terms – the complete surrender of Hungary and Transylvania and the dismantling of Turkish fortresses in Wallachia (modern southern Romania) – were unacceptable.

The Austrians developed links with rebellious Bulgarians and Serbs and began negotiations with the Prince of Wallachia, a client-ruler of the Turks. In 1689, Ludwig Wilhelm of Baden defeated the main Turkish army south of Belgrade and advanced to Nish. The Austrians pressed on to seize Vidin, Pristina and Skopje, and to reach Bucharest. The Serbian Patriarch of Pec was persuaded to take an oath of loyalty to Leopold, who, in April 1690, issued an appeal for the support of all Balkan peoples against the Turks and promised them liberty, under his rule as King of Hungary.

The late 1680s and early 1690s may have represented the best opportunity for driving the Turks out of all or most of the Balkans prior to the late nineteenth century. The Turkish empire and army were in chaos and faced by a powerful coalition. In this perspective, the crucial blow that saved the Turks was Louis XIV's invasion of the Rhineland in 1688, which distracted Austrian and German resources.

However, it is by no means clear that the advance of Austrian troops in 1689 indicated imminent Turkish collapse. Austrian and allied forces confronted formidable logistical problems, and the maintenance of large forces south of the lower Danube would have exacerbated these. Turkish resilience was more important than Austrian problems in explaining the failure of Austria to conquer more territory. More generally, the alacrity with which historians have used the concept of decline to categorize several 'states' in this period, particularly Poland, Spain and Turkey, is unhelpful. The Spanish empire was still the largest in the world in 1700, and in 1800. The Turkish empire took longer to disintegrate than the later Western European-based transoceanic empires.

The oscillating nature of Turkish fortunes at the end of the seventeenth century indicated the importance of leadership. The chaos that greeted Suleiman II (1687–91), including rebellious janissary troops in the capital and provincial disturbances, was quashed and a new grand vizier from the Köprülü family, Fazil Mustafa (1689–91), helped to restore order to the army and the central government. From 1688, the Austrians were distracted by the resumption of war in Western Europe, while the Orthodox population of areas now open to Catholicization by the Austrians was becoming restless. In 1690, there was a revolt in Transylvania, and most Austrian troops had to be withdrawn to face France. That year, Fazil Mustafa recaptured Nish and Belgrade after a short siege. Many of the Orthodox Serbs who had turned to Leopold fled north. In 1691, Fazil was killed in a major defeat at Zalánkemén that ended Turkish hopes of recapturing Hungary, but Austrian chances in Serbia and Wallachia were over. They now had heavy commitments against Louis XIV in northern Italy and the Rhineland.

Conflict over the next few years was indecisive and difficult, because of improved fortifications, the depletion of local sources of supply and the problems of fighting in undrained marshy lowlands. The Austrians recaptured Grosswardein in 1692, but in 1693 were forced to raise the siege of Belgrade. Matters moved to a climax after the energetic Mustafa II (1695–1703) replaced Ahmed II (1691–5). In 1695, he stormed Lippa and relieved Temesvár, and in 1696 outmanoeuvred the Austrian forces. However, the end of the war with France in Italy in 1696 enabled Leopold to transfer more troops and his rising general, Eugène of Savoy, to Hungary. At Zenta, in 1697, the Turks under Mustafa were caught by Eugène in the vulnerable position of crossing the river Tisza and routed with possibly 30,000 casualties. Although the victory was followed by a raid into Bosnia and the sacking of Sarajevo, the lateness of the campaigning season, combined with heavy rains, sickness and logistical problems, ensured that there were no significant gains that year.

In theory, the end of the Nine Years' War with France in 1697 should have released Austrian resources to resume the conquest of the Balkans, but victories won after several years' campaigning were rarely as decisive in creating new opportunities as those, such as Vienna in 1683, gained near the beginning of a war. The retention of Hungary appeared a viable goal, but not the conquest of the Balkans. In 1698, the Turkish forces refused to engage, while Eugène's army was affected by a mutiny caused by a lack of funds.

Furthermore, the shifts in European diplomacy that were likely to follow peace demanded Leopold's attention, especially as the disputed Spanish succession appeared more imminent. Peace in Western Europe also made French pressure on the Turks to continue the war less effective. In addition to unrealistic demands from both sides, this pressure had helped to thwart peace negotiations in 1688–9 and 1692–4. However, when, after the Treaty of Rijswijk of 1697, the French envoy promised that France would resume fighting Austria when Charles II of Spain died, his inability to offer documentary proof of French promises led the Turks to ignore the French overture.

The other attacks on the Turks were subsidiary strikes. Venice attacked the Turks in Bosnia, Dalmatia, Greece and the Aegean. An invasion of Bosnia was routed in 1685, but landings on the Dalmatian coast, initially repelled in 1685–7, were subsequently more successful, leading to Venetian gains. An anti-Turkish revolt in the Morea (the Peloponnese) was exploited by Venetian amphibious forces in 1685–6; Koron, Kalmata, Modon, Nauplia and Navarino fell and, in 1687, the Venetians moved north to capture Athens, Lepanto and Patras: the Turkish magazine in the Parthenon in Athens was blown up by a mortar shell. Thereafter, there were no lasting gains: the Venetians were unsuccessful on Euboea in 1689 and Crete in 1692, and, although they captured Chios in 1694, the unpopularity of their rule led to an uprising and their expulsion the following year.

The Poles campaigned in Podolia and Moldavia and, after Sobieski died in 1696, Austria and Russia cooperated to ensure that the Prince of Conti, the French candidate for the succession, was beaten by Frederick Augustus I of Saxony, who became Augustus II of Poland, in 1697. This failure prevented the breaching of the anti-Turkish alliance, for a protégé of Louis could be expected to support the Turks. Augustus's conversion to Catholicism in order to secure the Polish throne indicated the importance of religious issues in furthering domestic goals and, therefore, international power.

Confirmation in 1686 of the Andrusovo terms in a Treaty of Eternal Peace with Poland helped direct Russian attention southwards, encouraged by the fear that otherwise Russia would gain nothing from Turkish weakness. The Polish envoy was subsequently accused of having exceeded his instructions, but the Poles, who needed the promised Russian attack on the Tatars, were not in a position to challenge the treaty. In 1687 and 1689, Russian armies under Prince Golitsyn, the lover and chief minister of Alexis's daughter Sophia (regent 1682–9), advanced on the Crimea only to be thwarted by logistical problems and Tatar resistance, including scorched-earth policies. The failure of the 1689 offensive helped to ensure the overthrow of Sophia by her half-brother Peter (Peter I, the Great). This was followed by several years of relative inactivity, with the consequent danger that Russia would be ignored in the peace negotiations and possibly subsequently exposed to Turkish attack.

Under Peter, Russian attention shifted from the Crimea to the more vulnerable city of Azov, at the mouth of the river Don. Although in 1695 the forts at the mouth of the river Dnieper were captured, Peter's lengthy siege of Azov that year failed, partly because of the Turks' ability to reinforce Azov by sea. Peter returned the following year, and built a navy on the river Don with the help of which he was able to take Azov. He ordered the construction of a naval base at nearby Taganrog. Peter aimed to establish Russian power on the northern shores of the Black Sea. In 1697, he reached an agreement with Leopold I and Venice by which they agreed to continue the war until the Turks yield to Russia the port of Kerch, which controls the passage between the Sea of Azov and the Black Sea.

However, the negotiation of peace led to the unravelling of the alliance. Austria was the major beneficiary of the Treaty of Karlowitz (1699), the product of negotiations held under Anglo-Dutch mediation. The Austrians gained all Hungary except the Banat of Temesvár, which they had failed to conquer. An Austrian threat to resume hostilities led the Turks to abandon their demand for an Austrian evacuation of Transylvania and its reversion to its earlier autonomous status. Poland returned its conquests in Moldavia in return for the cession of Podolia. Turkish threats to reopen hostilities, Austrian pressure and the fear of isolation led Venice to abandon her gains on the northern shore of the Gulf of Corinth, and to content herself with the Morea and part of Dalmatia.

Peter I was unwilling to negotiate at Karlowitz and his envoy, instructed to demand Kerch which the Turks would not yield, was obliged to accept a two-year truce rather than a peace settlement. Peter failed to better his position and, in 1700, a peace was concluded under which he gained Azov, but not Kerch, and had to evacuate the newly erected fortresses on the lower Dnieper. Peter's demand for Kerch was unrealistic in light of the widespread use of the principle of *uti possidetis* (retaining what was held) in the treaty and the limited need of Russian cooperation for Leopold once the Turkish war had ended. Peter's gains did not compare to those of Leopold I. This reflected Russian failures in the late 1680s and inaction in the early 1690s, and also a lack of diplomatic clout.

Hungary had not been crucial to the Turkish economy, but its loss diminished Turkish prestige, and thus diplomatic credibility, while enhancing that of the Austrian Habsburgs. The new territories were devastated by war and their integration into the pluralistic structure of the Habsburg territories was to be delayed by rebellion in the 1700s. Nevertheless, the gain of Hungary was important not only because it provided security for the other territories and limited the feasibility of enlisting Eastern European powers against the Habsburgs, but also because Hungary was eventually to become a source of manpower and wealth. In the short term, it offered a prospect of further conquests. There was no reason to believe that future wars would not bring more gains. Whereas, in Western Europe, acquisitions by the Austrian Habsburgs were limited by dynastic circumstances, contested by the Bourbons and, to a considerable extent, dependent on the support of other rulers, in the Balkans the constraints were fewer. As yet, Russia did not appear to pose a challenge to the Habsburg claim and hope to act as the liberator of the Balkans.

The British Isles

Compared to Eastern Europe, territorial changes in the western half in the second half of the seventeenth century were modest. Scholarly attention commonly focuses on French policy under Louis XIV

(1643–1715). This is understandable as France was the most populous state in Western Europe and had the largest army. Furthermore, Louis XIV dominated contemporary attention. Important as France was in this period, however, changes in the British Isles were more significant. In the 1650s, unity was enforced by the New Model Army under Oliver Cromwell. Having tried and executed Charles I in 1649, England was declared a republic. In a tremendous display of military power, which contrasted with the indecisiveness of much conflict on the Continent, the republican forces conquered Ireland (1649–52), a success which had eluded English monarchs throughout history, and Scotland (1650–2), as well as the remaining English Royalist bases in the Channel Islands, the Isles of Scilly and the Isle of Man. Largely as a result of subsequent famine, plague and emigration, the conquest led to the loss of 40 per cent of the Irish population, and was followed by widespread expropriation of Catholic land as the Anglo-Irish Catholics lost power and status.

This 'achievement' was repeated in 1689–91 after William III of Orange seized power in England in 1688–9, driving James II (and VII of Scotland) from the throne. Scotland and Ireland did not fall so easily and, instead, provided support for James. Scottish Jacobites were initially successful, but their position collapsed in 1690–1. William III invaded Ireland in 1690 and defeated James at the river Boyne. After the defeat at Aughrim the following year, the remaining Jacobite positions fell.

These civil wars may not seem relevant for a book on international relations, but it is important not to assume that these relations should be seen in terms of a clear and obvious grouping of states. In the case of the British Isles, there was a struggle between a government based in southern England and resistance elsewhere. The former sought to monopolize sovereignty and diplomatic representation, and thus to treat what might otherwise be seen as international relations as internal affairs. Resistance provided opportunities to foreign opponents of the government, particularly France and Spain.

The consolidation of governmental authority in the British Isles was to be reaffirmed with the parliamentary Union of England and Scotland in 1707 and with the defeat of Jacobite uprisings in 1715–16 and 1745–6. This consolidation ensured that the British state enjoyed relatively safe control of an expanded home base, and this was an important help to British opposition to the Bourbons in a series of eighteenth-century wars. Thus, conflict on the 'periphery' of Europe, or at least of what can be seen as an European states system, helped to strengthen states – Austria and Britain – that were able to resist French policy within Europe.

Louis XIV 1661–71

French policy is usually discussed in terms of Louis XIV's aggression, but it is also necessary to note French anxieties about Spanish power.[7] Spanish security appeared to depend on French weakness, a situation that encouraged the French desire to harm Spain. In the 1520s, and from the 1560s, Spain had been able and willing to encourage disaffection within France, and thus to challenge the power of the crown, its ability to wage war and the appearance of stability that was so important to a successful foreign policy. In 1585, Philip II of Spain allied with the Guise family, the leaders of the Catholic League in France, in the Treaty of Joinville, and from 1648 Philip IV provided support for those aristocrats led by Condé who sought to overthrow Mazarin's government in the Fronde. A settlement of Condé's situation was an aspect of the Peace of the Pyrenees. Such sponsorship of aristocratic opposition was both dangerous and humiliating for French monarchs, and only Spain was well-placed to provide it.

Peace was followed in 1660 by Louis's marriage to Philip IV's daughter, Maria Teresa/Marie-Thérèse. Louis thus gained pretensions to the Spanish succession, for her renunciation of her rights was made conditional on the payment of a substantial dowry.

An awareness of Spanish resilience, which has recently been stressed for the 1690s,[8] helps explain why Louis took measures against Spain, a policy encapsulated by his frequent references to his grandfather, Henry IV (1589–1610), who had been an active opponent of Spain and had also faced Spanish support for aristocratic opponents. Honour and prestige were central values for Louis and, from the outset of his personal reign (1661), his concern for his *gloire* influenced policy. In 1661–2, a dispute over precedence between French and Spanish diplomats led Louis to bully Philip IV into backing down in a dispute that reflected his concern about prestige, his aggressive tactics, and his particular sensitivity about Franco-Spanish relations. Similarly, a quarrel with the Papacy in 1662–4 was not solely about prestige but was also related to French hopes of weakening the Spanish position in Italy. The foreign minister, Hugues de Lionne (1663–71), had been a trusted agent of Mazarin and helped to maintain a measure of continuity, but policy was very much set by

Louis. A series of treaties – with Sweden (1661), Denmark, Lorraine and the Dutch (1662), and the Swiss Cantons (1663) – reflected France's diplomatic presence and pressure, and the new opportunities opened up by the end of the war with Spain. In 1665, Frederick William of Brandenburg-Prussia (1640–88) joined the French-sponsored League of the Rhine.

The death of Philip IV in 1665 provided Louis with an opportunity to act, and served as a reminder of the challenges and volatility provided by dynastic chance. Had Philip's successor, Charles II (1665–1700), been a strong ruler, then traditional French fears of Spain might well have been renewed. However, the four-year-old Charles was mentally and physically weak and apparently unlikely to have children: he never did so, despite two marriages. His speedy death appeared sufficiently possible that Louis and Leopold I were to reach a secret agreement in 1668 to partition the Spanish inheritance. This agreement was not to be carried out and the two powers were to be at war by 1673, but, like other examples of French interest in better relations with Austria, it serves as a reminder of the volatility of the international system.[9]

The opportunity presented by Charles's succession appears clear in hindsight, especially considering Louis's exploitation of his position in order to seize part of the Spanish Netherlands in the War of Devolution (1667–8). Louis's claims themselves were tenuous: an application of private laws of inheritance in the Spanish Netherlands under which children of a first marriage, such as Louis's wife, took precedence over those of a second marriage, such as Charles.

There was also a danger. Apart from the possibility of Spanish regeneration if Louis did not act, there was the prospect that part of the inheritance would be acquired by another ruler. The likely candidate was a future child of Leopold: the Emperor was shortly to marry Philip IV's other daughter. Philip's will left the inheritance to this line in the event of Charles's death without children. Such a development would have led to a major establishment of Austrian power on France's borders, prefiguring and greatly exceeding that of Prussia after the fall of Napoleon.

There was also the risk of a close union between the Austrian and Spanish Habsburgs, which would limit French influence in the Empire and Italy and threaten her from the east. Far from simply being a Franco-Spanish duel, the French struggle with the Habsburgs involved an important Austrian dimension, not least in terms of the French reaction: sponsorship of Austria's leading German rival, Bavaria, and also of the Swedes. If French rivalry with Austria receded after 1648, when the two powers made peace, it was still present in French sponsorship of the League of the Rhine from 1657. Thus, the Spanish succession focused a long-standing French problem, that of Austro-Spanish cooperation.

The succession also served as a reminder that France's European opportunities and challenges were linked and the number of her options limited. Louis has traditionally been criticized for pushing his schemes for territorial expansion too hard. This analysis is open to a number of qualifications. It is difficult to assess how much expansion is 'enough'; and, therefore, questionable to suggest that, up to such a date or such a frontier, policy was justified and that, thereafter, folly had been embraced. To many Germans, any French expansion was not immutable, but, rather, the product of French strength that could be reversed. Ultimately, French hegemony over the lands between the Saône/Marne and Rhine depended on military strength, for the Dukes of Lorraine were traditional Habsburg allies, and the Emperor and Empire concerned to prevent the consolidation of the position the French had acquired in Alsace at the Peace of Westphalia.

Louis XIV sent troops into the Spanish Netherlands in 1667 to enforce his claims. The resulting War of Devolution was a major success for France militarily, but had an unfortunate diplomatic consequence. French successes led, in January 1668, to the conclusion of a Triple Alliance of England, Sweden and the Dutch Republic, each of which had been important allies of France during the previous quarter-century. The ostensible purpose of the Triple Alliance was to mediate between the combatants, in order to produce a compromise peace that would include some French concessions, but the Alliance secretly agreed to back Spain if Louis refused to compromise.[10]

Although his leading generals wished to fight on, the creation of the Triple Alliance led Louis to accept terms in the Treaty of Aix-la-Chapelle, signed on 2 March 1668. This extended France's frontiers in the Low Countries, in particular with the retention of conquered Lille and Tournai, but far less so than those of Russia, at the expense of Poland, in the Truce of Andrusovo of 1667.

The contrast between the two treaties is instructive; and reflected the differing nature of the international situation in the two halves of Europe. In Western Europe, where the number of independent states and density of their interests were greater, any advance of a certain distance potentially brought more powers into play. In Eastern Europe, where there were fewer players, there were major opportunities for territorial gain, but in the West this process appeared far less likely because of the number of second-rank powers willing to combine against any potential hegemon.

Yet Louis XIV did have a prospect of major gains in 1668, a prospect provided by dynastic claim. The prize was the Spanish succession. The secret partition agreement with Leopold I, signed on 19 January 1668, the Treaty of Grémonville, promised that, on the death of Charles II without children, Louis and his heirs would receive the Spanish Netherlands, Franche-Comté (the area round Besançon), Naples, Sicily, Navarre in northern Spain, and the Philippines. This was a rich prize, and an acceptance that Louis did have a claim to the Spanish succession, although the Austrian Habsburgs were left the New World, as well as Spain, Milan and Sardinia. As a permanent gain to the French royal house, the agreement promised much, especially as the Spanish Council of State felt obliged to concur. This seemed a more appropriate way to make gains than that of conquest. Austrian consent would prevent a lengthy war.

The existence of the Triple Alliance suggested that other powers might have a view on the Spanish succession, predictably irritating a monarch unused to compromise. Louis had found that his control of military developments was not matched by international deference. In May 1669, the powers of the Triple Alliance guaranteed the Spanish Netherlands. In planning an attack in the Dutch, Louis correctly anticipated their hostility to an extension of French power in the Spanish Netherlands, but, also, was swayed by scorn and spite. The United Provinces was a republican, Protestant, commercial state with a political culture to match, and there was a powerful element of instinctive hostility to this culture in Louis's aggressive approach. As a result, he misjudged the potential strength of the Dutch. Divisions within the United Provinces between the princely House of Orange, the traditional source of the stadtholders (provincial governors), who provided the monarchical element in Dutch politics, and the more republican town oligarchies of the wealthiest province, Holland, provided Louis with a chance to intervene. He indeed did so, but lacked the necessary acuteness to succeed in the long term.

Before pushing the criticism of Louis too far, it is worth noting that hostility to the Dutch that had what might be considered a degree of irrationality can also be seen in the case of England. Dutch economic power had been seen by some commentators in the 1650s as threatening to create the universal dominion that was more commonly regarded as stemming from Spanish power.[11]

Louis also sought to benefit from divisions within English politics, encouraging Charles II of England to abandon the Dutch and, by
the Treaty of Dover of 1670, to join with France against them in an
alliance that included secret clauses loosely committing Charles to
support the Catholic cause in England, and Louis to secret subsidies
that would improve Charles's position *vis-à-vis* Parliament.[12] The
French fleet greatly increased in size in the late 1660s and early
1670s, so that, by 1675, it was the largest in the world. In Germany,
the major rulers near the United Provinces were persuaded to provide
a route for French attack. By a treaty of neutrality of 1 November
1671, Leopold I promised not to intervene, so long as Spain was not
attacked. Louis would have liked such an attack, another triumphal
march into the Spanish Netherlands, but England was also against
such a step.

The Dutch War 1672–9

The French invaded the Dutch Republic in 1672, declaring war on 4
April. Thanks, in part, to the support of the local ruler, the Elector of
Cologne, French forces crossed the Rhine and invaded the United
Provinces from the east, only being stopped when the dykes were
breached on 20 June. The province of Holland had been saved, but
the French had made a far greater impact in one campaign than the
Spaniards had done in over a quarter-century of war (1621–48).

The Dutch offered terms, but an overconfident Louis, hopeful
that the war would widen to include Spain, issued excessive demands,
including major territorial gains and the acceptance of Catholic wor-
ship. This was unwise, not least because an Orangeist coup in Holland
in July 1672 brought the anti-French William III of Orange to power
as stadtholder. He was to prove Louis's staunchest opponent. William
was unwilling to accept a settlement under which he became hereditary ruler of the United Provinces in return for yielding to English and
French demands.

In 1673–4, the conflict changed shape, in part because of Louis's
overconfidence and maladroit handling of others, but also because the
coalition that Louis had created was unstable. He lost his ability to
manipulate German politics in order to create an important alliance
system, while the Austrians became increasingly successful at doing
so. A peace congress at Cologne failed, in part because Louis was

insufficiently conciliatory, and Spain, the Emperor and the Empire joined the struggle against him, while, in February 1674, angry at the lack of French naval support, Charles II abandoned the war, ending Anglo-French naval pressure on the Dutch. There was no Turkish attack on Austria to help Louis.

In August 1673, Leopold, the Dutch, Spain and Charles IV of Lorraine agreed to force Louis back to the frontiers laid down at the Peace of the Pyrenees. To try to undo both his gains in the War of Devolution and his conquests in 1672–3 was a bold objective, but France had not had to face a comparable coalition hitherto that century. In 1673 and 1675, French forces were pushed back by the skilful Austrian general Montecucculi. However, the threat to eastern France was resisted, lightly defended Franche-Comté was conquered by the French in 1674, and major advances were made in the Spanish Netherlands and Catalonia. A significant French fleet was sent to the Indian Ocean, but attacks on the Dutch in Sri Lanka and southern India failed, although, in 1674, a base was established at Pondicherry in India. The French fleet was sent to help the Messina revolt (1674–8) against Spanish rule in Sicily, although, thanks in large part to Dutch naval help, the revolt was quashed.

French trade and commercial networks were hit by the war. The French had relied on Dutch intermediaries in order to trade with the Baltic and to reexport their colonial products, but this system collapsed after war broke out. In 1669, Colbert had founded the Compagnie du Nord to limit the Dutch role as intermediaries, but it was unsuccessful and, after its ships were seized by the Dutch, folded in 1677. The number of ships sent to the Indian Ocean by the French East India Company fell after 1676.

The war was brought to a close by a series of treaties signed in 1678–9, known collectively as the Peace of Nijmegen. Their terms reflected the French military success that had led the Dutch to negotiate. Gains and exchanges gave France a far stronger frontier with the Spanish Netherlands. Gains included Bouchain, Bouillon, Charlemont, Condé, Longwy and Valenciennes. None was as important as Luxembourg or Namur would have been, but, individually and collectively, they altered the balance of vulnerability between France and the Spanish Netherlands. The gain of Franche-Comté consolidated French links with Alsace and weakened the position of the Duke of Lorraine. Within Alsace, the French replaced the ambiguous relationship established by the terms of their acquisitions there under the Peace of Westphalia by more clear-cut control. The gain of Freiburg in the

Black Forest took French power east of the Rhine, further strengthening Alsace and giving France greater influence in the Upper Rhineland.[13]

There was also a diplomatic victory. The Dutch War was very different to that with Spain in 1635–59 because it was fought against a coalition. The destruction of this coalition was instrumental to France's success, both in obtaining satisfactory peace terms and in launching a postwar diplomatic offensive. French diplomacy played on the divisions among her opponents, ensuring that there was no single treaty ending the war, but, instead, a number of agreements. The Dutch, who lost no territory, settled before the Spaniards, while Leopold I, who had hoped to push France out of Alsace, was isolated and forced to abandon his schemes. Frederick William of Brandenburg-Prussia was obliged by French military moves to return his gains from France's ally, Sweden, and felt it necessary to ally with France from October 1679.

Western Europe 1679–88

Louis's opponents were left divided and without strong leadership. This encouraged a reversion to the French intimidatory tactics of the 1660s. In the winter of 1678–9, French forces occupied much of the Spanish Netherlands, in order to collect contributions owed to the army, and also fortresses in the lower Rhineland, in order to exert pressure on the local rulers. Using force, Louis advanced a series of claims in a unilateral fashion. Claims to the dependencies of territories already ceded to the French crown led to demands for much of the Spanish Netherlands and of the Empire west of the Rhine and south of the Moselle. Many of these territories were reunited by force in the early 1680s, the *réunions*, named after the *Chambre de Réunion* at Metz. Other gains included the seizure of Strasbourg in 1681, an important strategic advantage, as Strasbourg was a major crossing place across the Rhine between Alsace and Germany. The seizure of Strasbourg was also part of Louis's replacement of Richelieu's more cautious approach to German politics by one of wholesale territorial advance. The French attitude to the German constitution had become more contemptuous.

The gain of Freiburg, and of the north Italian fortress of Casale, which was purchased from the Duke of Mantua in 1681, extended Louis's power far beyond what were subsequently seen as the natural frontiers of the Rhine and the Alps. They provided bases for the projection of force into southern Germany and northern Italy. Casale was a threat to Milan. French gains also made strategic sense in preventing the difficulties that had affected France during the Dutch War.

Louis's successes in these years were a product not simply of military power, but also of the strengths of France's diplomatic position. The wartime attempt to arouse and direct anti-hegemonic fears against France was not successfully sustained, despite the efforts of William III, who argued that Louis's strength and attitudes were a threat to what he presented as a European system in which sovereign powers, however weak, were guaranteed by the restraint of the powerful. Louis, a monarch who, to William, represented an absence of restraint, appeared the principal threat to such a situation. William negotiated a series of treaties against Louis, and, in 1682, the threat of Dutch attack led Louis to raise the siege of Luxembourg, the crucial military base in the Spanish Netherlands and one from which France could be threatened and links with Germany maintained.

William's position was weakened by French diplomacy, which included intervention in the factional politics of potential opponents. In the United Provinces, the French envoy was able to exploit the anti-Orangeist feeling of the Louvestein party and the sense that England and Spain were broken reeds, while favourable French tariff changes and the consequent revival of trade also influenced Dutch opinion. In England, Louis was willing in 1678 to help opposition politicians attack the government and bring down Charles II's leading minister, the Earl of Danby, when it appeared that English foreign policy would remain anti-French. In 1681, Louis switched to supporting Charles, providing him with funds to postpone calling Parliament.[14]

The weakness of potential opponents encouraged Louis to press his aggressive schemes. Intimidation seemed an end as much as a means, the creation of a situation in which diplomacy was not necessary other than to cement military gains. This was clearly seen in the Spanish Netherlands. In 1683, troops were sent into Spanish Flanders. Spanish responses led to an escalation of intimidation, to a Spanish declaration of war that December, and to the French capture of Luxembourg in June 1684.

No other power was in a position to help Spain. Many of the German princes had received subsidies; Charles II responded to his French subsidies, not to his treaty with Spain; and pressure from Amsterdam, encouraged by France, blocked William III's attempt to increase his army and paralysed his attempts to aid Spain. Although Brandenburg and Denmark did not act against William's allies in Brunswick, as Louis had hoped, they also did not support Louis's opponents. The dispatch of a fleet to the Baltic in 1683 reflected France's ability to challenge the Dutch in an area of traditional interest. That year, the Austrians had to focus on the Turkish attack.

Louis's success in negotiating with his rivals separately in 1684 brought him the twenty-year Truce of Regensburg, leaving him in possession of Strasbourg, Luxembourg and his *réunion* gains, which he was allowed to fortify; but not a definitive peace ceding them to France. The importance of this can be exaggerated. Although their gains from Poland under the Truce of Andrusovo (1667) were only those of a truce, the Russians made them permanent by the Treaty of Eternal Peace (1686). Unless Louis wanted a full-scale war in 1684, it was sensible for him to accept what could be obtained. Louis had to consider the danger of provoking Leopold to settle with the Turks, as he had done in 1664, and also to assess the effects of his policies on the Spanish government and on Charles II of Spain's likely will.

Louis's position was undermined in the mid-1680s by a series of developments. The order in which these are presented reflects a prioritization that is difficult to make. The Revocation of the Edict of Nantes in 1685, the consequences of Austrian victories over the Turks and the breakdown of France's position in the Rhineland were all of consequence, but possibly most important was the sense of power ebbing that affected Louis in the mid-1680s, and the consequences both of this, and of the king's continued insensitivity, for the handling of developments in an increasingly volatile situation.

Suspicion of French policy in Europe was accentuated by a belief that the Truce of Regensburg did not necessarily represent the conclusion of Louis's aggression and the end of French expansion. Louis, anyway, appeared to be unwilling to respect the provisions of the truce. This encouraged the creation, in 1686, of the League of Augsburg by which many of the princes of the Empire, including Leopold, guaranteed the public security of the Empire and the agreements of Westphalia, Nijmegen and Regensburg, and stipulated military quotas to support this guarantee. Although not in theory aimed at any particular ruler, the intention of the League was to prevent France from disrupting the struggle against the Turks. That the League was formed under Imperial sponsorship and was a vehicle for the revival of Austrian Habsburg influence within the Empire constituted an obvious contrast to Mazarin's sponsorship of the League of the Rhine less than thirty years earlier. Combined with the repulse of the Turks, the League was an occasion for the revival of the ideology as well as the mechanisms of the Empire.

The League reflected and strengthened a growing hostility towards France within the Empire and an increased tendency to rally to the Emperor, a marked reversal of the situation for most of the previous 150 years. This rallying was linked to Leopold's success against the Turks. It was also important to the eventual role of England and the Dutch, for their military capability against France was, in large part, to depend on their ability to hire and subsidize allied German forces. Aside from the League, Leopold and Frederick William I of Brandenburg signed an anti-French defensive alliance in March 1686.

Closer relations between Leopold and Max Emmanuel, Elector of Bavaria, indicated that the decline in France's position was not restricted to Louis's relations with Protestant powers.[15] In Protestant states, revocation of the privileges of the French Protestants, the Huguenots, as originally conferred by the Edict of Nantes of 1598, in the Edict of Fontainebleau of 1685, produced a mass of hostile propaganda. French envoys noted that Protestant groups who might hitherto have been sympathetic to France became hostile. The Revocation did not produce commensurate gains for Louis in Catholic Europe: because of his successes against the Turks, Leopold appeared a more convincing champion.

Dutch anger about the treatment of the Huguenots was exacerbated by a more hostile treatment of Dutch trade from the summer of 1687. Tariffs on cloth imports rose, and imports of herring were banned unless French salt was used in the curing. Having tried to solve the situation by diplomatic means, the Dutch retaliated. The Dutch were also concerned by the build-up of the French navy. Swedish anger was exacerbated by the impact of the *réunions* on the Duchy of Zweibrücken, a German possession of the house of Vasa adjudged to Louis in 1680. More generally, there was widespread resentment about the *réunions* and, especially, at the combination of force and legal chicanery.

As yet there was no specific issue to test the impact of these shifts. This issue was to be provided as tension mounted over uncertainty about Louis's intentions towards two contentious issues. In 1685, the succession of a new ruler to the Electorate of the Palatinate, the leading territory on the Middle Rhine, led Louis to advance claims on behalf of his Palatine sister-in-law. In addition, the apparently

imminent death of another Rhenish Elector, the Archbishop of Cologne, led Louis to seek the succession of a sympathetic cleric.[16] These
were crises in 'near'-Germany. Louis did not want war, but if he could
not determine developments there then he had little hope of having an
impact further afield in the Empire.

Neither issue, however, was really important to French power,
and it appears that irritation at an inability to determine events,
combined with a sense of being overshadowed by the Emperor and
overtaken by change, led Louis to resort to force. The disputes over
Cologne and the Palatinate became important tests of determination
at a time when the respective strength of the major powers appeared
to be altering considerably. Pope Innocent XI was unwilling to support
the French candidate for Cologne when the Archbishop died in June
1688. The Pope was hostile to Louis's policies towards the Church in
France and to his role in international relations. The Cologne dispute
showed how the Papacy could continue to be of considerable importance in key episodes in international relations.

The Nine Years' War 1688–97

Louis, possibly affected by a failure of nerve, decided that a military
demonstration was necessary in order to display his power and the
vulnerability of the Rhineland. French diplomats claimed that Louis's
gloire and honour were bound up with the Cologne election, and that
Innocent and German opponents needed to be overawed. The French
military were not prepared for a major war, but, in October 1688, a
large army, under the ostensible command of the Dauphin (the heir to
the French throne), besieged Philippsburg, the major fortress of the
Empire in the Middle Rhine. Another force occupied the papal enclave
of Avignon in southern France. Claiming that the League of Augsburg
was an aggressive coalition aimed against France, Louis issued an
ultimatum that Leopold and the Empire were to convert the Truce of
Regensburg into a treaty and to accept his candidate in Cologne
within three months. He was to be proved wrong in his expectation
that German rulers would desert Leopold, and that his attack would
lead to a limited, short and successful conflict, in which French triumphs would drive Leopold to terms.

Instead, Louis found himself in an intractable conflict. Philippsburg and Mannheim quickly fell, but German resistance gathered

pace. Reflecting a rise in German patriotism, the rulers of Brandenburg, Hanover, Hesse-Cassel and Saxony in October concluded a
treaty for the defence of the Middle Rhine. French generals resorted
to crude intimidation, devastating much of south-western Germany in
1689. These tactics touched off a guerrilla struggle in the Palatinate
and accentuated the anti-French nature of German patriotism. The
episode is evidence of the extent to which it is mistaken to see *ancien
régime* international relations as solely a matter of courts and cab-
inets.

The conflict was not restricted to Germany. In 1688–9, James II
of England, a Catholic with autocratic tendencies, was overthrown by
his nephew and son-in-law, William III of Orange, as the result of an
invasion that Louis XIV had failed to predict or prevent. James's
departure itself was not a crisis for Louis, as he had been unwilling
to associate himself too closely with France for both domestic and
international reasons, and had sought to win the support of other
Catholic powers: the Pope, Leopold and Spain. However, James's
replacement by William was a crisis for Louis as it led to the first
major war between England and France since the Hundred Years'
War had ended in 1453. William's commitment to the defence of
the Spanish Netherlands, a role that Spain was no longer able to
fulfil, played a crucial role in the continuation of the anti-French
coalition.

In November 1688, Louis declared war on the United Provinces.
The following May, William, as King of England, declared war on
Louis, while Leopold and the Dutch made an alliance with the declared aims of returning France to the frontiers stipulated by the
treaties of Westphalia and the Pyrenees and of returning Charles of
Lorraine to his duchy. The claims of the Austrian Habsburgs to the
entire Spanish succession were backed. As King of England, William
acceded to this Grand Alliance later in the year. The treaty also
provided for joint peace negotiations and for the continuation of the
alliance after the war.

The conflict itself widened. In April 1689, Louis declared war on
Spain, which had refused to promise to be neutral, and which presented a vulnerable target in the Spanish Netherlands. In May, an
Austro-Bavarian treaty brought Max Emmanuel into the war, and,
in 1690, Victor Amadeus II of Savoy-Piedmont, fed up with French
tutelage, and eager to dislodge the French from Pinerolo and Casale,
joined the alliance.[17] The opposition of most of Western Europe was a
comment not only on Louis's policies but also on the sense that he was

now vulnerable and that he would not determine any reordering of Europe. Princes keenly aware of shifts in the wind, such as Victor Amadeus and Max Emmanuel, now looked for opportunity at the expense of Louis. As later with Napoleon, when his position began to deteriorate, it no longer appeared prudent, or indeed wise, to accommodate Louis's pretensions and goals.

Louis sought to overcome the crisis by a string of victories that would divide his opponents, but was no more able to provide them than he had been in the Dutch War. Although successful in the Spanish Netherlands, winning victories at Fleurus (1690), Leuze (1691), Steenkerk (1692) and Neerwinden (1693), and able to defeat Victor Amadeus at Marsaglia (1693), Louis was unable to make significant inroads into the Empire or northern Italy, to maintain James II in Ireland,[18] or to sustain early naval success in the Channel. The Jacobites in Ireland surrendered in 1691 and an outnumbered French fleet was defeated by the English and Dutch at Barfleur–La Hogue in the Channel in 1692. Furthermore, French military prestige was damaged when Namur was recaptured by William III in 1695. French trade was harmed by commercial embargoes by England, the Dutch and the Empire. As in the 1670s, wine exports collapsed, affecting rents and wages.

The mixed fortunes of war encouraged negotiations, although French discussions with Leopold I, begun in 1692, were stalled by the English succession, while William's refusal to make it a topic of discussion ended talks with him begun in 1693. In 1695, facing the loss of Casale, Louis, by means of a secret deal with Victor Amadeus, ensured that it did not fall into the hands of Leopold. In a difficult situation in 1696, and with his war effort under great pressure, Louis bought off Victor Amadeus in the Treaty of Turin, at the price of Pinerolo. This enabled the French to transfer forces to Catalonia, where Barcelona fell in 1697, encouraging Spain to press for peace. Growing war-weariness among the combatants, and their interest in the Spanish succession, led to negotiations at Rijswijk, where all the powers signed on 20 September apart from Leopold. He still hoped to weaken France and to drive her from Alsace, but, now isolated, he had to abandon such hopes and to sign on 30 October.

The peace was no confirmation of the Truce of Regensburg. Louis got his way over neither Cologne nor the Palatinate and returned many *réunion* gains, as well as Freiburg and Luxembourg, although his position in Alsace, including Strasbourg, was recognized. Lorraine was restored to the Duke, although on terms that left it vulnerable to French occupation. William III was recognized as king and Louis promised not to support Jacobite schemes. The silence of the treaty about the interests and privileges of Ireland and Scotland reflected the inability of the French force sent to Ireland in 1689 to prevent Williamite conquest.[19]

The Spanish succession

Rijswijk was a prelude, not a conclusion, in that it left unsettled the future of the Spanish succession. By ending the war before the succession was thrown open, Rijswijk brought Louis back into a central role in negotiations, creating an opportunity for him to reach an agreement that both served his interests and divided the Grand Alliance. Such an option was to be presented by the unlikely combination of Louis and William III. They sought in 1698–1700 to create a diplomatic order, based on cooperation, that was able to surmount and settle the issue of the Spanish succession.

The role that dynastic considerations played in the diplomacy of the succession can be presented as an aspect of the conservatism of *ancien régime* international relations, and one that was at odds with a more pragmatic 'rationalism' represented by interest in partition, both as a means to avoid or resolve disputes and as a measure of strength. The subsequent War of the Spanish Succession (1701–14) can then be seen as the product of dynasticism, but one that led to an enforced partition. Although this is overly simple, it raises the question whether excessive weight is commonly placed on the details of dynastic claims. They were, however, important to the culture as well as content of the diplomacy of the period, and the claims to the Spanish succession represented the culmination of several important seventeenth-century dynastic strategies.

There were three principal claimants. The marriage of the daughters of Philip III of Spain to Louis XIII and the Emperor Ferdinand III, and of their sons, Louis XIV and Leopold I, to Philip IV's daughters produced important interests on the part of the Bourbons and the Austrian Habsburgs. Both the princesses who married into the Bourbon dynasty specifically renounced their rights of succession for themselves and their heirs, but it was by no means clear how acceptable this was to Spanish custom and law. When Louis XIV married Maria Teresa/ Marie-Thérèse in 1660 – part of the booty from the war with Spain, as Napoleon's second wife was to be from his with Austria – her renunciation was regarded, even then, as a matter of form only, entered into in order to allay international mistrust. Leopold's claim was better because his mother, Philip III's younger daughter, had not made any such renunciation. However, Leopold's sons, Joseph and Charles, were the sons not of his first, Spanish, wife, but of his third. By his first marriage, Leopold had only a daughter, Maria Antonia. Her Bavarian marriage produced a son, Joseph Ferdinand, who was the third major claimant.

The inheritance 'rules' of the period were a combination of positive law, traditions, and the testaments (wills) of rulers. National conventions were frequently ambiguous and they could clash with those of other countries. The relationship between dynastic and other inheritance practices was unclear. Legal claims played a major role in the diplomacy of 1698–1700, but such considerations did not greatly influence those rulers who had no dynastic claim to the succession and either wished to make gains for themselves or feared the consequences of acquisitions by others. Furthermore, the recent war suggested that compromise would be a likely consequence of any conflict.

Louis approached William in early 1698 to discuss the situation. He had correctly identified Leopold as likely to be his most obdurate opponent and had appreciated that the crucial point of tension in the Grand Alliance had been the relationship between Leopold and the Maritime Powers (England and the Dutch). Although Leopold had been willing to negotiate a partition treaty with Louis in 1668, success against the Turks since had made him more determined. In April 1698, Louis proposed that the bulk of the Spanish empire, including Spain, but not the Spanish Netherlands, should go to a French prince, but the treaty he signed with William that October was very different. Spain, her transoceanic empire, the Spanish Netherlands and Sardinia were allocated to Joseph Ferdinand of Bavaria, while Naples, Sicily, the *presidios* (Tuscan coastal forts) and the Basque province of Guipuzcoa would go to Louis's heir, the Dauphin Louis. The treaty provided that the signatories should impose it by force if any power refused to comply.[20]

Conclusions

Ending this chapter with what was to be the First Partition Treaty draws attention to the role of uncertainty in international relations and to the possibly misleading nature of periodization in modern treatments. Different impressions can be created if this section concludes with 1695, when war convulsed much of Europe; 1697, when peace came to Western Europe; 1698, when the First Partition Treaty was signed; 1699, when the Treaty of Karlowitz brought peace to Eastern Europe but the death of Joseph Ferdinand threw open the Spanish succession; 1700, when the Second Partition Treaty was signed; or 1701, when war broke out over the succession.

This list, which could be expanded to draw attention to other abrupt shifts, is an instructive reminder of the volatility of international relations. It is, however, useful to pause at the close of the century. Rijswijk and Karlowitz had brought an end to two major wars and, as yet, European international relations had not been affected by the rise of Russian power and assertiveness under Peter the Great. Instead, Leopold, Louis and William dominated relations within Christian Europe, and pursued diplomatic strategies focused on Western European issues, more particularly predominance in the international system; control of Italy, Germany and the Low Countries; the Spanish succession and the struggle for primacy between the Bourbons and the Habsburgs; and the ability to mould change. The events of the following decade were to provide no shortage of the latter.

Chapter 7

Conflict and Diplomacy in the Early Eighteenth Century 1700–40

Introduction

Some of the major themes of the period 1714–40, especially Franco-Spanish differences in 1717–29 and French sponsorship of anti-Austrian German princes, particularly the Wittelsbachs, both of which looked back to the seventeenth century, indicate that it is misleading to exaggerate the changes created by the War of the Spanish Succession (fighting 1701–14) and the subsequent peace treaties in 1713 and 1714. It has been suggested that these changes marked the end of French hegemony in Western Europe, but the existence of this hegemony can be queried, particularly in light of the willingness of so many rulers to defy Louis XIV in 1688. It was rather that French hegemony had been feared, though, even then, many Austrian ministers had been more concerned by Turkey and Hungary, while the Scandinavian and north German rulers were more interested in Baltic affairs. The predominance of one dynasty had been feared in 1700, when a Bourbon, Philip, Duke of Anjou, had been left the Spanish succession in Charles II's will, and this was, arguably, a more realistic anxiety than earlier fears of French hegemony. However, claims that the new Philip V of Spain would not follow the French lead were to be fully vindicated after the war ended, and it is easy to appreciate why many German and Italian princes were more concerned about Austrian, than Bourbon, power and intentions in the first three decades of the century. Their perspective was a valid one, was to be shared by the Maritime Powers in the 1720s, and should be placed alongside their earlier concern about the Bourbons.

The decades after 1714 have not received as much attention as the period 1680–1714 or the second half of the century. The diplomacy and wars of the 1720s and 1730s have appeared to be less important and more limited than their counterparts in 1680–1714 or such later episodes as the Seven Years' War and the First Partition of Poland. Furthermore, in so far as the period 1740–55 has appeared worthy of mention, it has largely been as preparation for the so-called Diplomatic Revolution, the Franco-Austrian *entente* of 1756. To a considerable extent, this situation has been matched in scholarly studies of the monarchs of the period. The Russian rulers of 1725–62 have never enjoyed the attention lavished on Peter the Great and Catherine the Great. The Emperor Charles VI (1711–40) and Frederick William I of Prussia (1713–40) have received insufficient attention compared to their successors and much Mediterranean history in this period is obscure. Ferdinand VI of Spain (1746–59) is scarcely a familiar figure and the same is true of Charles Emmanuel III, King of Sardinia (1730–73), as the rulers of Savoy-Piedmont were known after 1720. Partly as a result, the diplomatic history of the period has been both relatively neglected and presented in familiar terms: the Anglo-French alliance of 1716–31, the recovery of France in the 1730s and, for 1740–56, the Prussian attack on Austria and the background to the Diplomatic Revolution. Convenience, the need to present an orderly account of events and a sense that international relations had changed in the period 1680–1714 have combined to ensure that Europe after 1714 has been seen as essentially one political system, with the concomitant that it is realistic to write of an overall European-wide balance of power.

Contemporaries certainly argued that events were interconnected and that, once a conflict broke out, it was difficult to prevent it spreading to the whole of Europe. The image of a flame spreading was used, for example by the Dutch statesman Goslinga in 1715 and the French first minister Fleury in 1727. The idea that a European system existed was expressed by, among others, Frederick II of Prussia in 1748. The same year, he suggested that Britain and France were the powers that determined what happened in Europe. In 1723, his father, Frederick William I, had claimed 'that there was no doubt that if France and George I united', they 'could affect all the affairs of Europe'.[1]

The role of Britain and France in the Baltic crisis of 1748–50, both helping to restrain their respective allies Russia and Austria, and Sweden and Prussia, seemed to bear out Frederick's comment. The interrelationships of affairs were demonstrated by the concern of Western European powers to encourage or inhibit the march of Russian troops into Central Europe in 1730, 1735 and 1748. The direct military intervention by France in the War of the Polish Succession (1733–5), France's mediation of a Balkan peace in 1739 and her encouragement of Sweden to attack Russia in 1741 suggest that powerful countries did indeed seek a continent-wide reach for their diplomacy and their alliances.

However, the idea that international relations were in some fashion predictable and limited in their scope because of the operation of the balance of power, the principle of collective security and the supposed absence of serious issues at stake is misleading. The stability and predictability of these relations should not be emphasized. Instead, major efforts were made to overthrow dynasties, the Habsburgs in the Austrian Succession War (1740–8) and the Hanoverians in Britain in the French-supported Jacobite invasion attempts of 1744 and 1745–6. Substantial territorial changes were effected through warfare, particularly the establishment of two of Philip V's sons, by his second marriage, in Italy in 1734–48. The Turks recaptured the Morea and lost, and then regained, Serbia and Little Wallachia. Other plans were blocked through warfare, for example, Philip's attempt to regain much of Spanish Italy in 1717–20. Dynastic changes that would have created such dynastic groupings as Russia–Sweden and Russia–Prussia were actively considered. In 1737, Tsarina Anna made her lover Biron Duke of Courland. When she died in 1740, he became regent for the infant Ivan VI, but he was speedily disgraced both because his domestic position aroused envy and because he had planned enlisting Swedish help to create a state of Courland, Livonia and Estonia, which was to be placed under Swedish suzerainty. The creation of direct land bridges between Saxony and Poland, and Brandenburg and East Prussia was discussed, as were other changes at the expense of Poland.

The extent to which Europe was increasingly one system is open to qualification. Britain and France had intervened in both Baltic and

Balkan diplomacy prior to 1700. Russian policy had affected the course of the Thirty Years' War; Louis XIV had sought to place a protégé on the Polish throne in 1696. The principal changes helping to integrate European affairs in this period arose from the actions of Eastern, not Western, European powers. Contrary to the customary argument that Austria had become a Danubian monarchy as a result of her successes in the war of 1682–97, she made no Balkan gains between 1718 and 1878 with the exception of Dalmatia from Venice (1797–1805, 1815–) and the small and barren territory of Bukovina from the Turks (1775). Far from pursuing the theme of conquest in the Balkans, Austria was generally more concerned about Russian advances there, while in the period 1699–1740 she was more interested in Italy. Her acquisitions from the Spanish inheritance helped to make her a Western European power that had inherited from Spain the task of confronting the Bourbons in Italy and the Low Countries, adding it to the already existing conflict between Austria and France for influence in the Empire and for a secure Imperial barrier in the Rhineland.

Austria's new role was matched by that of Russia. Her defeat of Swedish and Polish aspirations, her territorial gains from both and the domestic weakness of both powers helped to destroy their role as buffers between Russia and the other European states. The new Russian diplomatic and military range was amply demonstrated in the 1710s and it ensured that resistance to her pretensions and power would have to involve other states. The weakness of Sweden and Poland helped, for example, to increase Prussian concern about Russia, and thus ensured that powers that wished to benefit from Prussia or prevent Prussian action had to consider Russian views.

However, the extent and impact of international relationships should not be exaggerated. Though power blocs were created by, for example, the Anglo-French alliance of 1716 and the Austro-Russian pact a decade later, there was a marked willingness to consider self-interest. Alliances were generally weak even if long-lasting, and powers that were forced to rely on them were swiftly disabused of hopes of assistance, as Austria was in the War of the Polish Succession and France in that of the Austrian Succession. Europe could act as a system when, in some circumstances, powers felt it necessary and were able to influence distant allies but, in general, the striking feature is the extent to which such influence was not only episodic but also ineffective unless it reflected shared views.

Accounts of diplomacy in this period tend to focus on Western Europe, especially the War of the Spanish Succession (1701–14) and, to a lesser extent, the complex diplomacy of the following quarter-century. However, in the long term, developments in Eastern Europe were more important, and they will take pride of place. The rise of Russian power transformed power relationships throughout the period. Sweden and Poland both suffered greatly and, in the long term, were unable to reverse the new system. The Turks proved better able to resist Peter the Great, but were defeated by Russia in the late 1730s. Similarly, in 1733–5, Russian forces confirmed Peter's earlier dominance of Poland. This helps provide a basic unity to the period.

The Great Northern War 1700–21

The major conflict that was eventually to deprive Sweden of most of her overseas empire began with a secret plan intended to achieve just that end. However, the three originators of the plan, Peter the Great, Augustus II of Saxony–Poland and Frederick IV of Denmark, were not all to be beneficiaries of the war; nor had they envisaged a conflict that would last for over two decades. The scheme for a joint attack on Sweden was not new, but a number of developments at the end of the 1690s appeared to suggest that it might prove successful. The accession of the young Charles XII in 1697 encouraged hopes of Swedish weakness, which were further sustained by overoptimistic reports of discontent among the Livonian nobility arising from Charles XI's policy of resuming crown lands. The end of the Turkish war released Russian forces, while the recent accession of Augustus, Elector of Saxony as King of Poland meant the arrival of a new ambitious element in Baltic diplomacy.

Although Russia was ultimately to be the greatest beneficiary of the war, the most active role in negotiating the alliance was taken by Denmark. Danish attempts over the previous quarter-century to re-conquer Skåne (Scania; now the southernmost section of Sweden), which had been lost to Sweden in 1658, and to dominate Holstein-Gottorp had suffered from the absence of any power to divert Swedish strength in the eastern Baltic. Danish approaches received a negative response in Moscow in 1697, as Peter was preoccupied with the possibilities arising out of the Turkish war, but Augustus was more receptive. He was uncertain what he would be able to make of Poland, where royal authority and power were heavily restricted, but his ideas included the growth of naval power and trade, both of which would challenge Sweden. Furthermore, he hoped to regain Livonia for the Polish crown and to use it as the basis for establishing a hereditary Saxon dynasty in Poland, rather as John Sobieski had earlier hoped to profit if he could gain Prussia or Moldavia. Augustus reached an agreement with some of the Livonian nobles who promised to raise an army and to accept his overlordship in return for a guarantee of Livonian autonomy and laws, an interesting indication of the factors that could be involved in 'state' formation and expansion. Between March 1698 and January 1700, a number of agreements were reached, creating an anti-Swedish coalition. It was agreed that, in 1700, Peter, his Turkish war over, would invade Ingria, Augustus Livonia, and Frederick first Holstein and then southern Sweden.

The wide-ranging plan assumed that coordinated attacks would divide the Swedish forces and thus ensure a speedy success, but both military fortune and the alliance's durability were swiftly to be proved limited. In early 1700, Augustus invaded Livonia and Frederick Holstein-Gottorp. The Swedes responded rapidly, landing on Zealand and threatening Copenhagen. Frederick abandoned the war, restoring the Duke of Holstein-Gottorp by the Treaty of Travendal. The guarantee of the treaty by Dutch, English and Lüneburg mediators protected Charles's back while he pursued his quarrel with Augustus and Peter. The quiescence of most of the Livonian nobility and the strength of Riga's defences had ended the Saxon invasion. Charles XII therefore attacked the Russian army under Peter besieging Narva. They were defeated by a smaller Swedish army that benefited from greater professionalism and from the snowstorm blowing in the face of the defenders. The Swedes lost 2000 dead and wounded, the Russians 8–10,000 and all their artillery. As with Vienna in 1683, Narva demonstrated the vulnerability of a poorly commanded and badly deployed siege army to a relief attempt.

The coalition had failed and Augustus appealed for the mediation of Louis XIV. Charles did not, however, trust the undefeated Augustus, and his appreciation of the danger that the Saxon–Polish union posed to Sweden led him to devise a plan to replace Augustus by a more pliable ruler. This led to Charles's embroilment for a number of years in the unsteady complexities of Polish politics. In 1701, Charles overran Courland and in 1702 captured Warsaw. Polish–Saxon armies were defeated at Klisów (1702), Pultusk (1703) and Punitz (1704). Charles had Augustus dethroned and his protégé, Stanislaus Leszczynski, crowned in 1705.

Swedish involvement in Poland allowed Peter to increase the size and improve the fighting quality of his army. Swedish forces in the Baltic provinces were defeated in 1701 and 1702, and in 1704 the Russians captured Narva and Dorpat. The previous year, Peter had founded St Petersburg to give Russia a Baltic port, his 'window on the West'.

Success in Poland increased Charles's ambitions. By a treaty of 1705 with Poland, he promised to help conquer the lands ceded to Russia in 1667. That year, Charles marched west, defeating the Saxons at Fraustadt, invading Saxony, and forcing Augustus, in the Treaty of Altranstadt, to recognize Stanislaus. Charles's presence in Saxony in the winter of 1706–7 led Austria and the Maritime Powers to fear that he would throw his weight behind France in the War of the Spanish Succession. However, Charles was more concerned about Peter, who had made it clear that he was unwilling to give up Ingria and his 'window on the West'. Charles may have been foolish to hope for a military solution against Peter, but a disadvantageous peace with Russia would possibly have encouraged Augustus and Frederick to plot anew. In addition, Peter, facing growing opposition in the Ukraine, did not appear to be very strong.

In 1708, Charles invaded Russia, successfully crossing the river lines that blocked his advance. At Holovzin, he defeated a much larger Russian army trying to block the route to Smolensk and Moscow, but the Russians fought better than they had done in 1700. Their scorched-earth policy of destroying crops and farms created grave supply problems for Charles. These, the severity of the winter of 1708–9, and the hope that Mazepa, Hetman (elected leader) of the Ukraine, would raise his people against Peter led Charles to turn south into the Ukraine. This lent military backing to the diplomatic threat, contained in the Swedo-Polish treaty of 1705, to undo the territorial stability of Russia's western and southern border. The possibility of winning the support of the Crimean Tatars and the Turks was considered. However, Mazepa's lack of preparation, combined with the swiftness and brutality of Peter's military response in the Ukraine and the severity of the winter, undermined the value of Charles's move south.

In March 1709, he won the backing of the Zaporozhian Cossacks, but the Don Cossacks, the Tatars and the Turks refused to help. Hopeful that he would regain the initiative with a major victory, Charles attacked the Russian army entrenched behind redoubts at Poltava on 27 June (old style), but was defeated with heavy casualties.

Defeat turned into disaster when most of the retreating Swedes surrendered three days later.

Charles succeeded in fleeing to Turkey, where he was to remain until 1714, but the Swedish position around the Baltic collapsed. Augustus remounted the Polish throne and Frederick of Denmark invaded Sweden, although the loyalty of Skåne and a decisive Swedish victory at Hälsingborg in Feburary 1710 forced Frederick to withdraw his troops. Peter had more success, occupying Courland in late 1709 and successfully besieging Viborg and Riga the following year. In 1711, Russian, Saxon and Danish troops attacked Swedish Pomerania. Charles's only hope appeared to be the Turks who were opposed to the Russian dominance of Poland which seemed to be an obvious consequence of Augustus's reinstatement as a result of Poltava.

Thanks in part to the influence of the Khan of the Crimean Tatars, Turkey declared war on Russia in November 1710 and was at war from then until the Peace of the Pruth of July 1711 and then again, as a consequence of Peter's failure to fulfil its terms, for most of the period between December 1711 and June 1713. Peter had sought to avoid war, Turkish neutrality being as important for him in the Great Northern War as it was for the Habsburgs in the War of the Spanish Succession, but he eventually responded by reviving his hopes of the late 1690s. In March 1711, Peter issued appeals for assistance in proclamations to 'the Christian People under Turkish Rule' and to 'the Montenegrin People'. The following month, a treaty was signed with Demetrius Cantemir, Hospodar of Moldavia, providing for Russian sovereignty over Moldavia, the preservation of Moldavian autonomy, Moldavian assistance against the Turks and the granting of the status of Hospadar as a hereditary right to Cantemir's family. As with Augustus in Poland, the desire to make a post hereditary played a major role in international relations.

Peter's planned invasion of the Balkans was, however, to prove a humiliating failure. Although he received Moldavian support, the speedy advance of a large Turkish army dissuaded the Hospodar of Wallachia from sending promised support to Peter and he blocked the march of Serbian reinforcements. Outnumbered, short of supplies and surrounded at the river Pruth, Peter was forced, in July 1711, to negotiate in a very disadvantageous position. He had expected to have to abandon Livonia and to recognize Leszczynski as King of Poland, but the Grand Vezier, Baltaji Mehmed, for reasons that are unclear, granted far less stringent terms. Azov was returned to Turkey and Peter promised not to interfere any more in Polish affairs. Though the war had proved a major disappointment for Peter, the peace was equally so for Charles, and indeed Baltaji Mehmed's distrust of him and his supporters may well have played a role in his readiness to negotiate. Peter temporarily withdrew most of his forces from Poland, but the Swedes were in no position to exploit this. Peter's supporters in the Balkans were abandoned. The Montenegrins held out until 1714, while Cantemir and several thousand Moldavians followed Peter back into Russia. The Turks consolidated their position in the Danubian Principalities, and the rule on their behalf of the Phanariots, reasonably reliable Greeks, rather than local aristocrats, began in Moldavia and Wallachia in 1716.

The restoration of stability to his southern frontier allowed Peter to return his attention to Sweden while leaving Charles in his Turkish exile. With Sweden's eastern Baltic territories securely in Russia's grip, Finland being conquered in 1713–14, attention now turned to her German possessions. Peter's overwhelming military superiority had ensured that there was no longer any doubt that Russia and not Poland would gain Livonia, but the situation in northern Germany was more complex. The Danes had traditionally sought to expand into the region, and they seized the Duchy of Bremen in 1712 and all of Holstein in 1713. The creation of a power vacuum with the collapse of Swedish power encouraged other rulers, hitherto neutral in the war, to intervene, a process facilitated by the end of the War of the Spanish Succession and the consequent freeing of the forces engaged in that struggle. To preempt a Danish invasion, George, Elector of Hanover occupied Verden in 1712 in collusion with the Swedes. The following year, the new King of Prussia, Frederick William I (1713–40), seized Stettin with Russian assistance. In 1715, both rulers declared war on Sweden. George's Electoral declaration of war (there was no declaration as George I of Britain) was forced on him by Denmark and Prussia, as only thus would the former vacate Bremen for his forces, and the latter suspend boundary disputes.

However, alongside the broadening of the anti-Swedish coalition, there were already signs of a new configuration in Baltic relations. The precarious and reactive nature of alliance diplomacy was to be demonstrated by the slow disintegration of the coalition and its replacement by an even more precarious one, directed this time against Russia. The Swedes had sought to split their rivals, suggesting in 1712 a triple alliance with Augustus and Prussia. However, Charles's approaches were hindered by his unwillingness to agree to territorial losses in return for alliances promising diplomatic support. Instead, he insisted on military support that might help him gain equivalents: comparable territorial acquisitions. The Emperor, Charles VI, had tried to settle the war by means of a congress at Brunswick, but Charles XII had refused to cooperate in 1712.

Charles's return from Turkey to the Pomeranian fortress of Stralsund in November 1714 was followed by reforms in the Swedish administration, but not by military success. Stralsund fell in November 1715, Wismar the following April. However, tension within the anti-Swedish alliance was increasing and there was particular opposition to the growth of Russian power in northern Germany. The collusive surrender of Wismar to the Danes and Hanoverians was effected in order to keep the Russians out. The marriage, that spring, of Charles-Leopold, Duke of Mecklenburg-Schwerin, to Peter's niece, Catherine, increased concern in neighbouring Hanover and in Denmark. Peter's postponement, possibly in response to Swedish peace-feelers but more likely for military reasons, of a planned invasion of Skåne left a large Russian army in Denmark in late 1716. Rumours flourished about Peter's plans. The Danes opposed the wintering of the Russian army in Denmark, and George of Hanover sought Prussian cooperation, without success, to block their wintering in Mecklenburg, while Hamburg feared attack. The Russians wintered in Mecklenburg. There was a real fear that Peter would establish a permanent Western outpost. This reinforces the general stress on the role of contingency since the fear and uncertainty surrounding Peter's plans were a significant influence on events.

The divisions in the coalition provided opportunities for Charles, who began separate secret negotiations with George and Peter. However, both rulers wanted recognition of most of their acquisitions, and Charles was unwilling to accept such terms while he was preparing a large new army. George I was certainly worried about the possibility of a Russo-Swedish alliance directed against him and he feared that it might lend support to his other opponents, the Jacobites and Philip V of Spain. The British fleet, sent to the Baltic to protect trade against Swedish privateers, was ordered in 1718 to prevent any joint naval action by Russia and Sweden. Aware of the extent to which policy could alter with a new ruler, Charles's minister Görtz also negotiated with the Jacobites, the supporters of the Stuart family. The increasing rift within the anti-Swedish coalition led to attempts by Peter and George to gain French and Austrian support. The period 1717–19 witnessed a diplomatic defeat for Peter. George beat him to the alliance of France, and, in January 1719, Hanover, the Emperor Charles

VI and, as a result of Austrian pressure, Augustus II, signed a Treaty of Vienna aimed against Prussia and Russia. Peter, who, in the summer of 1717, had felt obliged to withdraw most of his troops from Mecklenburg, and had been persuaded to do so by the French regent, the Duke of Orléans, who had been influenced by his ally, George I, now responded by withdrawing from Poland. Carrying out an Imperial legal decree, Hanoverian troops expelled the Duke from Mecklenburg, while Prussia abandoned Peter.

These developments reflected Peter's diplomatic weakness in the face of the hostility aroused by his success, and the difference between the precarious grasp provided by occupying the territories of allies and the firmer hold given by conquest. However, George's success led him to overestimate the extent to which Peter could be persuaded to yield his conquests from Sweden. This issue was to become serious during the developments that followed the death of Charles XII at the end of 1718, while besieging a Norwegian fortress, shortly after he had begun an offensive that was designed to lead to an invasion of Denmark and northern Germany, and to strengthen his hand when negotiating a settlement with Russia.[2] It is unclear what this would have led to in military and diplomatic terms, but the accession first of Charles's younger sister, Ulrika Eleonora, and then of her husband, Frederick I (1720–51), led to an attempt to regain some of Sweden's losses by diplomacy. With French support, George I negotiated treaties in 1719–20 by which Sweden ceded Bremen and Verden to Hanover, Stettin and Pomerania south of the Peene river line to Prussia, and her exemption from the Sound Dues at the entrance to the Baltic to Denmark, which also regained the Duke of Holstein-Gottorp's lands in Schleswig, under an Anglo-French guarantee.

In return, Sweden obtained peace and a guarded promise of British support against Russia. George I sought to create an alliance of Sweden's other former enemies plus France, Austria and Britain in order to impose a Russo-Swedish peace that would return most of Peter's conquests and alleviate northern European fears about Russian power. However, as so often, bold diplomatic plans proved unrealistic. Charles VI and Frederick William I proved unwilling to attack Peter, while the financial crises that affected Britain and France, the South Sea Bubble and its Mississippi equivalent, sapped the determination of both powers. Peter refused to be intimidated, while his galleys maintained pressure on the Swedes by raiding their coast.

As a result, Sweden signed a peace with Russia at Nystad in 1721. Peter kept the bulk of his conquests, Livonia, Estonia and Ingria and, although he returned Finland, he retained the strategic regions of Kexholm and part of Karelia. He promised to respect existing privileges in his acquisitions, and not to intervene in domestic struggles over the Swedish constitution or in the Swedish succession.[3]

The first promise was reasonably well-observed by Peter and his successors, but the other was not. Indeed, the Swedish constitution, which in the so-called Age of Liberty of 1719–72 considerably weakened royal power, a process that was helped by the absence for much of the period of a clear succession, helped to provide Russia, and other powers, with the means to influence Swedish conduct. The Diet and the embryonic political parties could be influenced. The existence of a rival claimant to the throne, Charles Frederick of Holstein-Gottorp, son of Charles XII's eldest sister, who took refuge in Russia after Ulrika Eleonora's victory over him in the succession struggle, and was in 1724 betrothed and in 1725 married to Peter's daughter Anna, further increased the possibilities of Russian intervention.[4]

Sweden had not lost all her gains from her age of greatness. Though Wismar and the small remaining section of Pomerania were of limited consequence, she had retained her Danish conquests. Furthermore, the possibility of regaining some of her losses to Russia, either through conquest or by means of a Holstein-Gottorp succession, continued to be entertained. Nevertheless, whatever the future might bring, the situation when Peter died in 1725 was clear. Sweden had been unable to resist Russia and the prospect of collective action had failed to intimidate Peter. In 1720, there was more substance in Frederick William's fears that, if he took action against Russia, Prussia would be attacked than in Polish hopes of obtaining Kiev and Smolensk.

Poland and the Baltic 1721–40

If Sweden was weakened in the international sphere by her constitution and the absence of a clear succession, the same was also true of Poland. Though plans for a partition in the 1720s proved abortive, and the territorial integrity of the country was preserved for many years, it was less able to take effective diplomatic and military initiatives. It did not matter that Sweden and Poland made no peace until 1731 because neither was in a position to fight the other or had anything important to fight about: Livonia was clearly in Russian hands. Though plans for a reordering of Eastern Europe in order to reduce Russian power were to play some role in European diplomacy in the period 1725–43, they were recognizably less plausible than in the previous quarter-century. Of the three powers that had competed with Russia for mastery in Eastern Europe, only Turkey remained strong and had succeeded in outmanoeuvring Peter. It was significant that powers further west, Britain, France and Austria, had had to play a major role in limiting Peter's advance. The weakness of Sweden and Poland was to help to bring Russia and these powers into closer contact.

In the last years of his reign, Peter I consolidated his powerful position in the Baltic and Eastern Europe. The collapse of the plan for a coalition to drive him from the Baltic did not prevent other anti-Russian initiatives, such as the Treaty of Charlottenburg between George I and Frederick William I in 1723, but it made it unlikely that a united anti-Russian front could be created, and this gave Peter opportunities for diplomatic initiatives. In February 1724, the Russo-Swedish Treaty of Stockholm provided a defensive alliance but also an agreement directed against Denmark for common action to return Schleswig to the Duke of Holstein. This helped to drive the two Scandinavian powers apart, and Scandinavian unity was to form as unrealistic a goal as the hopes of common action by the native-ruled Italian powers.

However, though Russia militarily dominated its neighbours, she was not to be free of anxiety on their count during the quarter-century after the death of Peter in 1725. Concern about the possibility that an unfriendly king of Poland would articulate anti-Russian tendencies in her borderlands, especially the Ukraine, led to intervention in the Polish crown election in 1733, helping to cause the War of the Polish Succession. Attempts to prevent hostile Swedish moves by manipulating Swedish politics were unsuccessful and, in 1741, Sweden attacked Russia, which was fortunately for her no longer at war with Turkey. The Russian victory was followed by the adoption of the same method that had been used for Poland, sponsorship of a monarch who would, it was hoped, act as a protégé. In Poland, Russian money and troops had helped Augustus III of Saxony to succeed his father. In Sweden, the favoured candidate was a member of the house of Holstein-Gottorp, Adolf Frederick (1751–71), though he rapidly proved a disappointment to his sponsor, the Tsarina Elizabeth (1741–62).

It would, however, be misleading to present the history of the region in terms of a struggle to enhance or restrict Russian power.

That would suggest a unity and consistency of purpose that was lacking, not least in Russia. Indeed one of the most interesting features of the period is the extent to which policy was debated in Russia, Sweden and Poland, although the domestic constitutional, political and institutional nature of the debates varied greatly. Within Russia there were a number of overlapping struggles: that of Westernizers, concerned to protect the legacy of Peter I, against opponents; disputes between those who thought attention should be concentrated in particular geographical directions; quarrels over the succession that reflected the absence of a clear succession law and the failure of any ruler until Catherine II to leave a son to succeed; and bitter ministerial disputes.[5] These disputes were both the despair of foreign envoys seeking favourable action on the part of Russia and an opportunity for others to seek to influence Russian politics and policies.

However, although to outsiders Russian politics and policy often appeared foolish and too easily manipulated, Russian rulers and ministers generally had a better appreciation of their varied territorial commitments than diplomats who tended to see Russian commitments in a narrower focus.[6] Russian policy was more cautious than many hoped or feared. This was not simply due to the replacement of Peter by more hesitant and domestically weaker successors. Peter himself had been less bold than his image: in the 1710s he had not invaded Skåne or resisted militarily the attempts to make him withdraw from Mecklenburg and Poland. His naval demonstrations against Denmark on behalf of Charles Frederick of Holstein-Gottorp in the early 1720s went no further.

This was equally true of his widow and successor Catherine I (1725–7). In 1726, a request from the Duke of Mecklenburg for the assistance of Russian troops was rejected. Catherine supported Holstein claims to Schleswig, but was thwarted by an absence of Swedish support, as well as by Danish firmness and a British naval demonstration in the Baltic. This was a failure of brinkmanship and intimidation, as there is little evidence of serious military preparations for war.

However, this Baltic dispute helped to affect other negotiations involving Russia. The collapse of the anti-Russian plan of 1720–1 had been followed by such negotiations as other powers sought to derive some benefit from Russia's rise. These became more serious as a consequence of the diplomatic revolution of 1725, the Austro-Spanish Alliance of Vienna and the response, the Anglo-French–Prussian Alliance of Hanover of that year. Though French unwillingness to guarantee Russia's Baltic and Turkish border was very important, a major restriction on French attempts to improve relations from the early 1720s was her alliance with George I, who had had no diplomatic relations with Russia since 1719. George's commitment to Danish control of Schleswig served in the mid-1720s to articulate anti-Russian action rather as his earlier commitment to the return of Sweden's Baltic provinces had done. The Russians in 1725–6 were more concerned about Turkish pressure on Persia and the possibility of war with Turkey, a prospect that made an alliance with Austria necessary. By a treaty of 1726, Russia was guaranteed Austrian support in the event of a Turkish attack.

Russian support was valuable to Austria as it helped to gain the alliance of Prussia and Saxony. In January 1730, Charles VI requested the dispatch of 30,000 Russian troops and, though they were not sent, hopes and concern about them led foreign commentators to follow carefully the political disputes that followed the death of Peter II (1727–30) and the accession of Tsarina Anna (1730–40). The Swedes revived their hopes of a reconquest of the Baltic provinces, but Anna was able to impose strong government and the alliance with Austria was reaffirmed. This reaffirmation helped to lead Frederick William I of Prussia to reject British diplomatic approaches in 1730. Thus, the Russo-Austrian–Prussian bloc, created in 1726 and based on the Russo-Austrian alliance, lasted, helped to bring stability to Eastern Europe and limited the influence of Western European powers. Though Frederick William I was not always happy with the policies of Russia and Austria, and was to be particularly offended by their support for a Saxon succession in Poland, he did not oppose the alliance. In contrast, his son Frederick II's defiance of it, his attempts to dissolve or counteract it and the responses of Austria and Russia were the fundamental causes of instability in Eastern Europe from 1740.

The unwillingness of any of the powers to push their disputes to the point of hostilities in the late 1720s and the strength of the Austro-Russian alliance ensured that proposals for action that would weaken the allies, such as Anglo-French-supported moves by Sweden or Turkey, were not pressed. The period 1722–31 was also a decade of peace in Europe because Austria–Russia did not use their military superiority for aggressive purposes. When Frederick William I planned an attack on Hanover in late 1729 he was discouraged by the refusal of his allies to provide assistance. Russian strength and the absence of any Russian territorial pretensions kept the peace in the Baltic, not any system of collective security. In contrast, Russian unwillingness to accept any limitation of her power within her sphere of interest was demonstrated in 1726 when force was used to reverse the election, as Duke of Courland, of Maurice of Saxe, one of Augustus II's numerous illegitimate progeny. However, a willingness to compromise elsewhere was revealed in the negotiations with Christian VI of Denmark that led to the Treaty of Copenhagen of May 1732. This guaranteed the European possessions of the two states and provided for Danish compensation for the Holstein claims to Schleswig, settling for the while the Holstein issue, ending the tension between the two powers, and helping to leave both Russia and Denmark as powers concerned to preserve the status quo in the Baltic, thus isolating Sweden.

The Treaty of Copenhagen was a prominent example of the strengthening of the Austro-Russian bloc that occurred in 1731–2. In 1731, Austria gained the alliance of Britain and Spain without losing that of any power. Improved Anglo-Russian relations followed the Anglo-Austrian treaty. French diplomacy sought to challenge the new arrangements, but the only apparent threat to the Russian position in Eastern Europe was the Polish succession. In 1730, the Austrians accepted a Russian proposal for joint action on the basis of the exclusion of Stanislaus and support of the future Augustus III if he was willing to accept conditions. Stanislaus was an unacceptable candidate because of his French and Swedish connections: there was no compartmentalization of history, based on notions such as the rise of Russia, or on chronological divisions, such as the Baltic after the Great Northern War. Russian views were made clear by the draft treaty offered to Augustus in the summer of 1733 which included a reciprocal guarantee of possessions, a renewal of all Polish–Russian treaties, and a promise that Augustus would not alter the Polish constitution.

However, the Polish Convocation Diet of May 1733 voted to exclude all foreign princes from the Election Diet. Stanislaus was elected in Warsaw before the arrival of Russian forces but, capturing the city, they had Augustus elected King on 5 October. This aroused outrage elsewhere, being seen as a clear infringement of Polish liberties. Count Gustaf Bonde, a Swedish Councillor, told the French envoy that 'if the Russians succeed in Poland, the same danger will menace Sweden all too closely, and that he would not give five pence to live under their form of government and to have their liberty'.[7] However, outrage was no more helpful to the Poles than it was to be at the time of the First Partition in 1772: the Swedes discussed sending troops, but a proposal to accept French subsidies to this end was rejected. The Poles proved unable to challenge the Russians successfully in the field and a small French force sent to relieve besieged Danzig in 1734 was easily defeated. The Russians were able to send troops to the assistance of Austria in 1735 and the provision in the peace treaty that Augustus should be recognized as King of Poland caused no surprise. The peace was accompanied by no Russian territorial acquisitions, for the Russians appreciated that that would compromise their effective protectorate over Poland.

From the mid-1730s, Poland did not present a serious problem for Russia for several decades. Instead, Sweden and Prussia attracted concern and the combination of the two at the end of the 1740s challenged Russian dominance of the Baltic. In 1735, this dominance had appeared clear. Denmark acknowledged Russia's right to the Baltic provinces by the Treaty of Copenhagen (1732), the War of the Polish Succession installed a Russian protégé in Poland, thus ensuring continued control over Courland, and, in 1735, the Russo-Swedish treaty of 1724 was renewed, with the exception of the Holstein article, for a further twelve years. However, this apparently pro-Russian step of the ministry of Count Horn in Sweden helped to lead to his fall at the Diet of 1738 when his rivals, increasingly known as the party of the Hats after the French tricorne which its younger members wore, used anti-Russian sentiment to achieve domestic power. A French subsidy treaty of December 1738 prevented Sweden from concluding any other alliance without first notifying France, and led to Russian fears of a French-financed Swedish naval build-up. In 1739, a French squadron appeared in the Baltic and the Russians were aware of Swedish attempts to obtain Polish help in the event of war. The Swedes hoped that the Turks would make the return of the Baltic provinces a goal in their war with Russia. Conflict between Sweden and Russia was delayed by the Russian willingness to ratify the Treaty of Belgrade, and thus end their war with Turkey, and by French attempts to maintain the peace, but that did not prevent the Hats from envisaging a war that would bring major territorial changes. In 1739, it was hoped that the dispatch of Swedish troops to Finland would persuade the Russians to yield Viborg, Ingria and St Petersburg.

Baltic affairs in the decades after Nystad have not received much attention in general works on eighteenth-century international relations. They were clearly less central than in the late 1710s and less far-reaching in their consequences than in the late 1700s, but it would be a mistake to assume that they were inconsequential, predictable or controlled by non-Baltic powers. Instead they reflected the uneasy relationship of local and distant influences that characterized all of European diplomacy and indicated the continued importance of dynastic factors and the widespread unwillingness to accept the settlements of 1713–21 that was to help lead Sweden to attack Russia in 1741 and Prussia in 1757.

War against Islam 1714–39

Having defeated the Russian challenge in 1711, the Turks next sought to regain from Venice the Morea, the most resented of the losses at Karlowitz. In 1714, they declared war and, the following year, overran the Morea; the Venetian garrisons enjoyed scant support from the predominantly Orthodox population. The Venetians turned for help to the Austrians but, aside from mutual hostility arising from Venetian opposition to Austrian dominance in Italy, the latter were more concerned about possible trouble with Spain. Furthermore, a Turkish embassy assured the Austrians in May 1715 that the Turks had no wish to attack Austria.

Austrian attitudes changed when the death of Louis XIV, on 1 September 1715, freed them from the fear of united Bourbon action and when Turkish success led to the prospect of an invasion of Venetian Dalmatia that might endanger the Austrian position in Croatia. Unlike in 1682, the Austrians were confident of a short and successful war and willing to fight without a major ally. In April 1716, the Turks were presented with an ultimatum demanding the return of their conquests from Venice and, on their failure to comply, Austria declared war in May. The Turkish army was crushed at Petrovaradin and the Grand Vizier killed, and Temesvár, the last major Turkish fortress north of the Danube, was captured.

Having ignored Turkish attempts for an armistice, Eugène besieged Belgrade in 1717 and, in August, defeated the Turkish relief army and captured the city. This spectacular success seemed to justify hopes of major conquests and to inspire new ones, including replacing the Turks in Moldavia and Wallachia, a move that would have closed the Balkans to Russia. However, there was little of the crusading spirit in Austrian ministerial circles. In 1716, appeals for liberation from Macedonia and Montenegro were slighted. Eugène was more concerned to consolidate the Austrian frontier and to dissuade the Turks from the idea of reconquering Hungary. Furthermore, the successful Spanish invasion of Sardinia in 1717 awakened fears that the rest of Austrian Italy would be attacked. Turkish proposals for negotiations were therefore heeded. Austrian pressure for a peace that would give them all of Serbia and the Bosnian fortresses was defeated by the Turkish insistence on *uti possidetis*, a principle that was also extended to Venice. The Peace of Passarowitz of July 1718 gave Austria the Banat of Temesvár, Little (western) Wallachia and northern Serbia. The Venetians lost the Morea, but their successful defence of Corfu in 1717 maintained their position in the Adriatic. The Venetian–Turkish frontier was thus stabilized for the rest of the century: the Turks ruled Greece, not the Adriatic. Similarly, though the Austro-Turkish war of 1737–9 was to alter the frontier, the essentials of the Austro-Turkish settlement were now clear. The Habsburgs were to rule the Hungarian plains, but not the Balkan mountains. The crucial area of tension on the frontier between Christendom and Islam was not to be the Adriatic or the Balkans, but the northern shores of the Black Sea.

If Austro-Turkish relations were relatively easy from 1718, the same was not true of Russo-Turkish relations. This was due not to any revival of Peter's hopes of Balkan conquest but to the clashing interests of the two powers in Persia (Iran). Persia was scarcely part of Europe but, in so far as there was a European international system, it was affected by the unpredictable and fast-changing developments in the 'sub-system' of Persia, Turkey and Russia. The volatility of eighteenth-century international relations and the major issues that could be at stake were amply illustrated by events in Persia. Whereas the Spanish empire had become the target of competing powers because of dynastic factors, and the Great Northern War arose through an alliance to despoil Sweden, Russo-Turkish competition over Persia was a consequence of a collapse of power there provoked by another outside force, an Afghan invasion.

In 1722, Peter I advanced into the region to see what he could gain and to block the Turks from the Caspian. Derbent and Rasht were occupied, Baku following in 1723, and, in September 1723, Shah Tahmasp of Persia was persuaded to yield the provinces along the southern and western shores of the Caspian. The Russians promised to aid Tahmasp in pacifying Persia and defeating the Afghans. The Shah, however, did not ratify the treaty, while Russian gains were in a traditional area of Turkish interest and the Turks advanced to benefit from Persian weakness. In June 1724, the Turks accepted, by the Treaty of Constantinople, Peter's proposal for a partition. Peter recognized Turkish occupation of Georgia and a number of Persian provinces, which the Turks had had to renounce in 1639, while the Turks accepted the Russian gains from their 1723 treaty. Both agreed that if the Shah refused to accept the terms, they could seize their allocated territories by force. Due to his failure to accept those allocated to the Turks, they attacked Persia in 1724–5. Initial Turkish successes, which worried the Russians, were followed, after a period of instability in Persia, by the emergence of a capable military leader, Tamas Kuli Khan (later known as Nadir Shah), and a Persian revival. By the Treaty of Rasht of 1729, the Russians promised to withdraw from some of their conquests and they were threatened with the loss of the rest unless they provided assistance against the Turks. Unwilling to fight the Persians and disillusioned by the cost of retaining their unhealthy Caspian provinces, the Russians signed another Treaty of Rasht in 1732 by which they agreed to evacuate most of Peter's gains.

However, the crucial struggle was not that involving the Russians, but the Turco-Persian war. This made fears of Turkish attack in, for example, Italy and Malta in 1723 unfounded, and plans by European diplomats to turn the Turks against Austria and/ or Russia impracticable. The British and French worked to this end in the late 1720s, and in the early 1730s the French sought to engage Turkish attention in the cause of Louis XV's father-in-law, Stanislaus, becoming the next king of Poland. Persian affairs, however, prevented any Turkish commitment. A Turkish complaint in April 1733 about apparent Russian intentions towards Poland was forwarded to St Petersburg by the Russian envoy, Nepluiev, with the assurance that the Turks were in no position to intervene. When, in August 1733, the Turks reminded Nepluiev of Peter I's promise not to intervene militarily in Poland, he reported that their willingness to act would depend on peace with Persia. However, Turkish peace proposals were rejected. In 1734, a special Russian envoy encouraged Persia to reject all Turkish peace proposals and the Russians provided the Persians with munitions. European diplomats generally presented Turkish policy as arising from court intrigues, Villeneuve, the French envoy, writing in 1735, 'it is difficult to base a solid system on Turkish intentions; changes are too frequent there and government maxims are not followed consistently enough for there to be any certainty'.[8] Such comments were the common response of diplomats throughout Europe faced by the difficulties of assessing court policies and intrigues.

War did break out between Russia and Turkey but it was over the unsettled frontier in the Caucasus rather than Poland, and it began not in 1733, when it would have helped Stanislaus, but in 1735. Neither power planned for a major conflict and both had responded in 1733–4 to what were regarded as provocative actions by the other without fighting. Far from following a 'forward' policy of aggression towards its Islamic neighbours, the Russians, by the Treaty of Gence of March 1735, had returned Baku and Derbent to Persia and recognized Persian suzerainty over the Daghestan region of the eastern Caucasus. The Turks responded by ordering the Crimean Tatars to assert the Turkish claim to Daghestan, a move that would take them through Kabardia, an area claimed by Russia, and that would repeat a step which had led to clashes in 1733. The Russians, unwilling to accept the Turkish claim to Daghestan and convinced that the Turks would not support the Tatars militarily, believed it necessary to help the Persians in order to prevent them settling with the Turks and either uniting against Russia or allowing the Turks to reestablish themselves on the Caspian.

Thus, far from there being any confident Russian plan for a long-term war to drive the Turks from Europe, consideration of the Russian situation in 1735 reveals anxiety over the views of others, and the defensive mentality that had led to a refusal to provide assistance for Vakhtang VI of Georgia in his struggle with the Turks in 1724–5 and to the withdrawal from Persia. A lack of Russian preparation ensured that the attempt to seize Azov in order to block the Tatars from expanding into Kabardia was unsuccessful in 1735. The following year, the Russians seized Azov and attacked the Crimea, but these steps were insufficient to persuade Tamas Kuli Khan, who made himself Shah in 1736, to continue his war with the Turks or to refuse a peace with them unless it included the Russians, as he had originally wished. Nadir Shah devoted 1737–9 to war with the Afghans and an invasion of India, conquering Kandahar, Ghazni, Kabul, Peshawar and crossing the Indus in 1738, and defeating the Mogul army at Karnal in February 1739 before seizing Delhi. Thus the Turkish–Persian peace was maintained sufficiently long to enable the Turks to devote the bulk of their resources to resisting Russia and Austria.

Deprived of the assistance of conflict between Persia and Turkey, the Russians devoted greater attention to ensuring that Austria, their ally since 1726, entered the war. In 1730, they had reached an agreement that if the Turks declared war on one of the allies, the other would consider itself at war. Though exhausted by the War of the Polish Succession (1733–5), the Austrians feared the loss of their only surviving major ally. Russia declared war on Turkey on 12 April 1736 and fought the first campaign alone. In October, however, the Austrians promised to honour their alliance commitments in what they hoped would be a short war.[9] Venice and Augustus III of Poland refused to provide assistance and the first Austrian campaign achieved little. Meanwhile, to the concern of the Austrians, Russian ambitions expanded. Veshniakov, their envoy in Constantinople, suggested an invasion of Moldavia and Wallachia and an advance as far as Adrianople. In unsuccessful negotiations at Nemirov in 1737, the Russians demanded the annexation of the Crimea and the Kuban, free trade for themselves throughout the Turkish empire and the bringing of Moldavia and Wallachia under Russian protection. The terms were rejected by the Turks. Though the Russians under Field Marshal Münnich took Ochakov at the mouth of the river Bug in 1737, logistical problems hindered both this campaign and the 1738 attempt to invade Moldavia and Wallachia. In 1739, they were more successful, capturing the Moldavian capital of Jassy, but the Austrians had followed their unsuccessful campaign of 1738 with a disastrous one in 1739. French mediation ended the conflict by the Treaty of Belgrade, Austria ceding to Turkey besieged Belgrade, as well as Little Wallachia and northern Serbia. Russia gained some of the southern steppe and was allowed to retain an unfortified Azov, while the Russian merchants were given freedom of trade in the Turkish empire. However, she still lacked a coastline on the Black Sea and was not permitted merchantmen or warships on it.

Turkey was not to fight Russia and Austria again until 1768 and 1788 respectively. Opponents of Austria and Russia attempted on a number of occasions, but without success, to inspire a Turkish attack on them. The mid-century, therefore, represented a clear break from the period that lasted from the early 1680s until 1739. However, rather than assuming that it represented a turning away from a long-term ambition to conquer lands from the Turks, it is more accurate to note the short-term causes of the individual conflicts: the responses to particular opportunities and fears that they represented. In place of a predictable system, the rulers and ministers of even the major powers felt themselves forced to respond to a number of challenges within the context of domestic and international problems that could not be predicted.

An assessment of the wars against the Turks suggest that it is essential to consider Persia as part of the 'system'. When, in the early 1740s, Austria turned to meet the challenges arising from the succession of Maria Theresa, and Russia to confront a Swedish attack and a contested succession, the Turks had to face the revival of their conflict with Persia which lasted until 1748, including a major siege of Mosul in 1743. The attempts of the Swedish envoy to turn the Turks against Russia, rather than Persia, were unsuccessful. Any account of European international relations in the period would necessarily depend on the perspective adopted, but the striking feature of accounts of the mid-century is how they generally omit the role of Persia and neglect the importance of Balkan peace.

The Spanish Succession

The likely consequences of Spanish opposition to a partition on the death of Charles II were still unclear when, after a short illness that gave rise to rumours of Austrian poisoning, Joseph Ferdinand of Bavaria died on 6 February 1699. This contingency had not been provided for. As there was no other suitable third party (Louis XIV rejected William III's suggestion of Pedro II of Portugal), Louis and William had in their negotiations for the Second Partition Treaty only to consider the distribution of territory among the Habsburgs and Bourbons. The treaty was not concluded until 25 March 1700. The delay reflected the problems created for William by the destruction of the solution of awarding contentious areas to a third party. As before, the fate of the Milanese was a difficult issue, and William emphasized the need to produce a solution that could be offered to Leopold I, who, however, refused to accede. The second treaty offered far more to the Habsburg claimant than the first though, as before, this was Leopold's second son, Charles, who was not, unlike the Dauphin, the direct heir to his father's territories. Spain, her transoceanic empire and the Spanish Netherlands were allocated to Charles. The Dauphin received the same portion as in the first treaty and was to receive Lorraine, while its Duke was allocated the Milanese.

Neither Leopold nor the Spaniards accepted the new treaty. The prospect of Austrian military action in Italy helped to encourage the French to begin military preparations while, in order to increase the strength of the partition pact, France sought the alliance of Victor Amadeus, an essential support in any conflict in northern Italy. In August 1700, the Spanish envoy pressed Louis to abandon the idea of partition, claiming that Charles II would live for a long time, only to meet with the reply that all were mortal and that Louis's only aim was to bring peace to Europe. In Spain, the idea that the monarchy could be preserved from partition only by France gained ground and was actively sponsored by Cardinal Portocarrero, the Archbishop of Toledo. The pious Charles, who disliked the partition, was pressed hard by clerical supporters of a French candidate. On 2 October, he signed a will leaving everything to the Dauphin's second son, Philip, Duke of Anjou, on condition that the crowns of France and Spain never be united in one person. If this was not accepted by the Bourbons, the whole empire was to be offered to Archduke Charles. Charles II added the suggestion that Philip marry an Austrian archduchess in order to ease tension.

On 1 November he died, and on 16 November Louis presented Philip to his court as King of Spain. Explaining this decision, the French argued that it should please Europe more than the partition treaty because, by accepting the will, France gained no territory. Louis was aware that Leopold would appreciate neither the will nor French acceptance of it, but, had he declined it and the inheritance been offered to Charles, Louis knew that the Austrians were not already bound to accept the partition treaty and he had no confidence that England and the United Provinces would oblige them to do so.

The outbreak of the War of the Spanish Succession 1700–2

Philip V, acclaimed throughout the Spanish empire, reached Madrid on 18 February 1701. He was recognized by England in April and the United Provinces in February, and the prospect of an Anglo-Dutch–French triple alliance was discussed in diplomatic circles. The process by which relations deteriorated between France and her possible allies has been thoroughly studied, but it was not itself responsible for the war. It was rather Austrian and French military preparations and initiatives that brought conflict near and eventually led, on 19 June 1701, to the first shots being exchanged as the French sought to block an Austrian invasion of the Milanese, which Leopold claimed as an escheated fief of the Empire. France was in a far stronger diplomatic position than she had been during the recent Nine Years' War. The Rijswijk negotiations and the partition treaties had clearly ended the Grand Alliance and this encouraged second-rank powers, such as Portugal, to regard France as a possible ally. In March 1701, Max Emmanuel of Bavaria made an alliance treaty with Louis by which the

French agreed to pay him to maintain 10,000 troops. His brother, the Archbishop-Elector whose election to Cologne Louis had sought to prevent in 1688, signed a similar treaty that spring. It was clear that other countries were preparing for war, irrespective of the actions of the Maritime Powers. Their attitude was not crucial to these preparations, for the key area of dispute was Spanish Italy, which Leopold did not intend to renounce. Having accepted Charles's will, Louis was in no position to negotiate: Philip had been accepted on the basis that there would not be any Spanish territorial losses. Leopold was prepared, in light of the will, to support a partition, but he was determined to gain Spanish Italy and on 18 November 1700, the night he heard of Charles's death, he ordered his ministers to plan the seizure of Milan. Three days later, Prince Eugène was appointed to command a force that was designed to undertake this task the following year.

French actions were considered provocative in both England and the United Provinces. The replacement of the Dutch garrisons in the Barrier fortresses in the Spanish Netherlands by French forces in February 1701 seemed to demonstrate the continued subservience of Philip to Louis and led to Dutch protests. The following month, French troops were moved towards the Dutch frontier. The Dutch unsuccessfully suggested that many of the major fortresses should be occupied by Anglo-Dutch forces in order to lessen French influence in the Spanish Netherlands. French merchants were granted better conditions in Spain, and the French Guinea Company was given, for ten years, the *Asiento* contract to transport slaves from West Africa to Spanish America, a lucrative opening into the protected trade of the Spanish empire. In January 1701, French warships were given permission to enter Spanish American ports and, that March, they were given permission to sell goods there. This was to be the basis of extensive and unregulated sales of French goods. These developments encouraged alarmist rumours. In England, a popular anti-French agitation combined with growing fears of French intentions to shift parliamentary attention from opposing William III's men and measures to resolving to support the king in his growing conviction that Louis's acceptance of the will had to be resisted.

The French responded not by conciliatory offers, but by military and diplomatic preparations for war that made it more likely. On 7 September 1701, the Grand Alliance of The Hague brought Austria and the Maritime Powers together to support a partition of the Spanish inheritance which was to award Spanish Italy to Leopold, create a

Barrier for the Dutch in the Spanish Netherlands, and allow England and the Dutch to retain their conquests in the Spanish Indies. At this time, the objectives of the Grand Alliance did not include dethroning Philip, much to Vienna's frustrated anger. Nine days later, before Louis knew of the treaty, the exiled James II of England died at his palace near Paris. His son was recognized as James III by Louis. Though this helped to end doubts about his intentions in England, Louis already saw William as a rival, and hoped that the step would win papal support which could be very important both in Italy and in the war already beginning between the Catholic powers. In theory the Treaty of the Grand Alliance was not an offensive alliance. It stipulated an attempt to achieve its ends by negotiation with France. However, Louis's move threatened to add to his conflict with Leopold, a revival of the British War of Succession of 1688–91. His attempt to ensure recognition of James III from his allies, such as Portugal, was unwelcome in England where, in January 1702, Parliament suggested an article in any treaties made by William 'that no peace shall be made with France, until His Majesty, and the nation, shall have reparation for the great indignity offered by the French king'.

Though William did not respond by declaring war, preferring to build up the anti-French alliance so that it could protect the United Provinces, the last months of peace were not spent in negotiation with Louis. Measures such as the French and Spanish prohibition of the import of British manufactures in the autumn of 1701 helped further to embitter relations. Louis's attempt to exploit William's death in March 1702 by opening negotiations with the Dutch was unsuccessful and, on 15 May, Austria and the Maritime Powers simultaneously declared war.

The War of the Spanish Succession 1701–14

The war was a complex struggle involving a variety of interests. For Austria, France and Spain, dynastic considerations were predominant. For England, which was constitutionally united with Scotland in 1707, the Protestant succession was involved, for the United Provinces the prevention of Bourbon control of the Spanish Netherlands, and, for both, colonial and commercial considerations, especially West Indian trade. The issues at stake became more serious in the years after war began as the result of commitments to allies. The support of most of the German princes was won by the Grand Alliance without excessive commitments, though at the cost of heavy subsidies. Elector Frederick III of Brandenburg was gained by Leopold's promise to recognize his new title of 'King in Prussia'. However, Pedro II of Portugal was only won from his Bourbon allies in 1703 by the promise of territorial gains in Spain, and of the candidature of Archduke Charles for the Spanish throne, both as a guarantee of support from the Allies and because he would be a less threatening neighbour than a Bourbon. Victor Amadeus II similarly deserted the Bourbons in 1703 in return for subsidies and part of the Milanese.

The opportunities that the conflict appeared to offer minor powers were illustrated by Max Emmanuel. His demands indicate the extent to which territorial divisions were not seen as fixed and the international system was seen as full of opportunity. As the Elector of Saxony had recently become King of Poland, the Elector of Brandenburg King in Prussia and the Duke of Brunswick–Lüneburg, in 1692, Elector of Hanover and, in 1701, had his place in the English succession recognized, it was not surprising that Max Emmanuel sought to turn the rivalry of the major rulers to his own advantage and, in 1701–4, negotiated with both sides. In the summer of 1702, the Austrian envoy offered territorial concessions in the Empire and the possibility of an exchange of Bavaria for Naples and Sicily. Max, who had been in the Habsburg camp from 1681 to 1697, demanded royal status for Bavaria, the cession of the Habsburg possessions of Tyrol and the Burgau, subsidies, the marriage of a daughter of Leopold's heir, Joseph, who had no sons, to his own heir, and the possible exchange of Bavaria and Naples and Sicily at his own option. Leopold was willing to offer money rather than Habsburg territories, but, in November 1702, Max demanded, in return for an offensive alliance, subsidies, the Milanese, the Burgau, and the Spanish Netherlands, either to keep or to exchange for the Lower Palatinate. He also used the opportunity to try to pursue the feud of the Bavarian Wittelsbachs with the Palatine Wittelsbachs, demanding Neuburg which was one of the possessions of Leopold's brother-in-law, John William, Elector Palatine. Max had already signed an offensive alliance with France in June 1702 by which he received subsidies and the promise of the Lower Palatinate or Spanish Gelderland. That summer, Max obliged Louis to persuade Philip V to rescind his elder brother's patent as Vicar General of the Spanish Netherlands and to award it to him. Concerned about the response in Spain, Philip promised Max Gelderland and the hereditary governorship of the Spanish Netherlands, but insisted on secrecy.[10]

Max's ambitions extended to neighbouring independent territories. In April 1702, he defined his goal as the Imperial Free Cities of Augsburg, Nuremberg, Regensburg, Rothenburg and Ulm, and in September he began hostilities in southern Germany with an unprovoked seizure of Ulm. Max's continued talks with Leopold and the French need for German allies in the face of Leopold's success in winning allies in the Empire led to a new treaty, in November 1702, by which Max gained the promise of the Palatinate and of full sovereignty over the Spanish Netherlands, with the exception of frontier fortresses reserved for France.

By 1703, therefore, the objectives of both alliances had increased greatly. France was committed to creating a German power that could rival the Habsburgs, while her opponents were now fighting to keep the Bourbons out of the entire Spanish inheritance. These commitments helped to make compromise difficult in the tentative and active negotiations that continued during more of the war. When, in February 1704, Prussia attempted to detach Bavaria from France, Max demanded the Milanese, a broad corridor to it through the Tyrol and his conquests in Swabia and Neuburg. Wide-ranging commitments also ensured that peace eventually came through exhaustion and the unilateral action of one of the members of the Grand Alliance, thus precipitating the collapse of the alliance.

Wartime diplomacy was both greatly affected by strategic considerations and intertwined with the fortunes of war. Initially these were mixed and, despite the Grand Alliance's success in overrunning Brunswick–Wolfenbüttel and the Electorate of Cologne (1702–3), the junction of French and Bavarian troops in southern Germany (1703) threatened the collapse of an Austria that was gravely weakened by a Hungarian rebellion. The arrival of Anglo-Dutch troops from the Low Countries under the Duke of Marlborough the following summer helped to rescue the situation and, on 13 August 1704, Marlborough and Eugène defeated the Franco-Bavarian army at Blenheim on the Danube, proof that decisive military verdicts were possible in the warfare of the period. This was followed by the retreat of the French from southern Germany and the overrunning of Bavaria. Thereafter, France's military position made it difficult to gain allies. Responding to pressure from John William of the Palatinate, Leopold's successor, his elder son Joseph I (1705–11), and the Imperial electors placed the Electors of Bavaria and Cologne under the imperial ban in 1706, depriving them of their rights and privileges. Fearing princely opposition, Joseph abandoned hopes of annexing Bavaria, though John William was invested with the Bavarian territory of the Upper Palatinate in 1708.

The conquest of Bavaria made the conflict more intractable. Max refused to renounce the idea of regaining the acquisitions he had made since 1702, and Louis believed that his honour was involved. In November 1704, a Franco-Bavarian treaty committed Louis to continue the war until Bavaria was retaken, made a kingdom and embellished with much of Swabia, conditions Louis pressed in negotiations with the Dutch in 1706. In contrast, John William sought to retain his gains and to add the Governorship of the Spanish Netherlands. Thus, Max's earlier Bourbon-supported determination to alter dramatically the territorial configuration of much of Europe was now matched.

The Bourbons were also driven from Italy. The French force besieging Turin was defeated by Eugène and Victor Amadeus in 1706 and the French evacuated Italy. Naples was seized by the Austrians the following year. Thanks to Marlborough's victories at Ramillies (1706) and Oudenaarde (1708), the French were driven from the Spanish Netherlands. However, the Grand Alliance had less success in conquering Spain and invading France. The attempt to establish Archduke Charles as Charles III of Spain failed, despite English naval power, support from the provinces of Catalonia and Valencia, and the intervention of English, German and Portuguese troops. Madrid was captured briefly in 1706 and 1710, but Castile, the key central area of Spain, remained loyal to Philip and his cause was increasingly identified with national independence despite his military dependence on French troops, who decisively defeated the Allies at Almanza (1707) and Brihuega (1710).

By the time that major attacks were launched on France, exhaustion was beginning to affect the Grand Alliance. Marlborough's plan to invade Lorraine up the Moselle in 1705 had to be abandoned due to a lack of German support. The Austrian invasions of Alsace in 1706 and Franche-Comté in 1709 and the combined Anglo-Austrian attack on Toulon in 1707 were unsuccessful. Marlborough's desire to follow up Oudenaarde by a march on Paris was thwarted by Dutch caution and he had to settle for the successful sieges of Lille (1708) and Tournai (1709). In defending France, Louis had reason to be grateful both for his earlier acquisitions and for Vauban's fortifications. All the powers were affected by financial problems and by the savage winter of 1708–9.

Peace negotiatons 1705–14

Initially, Louis's overtures had been largely designed to divide the Grand Alliance by winning over the Dutch, a course that Dutch determination to maintain their English alliance defeated. In 1705, he proposed a partition of the Spanish inheritance, awarding Naples and Sicily to Charles and a Barrier to the Dutch in a Spanish Netherlands that was to become an independent republic. English insistence on the allocation of Spain to Charles led to the failure of the negotiations but, after Ramillies, Louis tried again, proposing that Spain and the Indies go to Charles, Spanish Italy to Philip, and the Spanish Netherlands to the Dutch. These proposals came to nothing, not least because Joseph I, while willing to make concessions on behalf of his brother Charles, was determined to acquire the Milanese for Austria, in accordance with a secret agreement Charles had been obliged to make in 1703. The English were unprepared to accept the possible commercial consequences for their Mediterranean trade of a Bourbon acquisition of Naples and Sicily.

Nevertheless, the basis of the eventual settlement of 1713–14 was already present: a new partition treaty, accompanied by a Dutch Barrier and French recognition of the Protestant succession in England. Military developments, Oudenaarde and Lille, made Louis more eager to settle but they also left less room for manoeuvre. The likelihood that the Austrians would agree to concessions in Spanish Italy was lessened by their conquests there. In 1708, British naval power helped Charles conquer Sardinia and Minorca, and Charles promised Britain both Minorca and the *Asiento*. In negotiations in 1709, Louis abandoned his demands for an establishment for Philip, agreed to restore Lille and all he had taken in Alsace since 1648, including Strasbourg, met English wishes about their succession, and agreed that 'James III' should leave France. The sticking point was that Louis could not guarantee that Philip would accept any settlement, and was unwilling to promise to help depose him. Distrust of Louis played a major role in the formulation of this humiliating demand which was cited by Louis, in his appeals to the French public and his correspondence with Philip, as the reason why he rejected the preliminaries. However, Eugène attributed the decision to the provisions concerning Alsace, and it might also be suggested that the refusal to leave Philip any compensation for what Louis saw as his right to the Spanish inheritance was decisive.

The eventual peace terms were not as bad as Louis had been willing to consider. In part this reflected military developments. Charles was unsuccessful in Spain and Marlborough's victory at Malplaquet (1709) was followed by only slow progress in capturing French fortresses. Fresh negotiations in early 1710 collapsed on the Dutch insistence that Louis expel Philip before peace could be considered, but political changes in Britain, where the Whigs were replaced in 1710 by a Tory ministry that was prepared to compromise on its allies' demands in unilateral negotiations with France, made the terms offered in 1709 and early 1710 appear redundant. Dutch and Austrian demands were certainly more of a hindrance to peace than their British counterparts, for insularity ensured that Britain did not need to consider the strengthening of territorial frontiers. Instead she essentially sought, aside from the recognition of the Protestant succession, territorial gains in relatively uncontroversial regions: North America and isolated bases in the Mediterranean. In contrast, the Austrians sought a strong German barrier against France, demanding, for example, in 1709 the three bishoprics of Metz, Toul and Verdun, which the French had acquired in 1552, and the restoration of Lorraine's 1624 frontier with France. A meeting of the representatives of the Imperial circles required as a condition of any peace settlement a barrier that would include Strasbourg, Landau, Metz, Toul and Verdun. In October 1709, in response to Dutch pressure, the English Whig ministry had signed the Treaty of the Barrier by which they agreed that the Dutch were to make gains in French Flanders and to be allowed to garrison thirteen fortresses in the Spanish Netherlands which were to enjoy full autonomy from the government in Brussels.

Given such demands, it is understandable that the Tory ministry felt that it could proceed more successfully and gain more satisfactory terms for Britain if it negotiated alone, a clear breach of the terms of the Grand Alliance. In December 1710, following the defeat at Brihuega, English willingness to leave Philip in possession of Spain and the Indies was signalled. This was made more politically acceptable by the death of Joseph I on 17 April 1711. When Joseph's brother Charles VI died, also without a son, in 1740 his possessions passed to his elder daughter as a result of a special arrangement, the Pragmatic Sanction. No such arrangement existed in 1711 to prevent Charles succeeding his brother while maintaining his own pretensions to the Spanish empire. That represented, however, a strengthening of Austrian power that none of her allies sought, and this helped to ensure that the British initiative in beginning negotiations was followed by many powers. Most of the terms were settled in Anglo-French discussions in 1711, which served as the basis for the negotiations held at Utrecht in 1712–13. Affairs were complicated in February–March 1712 when Philip's elder brother, the Duke of Burgundy, and the latter's eldest son, the Duke of Brittany, both died, while Burgundy's other son, the infant Duke of Anjou, nearly died. This brought Philip very close to Louis's succession and revived fears of French influence in Spain. A dynastic union of France and Spain was as unwelcome as one of Austria and Spain. In June 1712, Henry St John, Viscount Bolingbroke, effectively the British foreign minister, warned his French counterpart, Torcy, that the need to prevent such a union was essential for Britain.[11] The French insisted that agreements could not contradict their fundamental laws, and that any renunciation by Philip of his claim to the French succession would be of no value, because France was a patrimony that the monarch received not from his predecessor or the people but in accordance with the law, which only God could change. It was stressed that as soon as one monarch died another succeeded, without his own personal choice or the consent of anyone being an issue. Torcy rejected the idea that any renunciation could be ratified by the Estates General or by the provincial Estates.

French insistence on Philip's right to succeed in France gave rise to discussions about the cession of Spain to another, possibly his cousin, the Duke of Orléans, or Victor Amadeus II in exchange for the latter's territories. Philip, however, made it clear that the only acceptable solution was, in the event of his nephew's death, his inheritance of France and his abdication then of Spain to his son. Dynastic considerations were not the only issues under negotiation. Indeed it is too easy to present the terms of the Peace of Utrecht as though they inevitably arose from the Anglo-French negotiations. In fact it proved difficult to settle many issues and the proposals advanced in 1711–13 indicate the unpredictable nature of the eventual settlement. The Barrier and the settlements for Max Emmanuel and Victor Amadeus proved especially contentious. Notions of honour and compensation were more important in these cases than any attempt to create a balance of power on a logical basis. Italy proved a rich field for proposals and new kingdoms. In 1711, the French proposed that Victor Amadeus be given the Milanese and made King of Lombardy; instead he was to receive Sicily as a kingdom. In the same year, they suggested that, in addition to the return of his dominions, Max Emmanuel should gain much of the Spanish Netherlands and in 1712, having pressed for him to receive Sicily or the Spanish Netherlands, they persuaded Bolingbroke to agree that he receive Sardinia and royal status. Torcy thought the idea plausible, despite the distance and the absence of links between Bavaria and Sardinia, because there was no diplomatic reason why they were incompatible. The gain of Bavaria and the Spanish Netherlands by Austria in return for Max acquiring Naples was also discussed in 1711.

Alongside the creation of kingdoms, the diplomats had to discuss frontiers. These discussions witnessed a mixture of strategic considerations and traditional bases for territorial claims, and again provide considerable insight into the attitudes that affected negotiations. Resisting Dutch demands that the Barrier include part of French Flanders, the French pressed for the return to them of Lille, Tournai, Aire and a number of other places. They argued that these places would close the French frontier without threatening their neighbours and claimed that Tournai was part of the ancient domain of the kingdom but, although they regained Lille, Valenciennes, Maubeuge and other forts promised to the Dutch by the Barrier Treaty of 1709, the French did not regain Tournai. Victor Amadeus's demands for an extended Alpine barrier were rejected by the French as leaving the Dauphiné vulnerable and, in a modern touch, Torcy urged Bolingbroke to consult a map. He also refused to accept the claim to Monaco, both because it was essential for the security of Provence and because it was important to protect the interests of the Duke of Monaco. Torcy also protested against the loss of any 'ancient domaine of the Crown' to Victor Amadeus, leading to Bolingbroke's sceptical observations, 'yet this point of honour is to be got over, and this domaine is to be parted with, provided the valley of Barcelonnette be given in exchange'.[12]

By early 1713, the Anglo-French negotiators had produced terms that would satisfy Victor Amadeus, the United Provinces, Portugal and Prussia, and, on 11 April, their plenipotentiaries signed the peace treaties. Britain gained the recognition of the Protestant succession, the value of which was increased by Queen Anne's ill health, as well as Nova Scotia, Newfoundland, St Kitts and the return of Hudson Bay. An Anglo-Spanish peace treaty, signed at Utrecht on 13 July, ceded to Britain Gibraltar, which she had captured in 1704, Minorca, the *Asiento*, and the right to send an annual 'permission ship' to the West Indies to trade with the hitherto closed Spanish territories. Britain and France agreed that Charles VI was to receive the Spanish

Netherlands and Spanish Italy bar Sicily which was to go to Victor Amadeus along with a settlement of his Alpine frontier that was less generous than he had sought but was more geographically consistent than the old frontier. The Dutch gained a Barrier, and the French privateering base of Dunkirk was to lose its fortifications. Philip V renounced his claims to the French succession, while the disposal of the less contentious Orange succession brought Louis XIV the enclave of Orange in southern France, and Frederick I of Prussia a scattering of small territories that bore little relation to his existing possessions. His claim to Neuchâtel, an enclave between France and Switzerland, was also recognized, an apt demonstration of the importance of dynastic pretensions in the peace settlement. Britain and France agreed on mutual territorial restitutions in Iberia between Spain and Portugal, though the two powers did not sign an agreement, the last of the Utrecht treaties, until February 1715.

Charles VI was willing to abandon his claims to Spain, where he still held Barcelona and Majorca, but insisted on the exclusion of Max Emmanuel from Bavaria. A short burst of fighting brought Charles and the Empire into the peace. The Imperial Diet at Regensburg declared in July 1713 that the French proposals would 'tarnish the glory of the German nation', but, outnumbered by the French and without promised supplies and funds from the exhausted Empire and the *Erblande* (Austrian hereditary lands), Eugène was forced to accept the loss of Freiburg and Landau and to press Charles for peace. Charles had hoped to attack Victor Amadeus in order to gain Sicily but, instead, he had to order Eugène to negotiate the Treaty of Rastatt. Desiring peace and fearful that a Hanoverian succession in Britain might lead to the revitalization of the Grand Alliance, Louis accepted terms that were favourable for Charles. Instead of pressing his demands for the eviction of Austria from Italy and for a kingdom for Max Emmanuel, Louis accepted the simple restitution of the Electors of Bavaria and Cologne and the acquisition of the Spanish Netherlands and all of Spanish Italy, bar Sicily and the cessions to Victor Amadeus, as well as the gain of the Duchy of Mantua by Charles. The German settlement was based on the Peace of Rijswijk, with France retaining Strasbourg and Alsace, but not any possessions on the right bank of the Rhine. Charles was obliged to sacrifice the ambitions of John William of the Palatinate. The terms agreed at Rastatt on 6 March 1714 served as the basis for the congress for the signing of peace between the Empire and France which met later that year and produced the Treaty of Baden, signed on 7 September 1714.

A host of rulers complained about the settlement, including those of Bavaria, Cologne, Lorraine and Spain, and several Italian princes concerned about the extent to which the Austrians were using their power in the peninsula to determine territorial and judicial disputes to their satisfaction. However, with the exception of Victor Amadeus, who benefited from British sponsorship of an apparently useful protégé, the expansionist views of the minor rulers were generally neglected in the settlements of 1713–14.

A common theme of the negotiations of the period was their dominance by the major powers. The growth in the size of armed forces in the second half of the seventeenth century, the true 'military revolution' of the century, in so far as there was one, and the wars of the period 1683–1721 had increased the distinction between major and minor powers and had witnessed the failure both of several second-rank rulers, such as Max Emmanuel, to achieve greater power, and of several regions that possessed a strong sense of identity to retain or gain independence. Moldavia, Wallachia, Scotland and the Ukraine had all seen their autonomy lessened. Hungary had not achieved independence during its 1703–11 uprising though it had distracted substantial Austrian forces from the war with Louis, to his pleasure and Anglo-Dutch fury. Philip V successfully besieged Barcelona with French troops in 1714 and Catalan privileges were dramatically limited. The new order was symbolized by the construction of a new citadel in the Catalan capital. Rebel causes were abandoned in the peace, including the Jacobites, for whose benefit the French had sent an invasion fleet to Scottish waters in 1708, and the Camisards, Protestants in southern France, who had rebelled during 1702–11 and received some, though very little, British help.

Philip did not sign any treaty with Charles and his (second) marriage in 1714 to Elizabeth Farnese, niece of the childless Duke of Parma, a duchy Vienna claimed as an Imperial fief, indicated that he was still interested in Italy. In 1715, his forces captured Majorca from Charles's supporters and the possibility that he would seek to disrupt the Utrecht settlement in Italy appeared strong. Similarly there was believed to be a danger that the accession of George I in Britain (1714) and the disgracing of Anne's Tory ministers would lead to a rekindling of Anglo-French tension and the revival of French support for the Jacobites.

The settlements of 1713–14 left a host of differences. Some, such as Austrian resistance to the demand by Cardinal Rohan, Bishop of Strasbourg, that his German possessions entitled him to representation at the Imperial Diet, were hardly threatening but rather indications of the extent to which local territorial and judicial disputes could become diplomatic issues because of the absence of any monopolization of sovereign powers by coherent states with clear frontiers. Others were more serious and the wars fought in Western Europe between 1717 and 1748 suggest that it is misleading to regard the settlements as having created a stable new international order.

The Italian Question 1714–52

There was no war between any of the signatories of the peace treaties ending the Great Northern War for twenty years. In contrast, hostilities broke out in Italy in 1717, with the Spanish invasion of Sardinia, only four years after the Peace of Utrecht. There was war in Italy in 1717–20, 1733–5 and 1741–8, and tension for the remainder of the period down to 1748. This was essentially due to the fact that, whereas in the Baltic the power that was dissatisfied with the status quo was now-weak Sweden, in the case of Italy both Austria and Spain were dissatisfied and the satisfied powers were the weak, small Italian states, such as Venice, that had nothing to gain from change. The prizes offered by the anticipated extinction of local dynasties, the Medici Grand Dukes of Tuscany and the Farnese Dukes of Parma, which ended in the male line in 1731 and 1737 respectively, exacerbated the dispute between the major powers, for Philip V sponsored the claims of Don Carlos, born in January 1716, his eldest son by his marriage to Elizabeth Farnese, while Charles VI sought to exercise jurisdiction over both territories as Imperial fiefs. The conflicts and diplomacy of the period were to result in the transfer of control over more than half of Italy, mostly with no attention to the wishes of local rulers or inhabitants. Italian rulers did seek through diplomatic means to advance and defend their interests, but they were generally unsuccessful. Cosimo III of Tuscany sought support in 1710 for the eventual reestablishment of republican government before deciding to support the succession of his daughter after that of his childless sons. In 1713, the latter was decreed and recognized by the Senate of Florence and the Council of Two Hundred but Cosimo was to have less success in achieving international guarantees for his daughter than Charles VI, who rejected Cosimo's claim in 1714. Charles's daughter, Maria Theresa, was to find these guarantees of limited value in 1740–1, but

Charles, unlike Cosimo, did not have to face the allocation of his territories to others being decided during his lifetime. In 1716, Cosimo chose the Este family of Modena as the successors to his daughter, hoping for a union of the territories. If Cosimo's wishes were ignored, so also were those of other Italian rulers. Charles VI refused to recognize Victor Amadeus II as King of Sicily, refused to guarantee the integrity of his possessions in the Treaty of Rastatt and, in 1716, sent troops into Novi in the Republic of Genoa in furtherance of a border dispute.

Some of the local population sometimes took a role. In the case of Naples, most opinion was loyal to Spain until the death of Charles II and accepted the succession of Philip V, though there was an abortive coup in favour of the Austrians in 1701. There was no opposition to the Austrian conquest of 1707. Pragmatism was matched by a consistent wish to secure as much autonomy as possible for the Kingdom of Naples and its elite under whoever came to be king. Full independence was not anticipated and its advent in 1734 was unexpected; the point was to avoid complete, direct subordination to an oppressive monarch.

This was not, however, the objective for independent Italian rulers, but their limited room for manoeuvre was indicated by the enforced exchange of Sicily for poorer Sardinia that Victor Amadeus was obliged to accept in November 1718. This satisfied Charles VI's wish to reunite Sicily to the Kingdom of Naples and thus rule all of Spain's former Italian territories. Meaningful resistance came not from Victor Amadeus but from more powerful rulers concerned to keep Charles out of Sicily. Victor Amadeus had owed the island to the support of France and, in particular, Britain. A British naval squadron took him there in late 1713, just as another was to escort Don Carlos to Tuscany in 1731. However, George I did not continue the anti-Austrian policies of Anne's Tory ministers while, after the death of Louis XIV, Victor Amadeus complained bitterly about the French failure to restrain Austria in Italy.

Victor Amadeus's diplomacy was rendered redundant by the unexpected Spanish invasion of Sicily on 1 July 1718, the failure of most Sicilians to support the king and the rapid conquest of most of the island. Spanish fortunes were affected not by Victor Amadeus but by the actions of other powers determined to ensure that changes to the Utrecht settlement took place only with their consent. The British fleet, whose preparation had failed to dissuade the Spaniards from invading, destroyed most of the Spanish fleet off Cape Passaro on 11 August. Meanwhile, on 2 August, Charles VI had signed a treaty with

Britain and France, a treaty mistakenly known as the Quadruple Alliance because the United Provinces did not adhere as anticipated. The treaty provided for an alliance between the powers, a settlement between Charles and Philip in line with the provisions of Utrecht, the exchange of Sicily and Sardinia, and Carlos's reversion to Parma and Tuscany to be guaranteed by Swiss garrisons. Philip refused to accept the terms and sought to effect, by means of a plot managed by his ambassador in Paris, the Cellamare conspiracy, the replacement of the pro-British regent, the Duke of Orléans, by more sympathetic courtiers led by the Duke of Maine. The conspiracy, broken in December 1718, in fact helped to win French domestic support for the declaration of war on Spain, published on 9 January 1719. Britain had declared war the previous month.

The war went badly for Spain. A poorly supplied Austrian force failed to drive the isolated Spaniards from Sicily but their position was weakened by British naval mastery. A French invasion of north-western Spain under James II's illegitimate son, the Duke of Berwick, revealed that Spain could not defend her frontier provinces and the major Spanish attempt to invade Britain on behalf of the Jacobites was thwarted by a storm off Cape Finisterre. A smaller force was defeated in Scotland. Philip finally acceded to the Quadruple Alliance in February 1720.

This was followed by the development of a Franco-Spanish alignment that led to a convention signed at Madrid on 27 March 1721, which stipulated support for the Treaties of Utrecht and London (the Quadruple Alliance), promised Franco-Spanish support for the Duke of Parma and French backing for Spanish pretensions to Gibraltar and invited Great Britain to accede, which she did by the Triple Alliance of Madrid of 13 June 1721, though without offering a firm promise to return Gibraltar. The alliance was cemented dynastically by the betrothal of Louis XV to Philip's daughter, Maria Anna, born in 1718, and by the marriage in January 1722 of Philip's heir, Louis, to one of Orléans's daughters. Philip hoped to use the new diplomatic alignment to isolate Austria at the peace congress that had been summoned at Cambrai to settle outstanding differences, but Anglo-French mediation failed Spain at Cambrai in 1724 and both powers rejected Spanish proposals for the coercion of Tuscany to establish Carlos's position.

As a result, in November 1724, the former Dutch diplomat Jan Willem, Baron van Ripperda, was instructed by Philip to go on a secret mission to Vienna to propose the marriage of Carlos and his brother

Philip to Charles VI's daughters, which would establish a Bourbon–Farnese claim to the Habsburg inheritance. This improbable scheme, typical of the adventurous dynastic diplomacy of the period, that was generally unsuccessful but introduced a powerful element of unpredictability, was helped by Austrian isolation and by a breach in Franco-Spanish relations. After Orléans's death in 1723, the Duke of Bourbon had become the chief French minister and, in order to weaken the position of his rival and Louis XV's heir, the new Duke of Orléans, he sought a speedy marriage for Louis, a policy that ill health on the king's part lent weight to. Maria Anna was therefore sent back to her parents in March 1725 and Louis married Maria Leszcynski, daughter of Stanislaus, that August.

Spain broke off diplomatic relations and recalled her plenipotentiaries from Cambrai. On 30 April 1725, Ripperda concluded treaties of peace and defensive alliance at Vienna with Charles VI's ministers, a commercial treaty following on 1 May. Carlos was granted the reversion of Tuscany and Parma. He and his brother gained the prospect of Habsburg marriages, while Spain guaranteed the Pragmatic Sanction and granted special privileges to the Ostend Company, a transoceanic trading company founded by Charles in 1722 that threatened Anglo-Dutch trade to the East Indies.

The treaties and the new alignment created a lot of unease in Britain and France. Bourbon's ministry was concerned about the prospect of Austrian support for Philip V's claim to succeed Louis XV and the British were worried by rumoured secret articles in support of the Jacobite Pretender, fears that were unfounded in so far as the actual agreements were concerned. Both powers feared that the challenge to their diplomatic influence represented by the new treaties could force them into making concessions in the myriad of disputes in which they were involved. On 3 September 1725, in response, Britain, France and Prussia signed the Treaty of Hanover guaranteeing each other's territories and rights inside and outside Europe. Austria and Spain responded with a secret treaty of marriage and offensive alliance, signed at Vienna on 5 November 1725. This stipulated a double marriage between Carlos and Philip and two of Charles's daughters, though stating that the crowns and territories of France, Spain and the Habsburg family would remain forever separate. Philip V promised to provide subsidies to Charles, who agreed to assist in the return of Gibraltar and Minorca to Spain.

Charles, however, did not want war, dynastic union with Spain or the establishment of Carlos in Italy. He concentrated on building up a powerful alliance, gaining the support of Russia and Prussia in 1726, and offered Cosimo III's successor, John Gaston, a private guarantee of grand-ducal sovereignty. The years 1725–7 witnessed major military mobilizations. Britain dispatched three large fleets, one to the Baltic to persuade Denmark and Sweden, successfully, that an accession to the Hanover alliance would not leave them vulnerable to Russia, one to the West Indies to blockade the Spanish treasure fleet, and thereby prevent Spain from being able to provide Austria with subsidies, and one to Spanish waters to menace attack and prevent a blockade of Gibraltar. The Spaniards fired the first shots when they began an unsuccessful siege of Gibraltar in February 1727. George I, anxious about Hanoverian vulnerability to Prussian and Austrian attack, persuaded France to move forces towards the Rhine.

Throughout, negotiations continued between some of the powers of the two alliances. Cardinal Fleury, Louis XV's former tutor, who became his chief minister in 1726, was determined to avoid war and he attempted to restrain the more aggressive British ministry, leading to British doubts about the degree of his commitment to the alliance. Aware that Austria was less interested in conflict than Spain, Fleury used an ultimatum to persuade Charles to settle. On 31 May 1727, the Preliminaries of Paris, the terms for a pacification of Europe, reaffirming the Treaty of the Quadruple Alliance and suspending the trade of the Ostend Company, were signed by the representatives of Britain, France, the United Provinces and Austria. Spain sought to defy the new agreement, but lack of Austrian support, the failure to woo France from her British alliance and Philip's ill health led Spain to settle by the Convention of the Pardo of 6 March 1728. This postponed contentious issues to a congress that opened at Soissons in June 1728, but that proved as unable to settle issues and consequently as much a cause of a new diplomatic alignment as Cambrai had been, indicating the limitations of the congress system in this period.

The Austrian rejection of Spanish pressure for Carlos's marriage in early 1729 led Spain to settle with Britain and France on condition that they supported Spanish garrisons in Parma and Tuscany. It might seem surprising that this apparently relatively minor issue was so important in the diplomacy of the period but for Spain, which had little confidence in international guarantees, they were the only secure basis for Carlos's succession, while, for the rest of Europe, they were seen not so much as a minor infraction of the Quadruple Alliance, but as a possible means by which Spain might destroy the existing Italian system and launch herself on a career of Italian conquest. The Treaty of Seville of 9 November 1729 settled most outstanding differences between Britain, France and Spain and committed them to accept the Spanish garrisons. The unfounded rumours that secret clauses stipulated the return of Gibraltar, Minorca, Naples and Sicily to Spain were typical of the world of distrust and rumour within which diplomats operated.

Charles refused to be intimidated and, as neither the Fleury nor Walpole ministries really wanted to fight, the Seville alliance quickly collapsed into recriminations. An Austrian attempt to link negotiations for the admission of the Spanish garrisons to a guarantee of the Pragmatic Sanction was rejected. As the French urged the need to plan for a general war in 1731, it was clear that the Anglo-French alliance had become, by the summer of 1730, under the stimulus of Spanish demands, the basis of a possible recasting of the European system tied to the abasement of Austria, which was to become a matter of planning and action, rather than speculation. This was unacceptable to the British, but they did not wish to lose the Spanish alliance and, when they opened secret unilateral negotiations with the Austrians, they insisted on the Spanish garrisons. In the Second Treaty of Vienna of 16 March 1731, Austria, Britain and the United Provinces mutually guaranteed each other's territories and rights and the last two guaranteed the Pragmatic Sanction on condition that the archduchesses should not marry Bourbon or Prussian princes. As security for Carlos's succession to Parma and Tuscany, 6000 Spanish troops were to be admitted immediately.

The British hoped to reconcile France and Spain to the new treaty, creating a new international order based on the Pragmatic Sanction to complement the new Italian order based on the Spanish garrisons. French refusal destroyed the Anglo-French alliance but the Spaniards rejected French approaches, leading to an Anglo-Austrian–Spanish agreement, signed at Vienna on 22 July, recognizing Spain's acceptance of the Second Treaty of Vienna. An Anglo-Spanish fleet convoyed the Spanish troops to Livorno (Leghorn) in October and Carlos, similarly escorted, followed. As the Duke of Parma had died on 20 January 1731 and the pregnancy of his widow, on which Europe's diplomats waited, had been shown to be false, Carlos became the new Duke.

France was opposed to the new European order based on the Anglo-Austrian–Spanish alliance. The extent of her success in the War of the Polish Succession (1733–5) was due to the rapid disintegration of this alliance and the eagerness of Spain to attack Austria. The Bourbon effort was to be aided by the alliance of Victor Amadeus's heir, Charles Emmanuel III. Austrian difficulties stemmed in large part from Italy where British diplomacy had failed to solve differences with Charles Emmanuel over the overlordship of the frontier region of the Langhes and differences with Spain over Carlos's vassalage and the size of the Spanish forces. These issues were serious irritants in a society where rank and recognition were crucial indicators of status and power, but it is also clear that Philip and his wife were looking for an opportunity to return Italy to the Spanish sphere of influence. In addition, however critical some commentators might be of their condition and however much their pay might be in arrears, the Spanish armed forces were large, while the vigour of Spanish policy had been amply displayed in 1732 when an expedition, having aroused fears of invasion in Austrian Italy, the island of Sardinia and Britain, seized Oran in North Africa. Spain was too powerful, and her ruler too volatile, to be regarded as a client state or a power following predictable policies. The French did not manage to ally with the Spaniards in the Treaty of the Escorial, later known as the First Family Compact, until 7 November 1733, after the French declaration of war on Charles VI of 10 October and the beginning of operations by French and Sardinian troops. The Treaty of Turin, signed with Charles Emmanuel on 26 September, provided that Carlos should have Naples and Sicily, Charles Emmanuel the Milanese.

French and Sardinian forces easily overran the Milanese that winter. The following summer, Carlos conquered Naples, the city falling on 10 May, and the Austrian forces in southern Italy were defeated at Bitonto on 25 May. This was one of the most decisive campaigns of the century. Austrian pressure on Britain to send naval assistance in accordance with the Second Treaty of Vienna was evaded with the argument that Charles's role in the Polish dispute was not blameless, though that had little bearing on Spanish operations. Philip V ceded his rights in Naples and Sicily to Carlos, who in consequence proclaimed himself King of Naples. Though Charles Emmanuel was already governing the Milanese under the Treaty of Turin, and sought Mantua, still held for Charles VI, Philip V wanted both and his wife thought that Parma, Tuscany, Naples and Sicily should be the inheritance of her sons. To a certain extent such demands were negotiating counters but they also indicated the bold wish to reallocate territories that characterized some of the diplomacy of this period. The wide-ranging schemes of 1741–2 after the death of Charles VI to partition his territories were prefigured in 1733–5 by discussions about the fate of his Italian possessions.

That Charles VI finally obtained better terms in the Preliminary Articles of 3 October 1735, that served as the basis of the Third Treaty of Vienna of 18 November 1738, owed little to his forces. Their attempt to reconquer northern Italy was defeated at Parma on 29 June and Guastalla on 19 September 1734, and in 1735 they were reduced to the defence of Mantua, in which they were aided by serious Sardinian–Spanish differences. However, French determination to beat their allies to a separate peace was aided by their willingness to compromise over Italy. Compromise and equivalents were an integral feature of the treaties of the period but that of 1738 depended on Sardinian weakness and Spanish inability to continue fighting on her own. The peace left Carlos with Naples, Sicily and the *presidios* but, in exchange, Parma went to Charles and the Tuscan reversion to Duke Francis of Lorraine in return for the acquisition of Lorraine by Stanislaus. As in the Partition Treaties, Italy was required to provide the equivalents and the equalling-out that compensated for gains elsewhere. With the death of John Gaston in July 1737, Francis, who had married Maria Theresa in February 1736, succeeded to Tuscany. Charles Emmanuel had to return the Milanese but his gains included some of it, not least the area around Novara, increasing the vulnerability of what remained with Charles.[13]

France, the Empire and Britain 1714–39

The central relationship in Western Europe was that between France and Austria. Generally it was one of rivalry and hostility but that did not preclude periods of cooperation, as in 1718–20 and 1736–9, and suggestions that relations might improve. Militarily, Western Europe was dominated by the armies of the two powers and the most serious conflict was the War of the Polish Succession between them in 1733–5. However, though their relationship was the dominant one in the diplomatic and military spheres, it was affected by independent initiatives by other powers, particularly Britain, Spain and the leading German powers.

Uneasy peace 1714–31

Austria, Britain and France all had in common an uncertain dynastic position. Louis XV, who succeeded his great-grandfather in 1715, was born in 1710. He did not marry until 1725 or have a son until 1729, and it was not until the late 1750s that the succession to the throne was firmly assured in his line. The claims of his uncle, Philip V, to the succession placed the regent, the Duke of Orléans, who controlled France from 1715 until his death in 1723, in a precarious position and encouraged him to look abroad for allies who could counteract the Spanish threat to intervene if Louis died. Philip doubted the validity of the Utrecht renunciation of his claims to the French throne, which placed Orléans, Louis XIV's nephew, next in line. When, in October 1728, Louis XV contracted smallpox, Philip prepared for the seizure of power in France and rumours spread of a possible civil war between his supporters and those of the then Duke of Orléans, the son of the former regent. Louis recovered swiftly, but the vulnerability of the situation is suggested by the political crisis that affected Russia in early 1730 when the childless Peter II (1727–30) died of smallpox.

The challenge of Jacobitism posed a major problem for successive British governments. It was suggested at the time that the threat of Jacobitism was deliberately exaggerated to discredit the principal opposition group, the Tories, and it had been suggested recently that they were largely free from Jacobitism. Such a view would have found little support from George I (1714–27) and George II (1727–60), both of whom believed that, although individual Tories were loyal and could be trusted, the party as a whole was factious and disloyal. Equally serious was the manner in which hostile rulers could be encouraged to support Jacobitism, and were themselves encouraged in their stance by a belief in the strength of Jacobitism. Jacobite chances were seen to depend on help from European powers.

The only children of the Emperor Charles VI (1711–40) to survive for any length of time were three daughters, the youngest of whom died in 1730 aged four. Charles hoped to secure the undivided succession of his various territories for his eldest daughter Maria Theresa, rather than for the daughters of his elder brother, Joseph I (1705–11). This, as much as the stipulations of the indivisibility of the inheritance and the reversion to female in the absence of male descendants, was the most troublesome aspect of Charles's promulgation of the Pragmatic Sanction in 1713, which assigned the succession to his own daughters in default of male heirs and, for the first time, asserted the indivisibility of the inheritance. Joseph's daughters, Maria Josepha and Maria Amalia, born in 1699 and 1701, were considerably older than Charles's two eldest daughters, Maria Theresa and Maria Anna, born in 1717 and 1718. Charles had a son in 1716 but he died that year. To reinforce the exclusion of the Josephine archduchesses, Charles ensured that their marriages were accompanied by solemn renunciations of all claims to the succession. In 1719, the marriage of Maria Josepha and the heir to the Electorate of Saxony, the future Augustus III, was preceded by a renunciation sworn to by bride, groom and groom's father. In 1722, the marriage of Maria Amalia to the heir to Bavaria, Charles Albert, was preceded by a similar renunciation. However, both the Saxons and the Bavarians believed that neither the acts of parents nor renunciations could abnegate inalienable rights. In 1725, to fortify the position of the Bavarians, who had only won the younger of the Josephine archduchesses, Charles Albert's father, Max Emmanuel, forged a copy of Emperor Ferdinand I's will, purportedly awarding them the Austrian hereditary lands upon the extinction of the dynasty's male line. Charles VI's continued failure to produce a male heir and his efforts to secure European support for the Pragmatic Sanction helped to make the Austrian succession a more critical issue. Under Charles, it increasingly dominated Austrian policy, while powers opposed to Austria resorted to the device of encouraging pretensions upon the succession.

These dynastic weaknesses played a major role in the diplomacy of the decades beginning with the Hanoverian succession in Britain in 1714. They led the rulers of the three states to seek guarantees of their position, while, at the same time, providing a possible means for intervention by hostile monarchs. In the case of the Habsburg dominions, they offered the possibility of a territorial recasting of central Europe. Within the Empire, Bavaria fostered the development of a close alliance, a *Hausunion*, between the closely related Wittelsbach Electors of Bavaria, Cologne, the Palatinate and Trier, and made it clear, in response to Anglo-French efforts in 1725–6 to secure their alliance against Austria, that a commitment to Bavarian pretensions was expected.

Dynastic weaknesses were not the only threat to stability. The Utrecht settlements had left a number of issues unsettled and several rulers unsatisfied and, although the principal sphere of tension was Italy, this affected other powers because of their interests there and their concern about how changes would affect the rest of Europe. A bigger cause of change was the very coming of peace. This dissolved wartime coalitions and created opportunities for new alliances. Within four years of the peace, Louis XIV was to approach Charles VI for better relations, and Orléans to negotiate an alliance with George I. The French approach to Charles was a tentative one, due in part to Austro-Spanish differences in Italy. Stressing common Catholicism, Louis sought to limit the possibility of Anglo-Austrian action against France. The accession of George I in August 1714 and the replacement of the Tory ministry by a Whig one threatened a reversal of the Austrian isolation that had obliged her to accept the Utrecht settlement, and forced Louis to reconsider his diplomatic position. Because the Whigs had bitterly opposed the Utrecht settlement and played a major role in ensuring the parliamentary rejection of Bolingbroke's plan for improving Anglo-French commercial relations, many assumed in 1714 that the accession of George would lead to poor relations with France, if not war, while, in Britain, French action in support of the Jacobites was believed imminent. Relations between the two countries were very poor in late 1714 and early 1715. The French failure to wreck the harbour of the privateering base at Dunkirk, as stipulated at Utrecht, had already caused tension between the Tory ministry and France. The issue was pressed with vigour by the new Whig government. In itself, the destruction of the sluices that prevented the harbour of Dunkirk from silting up was not of great importance, but it was seen as an indication of French willingness to obey and British ability to enforce the provisions of Utrecht. Furthermore, it provided a concrete instance by which French professions of good intentions could be judged.

The Whig ministry sought to recreate the Grand Alliance with Austria and the United Provinces, but their failure to do so, which was due in part to strong differences between the Dutch and the Austrians over the Austrian Netherlands, cleared the path towards better Anglo-French relations, a course that the Dutch supported. It might appear inevitable that the two weak rulers, George and Orléans, should unite. The Jacobite and Spanish threats made a resolution of Anglo-French diplomatic difficulties urgent. However, distrust was strong in ministerial and diplomatic circles in both countries. In addition, the state of Anglo-French relations was linked closely to political struggles in London and Paris. The British ministry watched anxiously the fate of French factional struggles, fearing that d'Huxelles or Torcy would defeat Dubois in the battle to influence Orléans or that Orléans himself would fall.

The negotiation of the Anglo-French alliance was conducted in a strained atmosphere and its frenetic and secretive nature suggests that it is wrong to argue that the alliance was an obvious matter of cooperation for mutual protection. It was to be royal pressure, stemming from Hanoverian vulnerability in the face of the collapse of relations with Peter the Great, that persuaded the British ministry to settle with France. By the alliance, signed on 28 November 1716, France guaranteed Hanover and the Protestant succession, and undertook to ensure that James Stuart went beyond the Alps, while George promised military support if Philip should seek to rescind his renunciation of his claims to the French throne. Thanks to the Dutch accession on 4 January 1717, this became a Triple Alliance.

The Anglo-French alliance was to persist until March 1731 when, with the Second Treaty of Vienna, Britain reached a unilateral agreement with Austria that France both resented and refused to support. Though there were periods during the alliance when both powers were far from satisfied with the conduct of the other, especially in 1721–2 and 1728–30, the alliance, nevertheless, remained the basis of their respective foreign policies. While the treaty was fairly clear in its aims, the maintenance of the essentials of the Utrecht settlement, it was less clear about what should be done to enforce these provisions. Both powers unilaterally developed good relations with third parties – Britain with Prussia in 1723 – and often sought to persuade their alliance partner to yield in disputes with other powers, France supporting Russian claims against Britain in 1724. Nevertheless, they avoided supporting the interests of the other powers when they threatened the vital concerns of their partner.

This was particularly clear in the case of relations with Spain in the 1720s. France felt little support for the commercial privileges Britain had gained in the Spanish empire at Utrecht, which led to persistent complaints from French mercantile circles, or for her retention of Gibraltar, but was unwilling to break with Britain over either issue. French support for Spanish pretensions in Italy reflected wider concerns. Though some French ministers supported better relations with Austria, and France was to be allied with her in the Quadruple Alliance, and to seek to make an Austro-French understanding the basis of the Congress of Soissons in 1728, a major theme of French policy was opposition to Austria, the power that had both gained most from the Utrecht settlement and threatened to dominate post-Utrecht Germany and Italy. Britain was most suspicious of France in the case of Franco-Spanish relations, but the French were willing at moments of crisis in relations with Spain to follow the British lead, as in 1718–19 and 1727.

Thus, as in any alliance between major powers, there was tension within the Anglo-French alliance, and this was concentrated on, and rendered specific by, relations with third parties. It had been possible to reach agreement in 1716 over constructing the alliance, when it was a matter of mutual guarantees and a defensive mentality. However, attempts to expand the alliance, both in intention and by means of negotiating additional agreements with other powers, proved to be very difficult, and productive of strain and quarrels. The two periods when the alliance worked best were those when it was clearly defensive, in 1716–17 and 1725–7. In the latter case the alliance was threatened by a new, dramatic and unpredictable international grouping, the Austro-Spanish alliance, created in the negotiations leading up to the First Treaty of Vienna in the spring of 1725, and fortified, the following year, by the accessions of Prussia and Russia. This pact represented a formidable military threat, especially to Hanover, and it led to the reassertion of the Anglo-French alliance, first in the Treaty of Hanover in September 1725, and, second, in joint efforts to gain allies and to plan for war. The Austro-Russian alliance of 1726 helped to produce poor Franco-Russian relations, ensuring that negotiations with Russia were no longer a point at issue between Britain and France.

France and Britain appreciated their mutual need, and the unilateral policy-making that had characterized the early 1720s was replaced by cooperation. This was not free of dispute, but the general theme of these years was of an alliance strengthened by outside threat. In 1727 and 1730, the alliance's plans for war with Austria and her allies included as a significant element, to which the British negotiators attached great importance, the movement of a French army into the Empire to protect Hanover from attack. In 1729 and 1730, when Prussian attacks on Hanover were threatened, the French position was again crucial. George ascribed the Prussian decision not to attack in 1729 to the assistance of his allies.

In 1729–30, French diplomats stressed Hanoverian vulnerability in order to press the British ministry to support French policy initiatives. French pressure to ally with the Wittelsbachs was especially important, for such an alliance would entail unpopular peacetime subsidies and would have committed Britain to a long-term anti-Austrian policy that was at variance with the Anglo-Hanoverian policy of bullying Austria into being an ally on acceptable terms. George II and his ministers did not wish to become tied down in a system for supporting Charles Albert of Bavaria's claims on the Austrian succession. Far from being trapped in rigid conceptions of international relations, neither the British nor the French ministries saw the alliance in the 1720s as much more than an expedient that should be used to further aims as long as it served that purpose, and discarded if there was a change of circumstances. Possibly James Stanhope, the minister who played the major role in formulating policy in the late 1710s, had genuinely hoped to make the alliance permanent and use it as the basis for the system of mutual guarantees and collective security he so favoured. However, this idea had won little support in British policy-making circles, where suspicion of France was never absent, and it was abandoned with his death in 1721.

This was a realistic view, given the kaleidoscopic nature of international relations in this period, and the fragility of French support for the alliance. Dependent in the late 1710s on the position of Orléans and his confidential adviser Dubois, who was foreign minister from September 1718 until his death in August 1723, it was based on little more than the life of Bourbon's successor, the elderly Cardinal Fleury (1726–43), a decade later. British policy-makers responded with fear to reports of Fleury's ill health or impending fall. They were well-aware that support for the alliance in France was limited, just as French ministers were concerned about the stability of the British government and the influence of ministers and diplomats deemed anti-French.

Anxious about Hanoverian security, fearful of the prospect of unilateral French and Spanish approaches to Austria and conscious of domestic criticism of their foreign policy, the British ministry began negotiations with Austria in the early autumn of 1730. Disquiet over both long- and short-term French policies played a role, but there was no wish to end good relations with France and the British hoped wrongly that France would accept the new alignment. Unilateral British negotiations with Austria were not new. They had been considered in 1728 and conducted in 1729. The commitment to the French alliance had never been so total as to preclude consideration of better relations with Austria. In 1730–1, the negotiations succeeded because Austria, having lost her Spanish ally in November 1729, felt more vulnerable, the British ministry was willing to make a greater effort to achieve a settlement, probably because of the battering its French alliance had taken in the 1730 parliamentary session over illegal repairs to Dunkirk, and George II was willing to shelve Hanoverian demands, in order to secure Hanoverian security through an alliance with Austria that would lead to Austrian restraint of Prussia. By the Second Treaty of Vienna of 16 March 1731, George II, the United Provinces and Charles VI mutually guaranteed each other's territories and the first two guaranteed the Pragmatic Sanction as long as no Bourbon or Prussian marriage for Charles's daughters was involved. In a separate, later, agreement on the Hanoverian issues George was granted the investitures of Bremen and Verden, but Charles refused to support his attempt to maintain his influence and limit that of Prussia in Mecklenburg.

France could not be expected to welcome the guarantee of the Pragmatic Sanction, a policy she had strongly opposed in early 1730. Conversely, the Austrians were opposed to the British idea of reassuring Fleury about the intentions of the new alliance. A French entry into the new system would have weakened Anglo-Austrian and strengthened Franco-Spanish ties and the unsuccessful attempts to ensure the cooperation of the four powers in 1717–24 hardly provided an encouraging precedent for Austria. In 1731, the possibility of Britain using the Vienna alliance as a stepping stone for a European peace and of persuading France to assent to the new arrangements was lost. Possibly such an attempt would have failed, defeated by French unwillingess to accept a dictated settlement. However, without French consent, no European peace settlement could be secure or long-lasting. Whilst France was isolated, her diplomatic efforts, such as the attempts to gain the alliance of Sweden, Denmark, Saxony and Bavaria and to prevent the Imperial Diet accepting the Pragmatic Sanction, were a threat to European tranquillity. As soon as France could gain powerful allies who were willing to act, as in late 1733 with Sardinia and Spain, she was to prove a major threat.

The basis for any French accession to the Anglo-Austrian agreement was asumed to be a guarantee of the Pragmatic Sanction. France was unwilling to provide such a guarantee, but the eventual solution of the Third Treaty of Vienna (1738), the acquisition of Lorraine for the French royal family in return for the guarantee, had been considered before 1733. Should Maria Theresa marry Duke Francis of Lorraine, as she was to do in 1736, the dynastic union of Lorraine and Austria would become a strong possibility, unacceptable to the French, not least as it would revive the strategic fears of the seventeenth century. However, the British ministry, which had pressed Austria to satisfy Spain and accept the introduction of the Spanish garrisons, was unwilling to press Austria to satisfy France over Lorraine. It was not until later in the decade that France and Austria were to settle their differences, including the Lorraine question and the French guarantee of the Pragmatic Sanction, and they did so without British mediation.

From the Second Treaty of Vienna to the War of the Austrian Succession 1731–40

By 1731 the dynastic weakness that had characterized Austria, Britain and France in 1715 was apparently over. Louis XV was an adult with a son, while the Hanoverian dynasty had survived the Jacobite rising of 1715 and the succession of George II in 1727 had been peaceful. Charles VI had obtained the alliance of all the major powers bar France and their guarantee of the Pragmatic Sanction. The diplomatic realignment of 1731 had eased some tensions while creating others but circumstances rather than any rigid system determined relations in the following decade. The Second Treaty of Vienna did not lead to an immediate breakdown of Anglo-French relations, though the summer of 1731 saw a war-panic, each power fearing attack from the other. Though their relations until the outbreak of formal hostilities in 1744 were poor, fighting was avoided until 1743. Britain did not honour her treaty commitments by supporting Austria against France in the War of the Polish Succession, while France ignored Jacobite requests for assistance until 1744, and refused to support Spain fully in her war with Britain, the War of Jenkins' Ear that began in 1739, by declaring war, as had been feared in London. Both states vied for influence in other countries, particularly in Denmark, Portugal, Sweden and the United Provinces, and competed in colonial and commercial affairs, but they took care to maintain a peaceful rivalry.

A similar rivalry characterized Austro-French relations in 1731–2. It centred on the Empire where, on 11 January 1732, Charles VI obtained the support of the Electoral College for the Pragmatic Sanction. France encouraged the opposition of Augustus II of Saxony, with whom a subsidy treaty was concluded on 25 May 1732, and Charles Albert of Bavaria, and a Saxon–Bavarian treaty was signed on 4 July 1732. These moves, though peaceful, were essentially preparatory for a future conflict over the Austrian succession. That was the prime issue in German diplomacy in 1731–2. War, though, was threatened by another succession dispute, those to the Rhenish duchies of Jülich and Berg, part of the territories of the childless Karl Phillip, Elector Palatine. The rights of his heirs in the Palatinate, the house of Palatine–Sülzbach, to succeed in Jülich–Berg were contested by Frederick William I, who, in 1732, responded to Karl Phillip's ill-health by preparing to fight. Karl Phillip's recovery ended the crisis and he was to survive until 1742, being peacefully succeeded at a time when

Prussian attentions were concentrated on the larger prize of the Austrian succession.

The Polish succession agitated diplomats well before 1733. The elective nature of the monarchy, the contentious nature of the last election and the conflicting interests of several major powers suggested that the issue might produce war. It was generally accepted that trouble would follow Augustus II's death, but although that was widely reported as imminent in the 1720s, he survived until 1733. The crucial differences between 1733, with its outbreak of a major war, and 1721–32, when serious differences between the powers failed to lead to war, were the willingness of France to fight and the beginning of hostilities in Eastern Europe. The international situation was favourable for a French attack on Charles in 1733. British attempts to settle Austro-Spanish and Austro-Sardinian disputes were clearly unsuccessful, the Anglo-Austrian relationship was tense, the United Provinces weak and, according to Chavigny, the French envoy in London, the Hanoverian monarchy was in danger of collapsing before Jacobitism, national indebtedness and contentious financial legislation, the Excise Crisis.

That the international situation became favourable for an attack does not mean that it caused it: France had not attacked Austria in 1730, when Britain, Spain and the United Provinces were also committed to do so and Austria's leading ally, Russia, was affected by domestic political turmoil. The French Council of State decided on 20 May 1733 that war would be declared before they were sure of the support of Sardinia and Spain. Given the significance of royal and national dignity and honour in this era and of dynastic pride, it is understandable that Louis XV should both support the candidature of his father-in-law, Stanislaus Leszczynski, for the Polish throne and oppose the attempt to prevent it. On 17 March 1733, Louis declared that he would not tolerate any interference with the free choice of the Polish nation. Royal honour was involved, as it had been for Philip V of Spain in 1725, when Louis XV sent back his intended bride and, as in the latter case, the reaction was violent. The effect of this on French policy is incalculable, as is the wish to take revenge for the diplomatic isolation of 1731, while it is not clear what the relation between the domestic political problems of 1732 and the aggressive diplomatic strategy of the following year may have been. That France went to war probably owed more to a conviction that she must fight for royal honour and to prevent humiliation and isolation than to any wish to establish her power in Eastern Europe. The conviction that France was prepared to fight led Charles Emmanuel III of Sardinia and Philip V to reject attempts to keep them allied to Britain and Austria.

On 10 October 1733, Louis XV declared war on Charles VI, holding him responsible for the actions of his Russian ally in Poland. Lorraine was overrun and the Rhenish fort of Kehl seized that year, but the French concentrated their war effort in Italy. A Franco-Dutch neutrality agreement of 1733 prevented the French from attacking the Austrian Netherlands, and concern about the reaction of neutral Britain and the United Provinces may well have limited French operations in the Empire.

Prefiguring the later failure of numerous rulers to fulfil their guarantees of the Pragmatic Sanction, a number of powers failed to come to Charles VI's assistance. Britain and the United Provinces were more concerned by their domestic situation. Their governments feared the costs of a war, while the Walpole ministry was concerned about the general election due in 1734 and the danger of French support for the Jacobites. However, a substantial British naval armament was prepared, both in 1734 and 1735, and the policy of the late 1720s of negotiating subsidy treaties was resumed. The increase in military strength enabled the ministry to offer its good offices in finding terms upon which the war could be ended, with the implicit threat that a refusal to accept either good offices or the subsequent terms would lead to conflict. When, in 1735, Spain threatened to invade Portugal, Britain sent a substantial squadron to the Tagus to protect her ally. The British also intervened actively to prevent other powers from supporting France, influencing Danish and Swedish policy, as well as to foster antagonism between Spain and Sardinia, and to coax the United Provinces into military preparations. Fleury's decision to accept and seek to manipulate Britain's decision to use her good offices, rather than to ignore it contemptuously, reflected his appreciation of British determination to influence the conflict.

The negotiations at The Hague in the winter of 1734–5 failed, but British neutrality was aided by French moderation. France did not support the Jacobites or make military moves against the centres of government of her enemies, as she had done in 1703–4 and was to do in 1741 (Austria) and 1744 (Britain). The peace she negotiated with Austria did not stipulate excessive Bourbon gains. Stanislaus's acquisition of Lorraine with its reversion to France did not represent a fundamental alteration in the balance of power, a difficult concept to apply with precision anyway. Lorraine had been militarily vulnerable to France for a long time, having been gained by them at the start of every major war. The territorial changes in Italy were not as detrimental to Austria as had been feared.

The British ministry has been criticized for failing to enter the war, but it is difficult to support claims that this was an error. Austrian weakness in the early 1740s reflected her unsuccessful war with Turkey (1737–9), the unpredictable policy of Frederick II and the Russian inability to help, rather than any earlier British failure to support her. The experience of the War of the Spanish Succession suggests that had Britain joined in, she would have found Austria committing her energies to Italy and demanding subsidies, whilst leaving Britain with the difficult task of holding the Austrian Netherlands against the principal French war effort, as was indeed to happen in 1745–8.

The preliminary treaty signed by Austria and France, which led to the Third Treaty of Vienna of 1738, produced an *entente* between the two powers centred on a French guarantee of the Pragmatic Sanction. French diplomatic support for Austria forced an unwilling Sardinia and, in particular, Spain to accept an Italian settlement less favourable than they had militarily secured. The aggressively anti-Austrian French foreign minister Chauvelin was dismissed in February 1737 and the most vociferous contender for a share of the Austrian inheritance, Charles Albert of Bavaria, was consigned to a diplomatic limbo, his freedom of manoeuvre destroyed by the understanding of his two powerful neighbours. In place of her alliance with Austria, Britain became more interested in winning over Prussia and Russia. It was expected that the future Frederick II, who secretly received funds from his uncle, George II, would support Britain when he came to the throne. The exchange of envoys with Russia in 1732 was followed by a commercial treaty in 1734 and by a British diplomatic initiative launched in 1738 to negotiate an Anglo-Russian alliance. That such a treaty was not signed until April 1741 was due to Russian rather than British obduracy.

Many eighteenth-century wars ended in secret unilateral negotiations, but the terms France accepted in 1735 were completely unacceptable to her allies and, by unilaterally abandoning them, she destroyed the alliance that supported her in the War of the Polish Succession, not that Sardinia and Spain had failed to engage in secret diplomacy. Distrust between the powers that had plotted or acted against Austria in 1732–5 made a successful resumption of such action appear less likely. When France guaranteed the Pragmatic Sanction she had saved the prior rights of third parties such as Bavaria, and, on 16

May 1738, France secretly signed an agreement with Bavaria promising to support her just claims. Nevertheless, the late 1730s did not witness a repetition of the French diplomatic offensive against Austria of 1731–3, and it was in line with his general policy that Fleury responded to Charles VI's death on 20 October 1740 by assuring the Austrian envoy Prince Liechtenstein that Louis XV would observe all his engagements with Austria.

Chapter 8

From Frederick the Great to American Independence 1740–83

The period from Frederick the Great's invasion of Silesia to the acceptance of American independence saw a major transformation both in Europe's place in the world and in the European world. Britain's defeat of France, making her the leading European global power, was matched by the creation of a strong British territorial presence in India that was to be the basis of subsequent expansion in South Asia. The American Revolution, in turn, shattered the unity of the English-speaking world and created the first of the European 'successor states': inhabited by independent people of European descent. The relationship between these developments and international shifts within Europe were frequently limited and indirect, and it is easy to understand why, in comparison, international relations within Europe may appear inconsequential. However, there were significant links, and, in order to understand contemporary concerns and attitudes, it is appropriate to devote considerable weight to developments within Europe. The period began and closed with war. Conflict ranged widely. In 1740, Prussia invaded Silesia, while the British unsuccessfully pressed the Spaniards in the New World. In 1783, the Russians occupied the Crimea and American independence was recognized.

The War of the Austrian Succession 1740–8

It is not clear what France would have done had the recently crowned Frederick II not attacked Maria Theresa by invading her duchy of Silesia on 16 December 1740. Fleury was aware that other rulers saw the death of Charles VI as an opportunity for action, but his early plans were restricted to a scheme to deny the Imperial election to Francis of Lorraine, rather than to eternalize the glory of Louis XV by heeding Providence's call to reestablish a just European balance of power, as Charles Albert suggested. The Prussian invasion of Silesia dramatically altered the situation by substituting action for negotiation and by forcing other European powers to define their position. It is possible to suggest that France would have gone to war with Austria anyway, but it was equally the case that France in 1740 was moving towards war with Britain in order to prevent the latter from conquering Spanish territories in the West Indies and, by defeating Spain, destroying any maritime balance of power. Britain and Spain had gone to war in 1739 over British grievances about Spanish restrictions on British trade in the Caribbean. War between Britain and France was widely anticipated and in August the French sent a fleet to the West Indies to prevent British conquests. However, the French did not attack Britain in the West Indies. As in the War of the Polish Succession, when France had taken care to avoid hostilities, so, in 1740, an uneasy balance, short of war, was maintained.

Frederick II was unable to achieve such a balance. His invasion of Silesia was not intended as the opening move of a major European war, a step that would precipitate attempts to enforce claims on the Austrian inheritance by other rulers. Frederick hoped that Maria Theresa would respond to a successful attack by agreeing to buy him off and, in many respects, his invasion can be seen as the action of an opportunist, seeking to benefit from a temporarily favourable European situation. Frederick offered, in return for Silesia, a guarantee for all the other German possessions of the Habsburgs, troops to serve in Italy or the Low Countries, support for Francis of Lorraine's imperial candidature (as a woman, Maria Theresa was not eligible to be Emperor) and a cash indemnity. Subsequently Frederick proposed a partition of Silesia. He hoped that Anglo-French hostility would lead both powers to bid for his support.[1] Frederick's opportunism can be regarded as a rash move, for, though the conquest of Silesia proved relatively easy, its retention in the face of persistent Austrian hostility was to be a major burden for Prussia. The French envoy felt that Frederick had attacked carelessly, without allies.

Combined with a duplicity characteristic of many rulers of the period, including his more religious father, was the rashness that led Frederick to declare that he would sooner perish than desist from his undertaking. The attack on Austria was to some extent fortuitous. In the autumn of 1740, Frederick had expressed more interest in Jülich–Berg and, just as he toyed with approaches from Britain and France, so he was clearly unsure whither to direct his aggressive instincts. Had Charles VI died a year later, then it is quite possible that Frederick would already have invaded Jülich–Berg, as his father had planned to do in 1732 and 1738. The consequence might have been a major war but one that pitched France, a traditional patron of the Wittelsbachs, against Protestant Prussia, as had been envisaged in the late 1730s. Thus, the combination of Frederick's aggression, rash or prudent, and the European situation at his accession did not make a War of Austrian Succession precipitated by Prussian action inevitable. Frederick was helped by the death of the Tsarina Anna, three days before that of Charles VI, and the succession of her two-month-old great-nephew Ivan VI and a weak and divided regency. Frederick predicted that her death would leave the Russians too concerned with domestic affairs to think of foreign policy.[2]

Prussian aggression helped to precipitate a major war. Despite British pressure, the Austrians were unwilling to accept Prussian claims, arguing that the cession of Silesia would be followed by demands on the Habsburg lands from other rulers. The failure to settle Austro-Prussian differences speedily had the same effect. Frederick overran Silesia and defeated the Austrians at Mollwitz on 10 April 1741. Maria Theresa's refusal to cede Silesia led Frederick to sign the Treaty of Breslau with France on 5 June. He renounced his claim to Jülich–Berg and agreed to support the Imperial candidature of Charles Albert in return for a French guarantee of Lower Silesia and French promises of military assistance for Bavaria and diplomatic pressure on Sweden to attack Russia. Fleury was affected by pressure at court from aristocratic circles eager for conflict. France and Frederick encouraged other powers to act, and they did so realizing the opportunities presented by what appeared to be a Europe in flux. On 15 August 1741, French troops began to cross the Rhine and, on 19 September, Marshal Belle-Isle, the principal French protagonist for war, obtained an offensive alliance between Charles Albert and Augustus III of Saxony: Charles Albert was to become Emperor and receive the Habsburg provinces of Bohemia, Upper Austria and the Tyrol. Augustus was to become King of Moravia and to gain Moravia and Upper Silesia. The threat of a French invasion of Hanover led George II to abandon his attempt to create an anti-French coalition and, on 25 September 1741, to promise his neutrality and his support for Charles Albert's imperial candidacy.

The Habsburgs appeared prostrate, an impression reinforced by signs of support for Charles Albert in Bohemia and Austria. Their traditional allies, Britain and the United Provinces, were weak and disunited domestically and unwilling to aid Austria with troops, while Austria's allies of the post-1726 period, Prussia and Russia, were respectively an enemy and affected by ministerial and dynastic instability. In contrast, a well-developed and well-motivated alliance was able to give military teeth to French diplomatic conceptions. On 14 September, Linz fell, and Charles Albert received the homage of the Upper Austrian Estates. On 21 October, French and Bavarian troops camped at Saint Polten and Vienna prepared for a siege. Maria Theresa and her ministers had already left for Hungary. However, fearing that Augustus and Frederick would seize Bohemia, Charles Albert decided to preempt them by reverting to Belle-Isle's original plan to concentrate efforts on gaining Prague, which fell on 26 November to Bavarian, French and Saxon forces. Charles Albert was proclaimed King of Bohemia at Prague on 7 December and crowned as Emperor Charles VII at Frankfurt on 12 February 1742, the first non-Habsburg Emperor since 1438.

And yet France failed in her attempt to create a new territorial order in the Empire. This was due to a variety of factors including underrating Austrian resilience and Russia's refusal to enter the French system. Unable to dominate Europe militarily on her own, France was forced, as was every other power considering a major conflict, to seek the assistance of others, but the very resort to war made it less easy to retain the support of allies. Powers that were willing to accept subsidies regularly in peacetime and, in return, promised support proved only too willing to vary their policies to meet wartime exigencies. War made the position of second-rank powers more crucial and, accordingly, it led to an increase in bids for their support, a significant corrosive of alliances that tended to lack any ideological, religious, sentimental, popular or economic bonds. The British envoy in Turin complained in December 1741 that 'the general system of politics at present reaches no farther with most princes, than to come in for a share of the spoil',[3] and, on 9 October 1741, British mediation helped to produce the secret Austro-Prussian Convention of Kleinschnellen-dorf, by which the ground was laid for a separate peace in which Austria would cede Lower Silesia. Though Frederick's path from there to the Peace of Breslau, concluded on 11 June 1742, by which he gained most of Silesia, was far from straight, his betrayal of France fatally weakened her cause. Augustus followed him into the Austrian camp on 23 July. Remarking, in November 1741, that experience should have taught people to distrust guarantees, Frederick observed that all men were fools.[4]

It was not Frederick alone, however, who was responsible for the collapse of the French cause. Far from the fall of Prague being followed by the collapse of the Austrians, they recaptured Linz in late January 1742, Munich on 12 February and, in July, began to besiege Prague, which the French abandoned on 16 December. The replacement of Walpole by the bellicose Lord Carteret in February 1742 was followed by the arrival of British troops in the Austrian Netherlands on 20 May and the abandonment of Hanoverian neutral-ity. Carteret hoped to recreate the Grand Alliance and believed that a strong Austria was essential. Seeking to benefit from the new more interventionist British policy, Charles VII sought help in negotiating a peace with Austria, arguing, in June 1742, that the growth of Bavarian power could help to provide Britain with a counterweight to France that was more effective than Austria. Alongside Charles's complaints about his rights was his vision of a new order in Central Europe. He argued that instead of preserving the preponderance of a single member of the Empire, who could become dangerous, it was necessary to preserve the power of the entire Empire. In September, he claimed that neither the theory of a balance of power nor the guarantee of the Pragmatic Sanction could protect just rights, but that only the force of the entire Empire united with that of the neighbouring powers could form and support the balance. He argued that experience had revealed that the preponderance of a single family led to abuses, including blows to the states and constitution of the Empire.[5]

Defeat obliged Charles's language to be that of rights, not power, a marked contrast to that of Frederick. However, the prospect of major territorial changes, such as the British idea in 1743 that Charles join the Anglo-Austrian alliance and, in return, make gains in Alsace, was rendered increasingly unlikely by the progress of the war. George II led an Anglo-German army into the Empire in 1743, defeating the French at Dettingen on 27 June, but his attempts that year, and those of the Austrians under Francis's brother, Charles of Lorraine, in 1744, to make a major impact on France's eastern frontier were unsuccessful. As after 1704, the Austrians dominated the Empire, but the French held their Rhine frontier, helped in August 1744 by Frederick's invasion of Bohemia. He began the Second Silesian War (1744–5) because of his concern about Austrian strength and when it ended, on 25 December 1745, with the Peace of Dresden, he retained Silesia, having demonstrated once more his ability to defeat Austria and having overrun Saxony.

Unlike in the War of the Spanish Succession, the French retained the initiative in the Low Countries, while the control of Britain itself became an issue. The French decision to risk an invasion of Britain in 1744 was a measure of how determined they were to prevent the British from blocking their Continental schemes. Dependent on favourable winds and tides, amphibious operations were notoriously difficult and the French plan was defeated by bad weather, but it was a reminder of the extent to which limited military forces obliged the British to keep much of their navy in home waters.

The Jacobite rising of 1745 led by James III's son, Bonnie Prince Charlie (Charles Edward Stuart), helped France considerably. British and British-subsidized troops had to be transported from the Austrian Netherlands, and their failure to defeat the outnumbered prince in late 1745 ensured that they could not be sent back to the Continent in time for the start of the 1746 campaign. George II was fortunate that Ireland was quiescent and that the French did not invade, as had been feared. On 24 October 1745, Louis XV signed the Treaty of Fontainebleau with the Pretender, by which he recognized him as King of Scotland and promised to send military assistance and to recognize him as King of England as soon as this could be shown to be the wish of the nation. An expeditionary force was prepared at Dunkirk, but delays in its preparation, the Jacobite retreat from Derby and British control of the Channel led to its cancellation. The French had better success in the Low Countries. British hopes that they could serve as the base for an invasion of France proved misplaced as the French under Marshal Saxe won the battle of Fontenoy and captured much of the Austrian Netherlands in 1745. In 1747, France declared war on the United Provinces and British hopes that the coup that brought William IV of Orange to power in the provinces of Zeeland and Holland in May would revitalize the Dutch were proved wrong, the major fortress of Bergen-op-Zoom falling to the French in September. The danger that the United Provinces would be overrun – in May 1748 the French took Maastricht – helped to lead the British to negotiate for peace seriously.

Negotiations had in fact been conducted during much of the war, but most of the powers had fought on, hopeful of success, fearful of the consequences of abandoning their allies and distrustful of their enemies. Nevertheless, 1745 had brought peace to the Empire with the Peace of Dresden and the death of Charles VII in January. The succession of Maximilian Joseph freed Bavarian policy from the burden of commitments and expectations associated with Charles and bound up with his French alliance and Imperial status. Austrian strength helped to persuade the new ruler to sign the Treaty of Füssen, abandoning France, on 22 April 1745. France supported Augustus III for the vacant Imperial throne but Maria Theresa's husband was elected as Francis I. For Austria thereafter the war centred on Italy.

Philip V of Spain had played a major role in challenging the Habsburgs. He supported French attempts to coordinate anti-Austrian actions in the Empire, signing a subsidy treaty with Charles Albert of Bavaria, the Treaty of Nymphenburg, on 28 May and a treaty with Saxony on 20 September 1741. However, Bourbon action in Italy was hindered by British naval action, the threat of the bombardment of Naples forcing Carlos on 18 August 1742 to declare his neutrality in one of the most striking displays of naval effectiveness that century; and by Charles Emmanuel's hesitant decision to gain concessions in the Milanese by alliance with Austria and Britain, rather than opposition to them. Initially Charles Emmanuel had sided with the anti-Austrian alliance, but British pressure on Maria Theresa obtained the promise of Piacenza and part of the Milanese for him by the Treaty of Worms of September 1743. A month later, the Second Family Compact committed France to help conquer Milan, Parma and Piacenza for the benefit of Philip V's second son, Don Philip. Spanish forces occupied Charles Emmanuel's Duchy of Savoy in 1743, holding it for the rest of the war, but Bourbon attempts to storm his Alpine defences failed. The Italian war was far from static. Winning the alliance of Genoa in April 1745, the Bourbons defeated Charles Emmanuel at Bassignano in September, captured Asti, Casale and Milan before the end of the year and signed a secret armistice with Sardinia in February 1746. Keen to expel the Austrians from Italy, the French foreign minister, d'Argenson, proposed that Charles Emmanuel become King of Lombardy and leader of an Italian federation or league. D'Argenson's argument that the Italian rulers sought liberty against the excessive and tyrannical power of Austria and that the Bourbons should exploit this was countered by Philip V with the claim that the league was impossible or would take many years to negotiate, that it would depend on Bourbon armed support, that any league required a number of near equal powers which Sardinian strength prevented, that Charles Emmanuel would not maintain the projected 'Republic of Sovereigns' but would seek to despoil it, and that he would despoil, not help, Don Philip.[6]

The project was rendered academic by Charles Emmanuel's decision to rejoin the Austrians which led in March 1746 to the recapture of Asti, Casale and Milan and to the Austro-Sardinian victory at Piacenza on 16 June 1746, another of the century's decisive battles. However, the Austro-Sardinian invasion of Provence at the end of the year was a failure. In addition, the Austrians did not drive Carlos from Naples as they had hoped, and, after they had been expelled from captured Genoa by a popular revolt in December 1746, they failed to regain the city.

Britain, despite her naval victories over France in 1747 and the capture of Louisbourg in Canada in 1745, was most concerned about the Low Countries, while France, her foreign trade harmed by the British, her economy hit by a poor harvest and her finances by the costly war, wanted peace. The French were also concerned at the prospect of British-subsidized Russian intervention on the Rhine. Britain and France were responsible for the Treaty of Aix-la-Chapelle, the preliminaries of which were signed on 30 April and the definitive treaty on 18 October 1748. Neither Austria nor Sardinia was happy about the terms and they did not sign until 23 October and 20 November 1748. There was to be a restoration of all conquests and, in comparison to the Wars of the Spanish and Polish Successions, relatively little land changed hands. Despite Austrian reluctance, Charles Emmanuel received the lands he had been ceded at Worms, bar Piacenza, while Don Philip gained Parma, Piacenza and Guastalla. The Pragmatic Sanction was renewed for the remaining Habsburg territories, while the French had to agree to recognize the Protestant succession in Britain and to expel Bonnie Prince Charlie. The disputed Canadian border was referred to commissioners. In August 1745, the French had demanded Furnes and Ypres in a secret approach to the Austrians, to which they added Nieuport and Tournai a month later, but, in 1748, they agreed to restore the whole of the Austrian Netherlands, while suggestions that the British gain Ostend were abandoned.[7]

Like all compromise peaces, that of Aix-la-Chapelle was criticized. In Britain the return of Louisbourg was seen as a fatal indictment of the consequences of subordinating policy to the interests of allies, while in France there was criticism of an inglorious peace that had failed to bring any gains. The war has generally received less attention than the succeeding Seven Years' War but in fact it was in many ways more decisive. The last attempt in *ancien régime* Europe to reorder Central Europe drastically had been defeated. Bavaria had failed to become a great power, while Prussia had succeeded, though this verdict was to be challenged in the Seven Years' War. The Protestant succession had survived its most major challenge, and a new and lasting territorial settlement was created in Italy. The attempt to contest the Russian position in the eastern Baltic had also been unsuccessful and was not to be repeated until 1788. Thus the war and the subsequent peace set the territorial division of much of Europe for the remainder of the *ancien régime*.

Political tension within Russia following the death of Anna in 1740 had helped to encourage the Swedes to attack in 1741. Peter I's daughter Elizabeth promised concessions in return for Swedish support for her plans for a coup. The Swedes hoped that war would bring the return of all the Baltic provinces and the gain of the territory between Lake Ladoga and the White Sea. The French, hoping to prevent Russia from helping Austria, then attacked by Frederick II, encouraged the attack. The discovery that the opposition grouping known as the Caps – after the epithet 'Night-caps' applied to them by critics who accused them of inertia – had suggested a Russian occupation of Swedish-ruled Finland for their domestic ends, helped to lead to a declaration of war in July 1741. The invading Swedes issued a manifesto in support of Elizabeth who, in November, carried out a coup against the infant Ivan VI. However, negotiations in which she refused the cession of any territory were followed in 1742 by a Russian manifesto urging the Finns to establish an independent state to serve as a buffer between Russia and Sweden, a successful Russian invasion of Finland and the capitulation of the Swedish army, at the end of one of the most decisive campaigns of the century.

Under the Treaty of Åbo of August 1743, Finland was returned to Sweden with the exception of Karelia, which created a stronger defensive shield around St Petersburg, and the Nystad clause giving Russia the right to prevent changes in Sweden's constitution was dropped. Frederick I of Sweden had no legitimate children and Elizabeth saw this as an opportunity and a danger. Christian VI of Denmark hoped to secure the election of his eldest son as successor in order to restore the Union of Kalmar, the Swedo-Danish dynastic union of 1397–1523. There was support for this within Sweden and, in March 1743, the Danish crown prince was elected by the peasant estate. Christian VI promised Danish help in the reconquest of Finland. The upper Estates, however, held back, the nobles fearing an alliance of the peasantry and a strong monarchy on the Danish model. Elizabeth, as a condition of the lenient peace, insisted that the Swedes elect as successor Adolf Frederick, cousin and heir of her nephew and adopted heir, Charles Peter of Holstein-Gottorp, the future Peter III. The prospect of Holsteiners in Russia and Sweden, and Adolph Frederick's refusal to give up any claims on Schleswig-Holstein that he might inherit, led Christian VI to prepare an invasion of Sweden in 1743. He was dissuaded when it became clear that he would receive no foreign support and when the Russians, in response to Swedish appeals, sent 12,000 troops in the autumn of 1743. These remained in Sweden until the following summer and in 1745 she signed a new defensive alliance with Russia.

Adolf Frederick, however, refused to act as a protégé of Elizabeth, a course that was encouraged by his 1744 marriage to the dynamic sister of Frederick II and her sponsorship of the Hats. Russian pressure on Adolf Frederick and the Russian attempt in 1746 to secure the overthrow of the Hats were unsuccessful and in 1747, despite Russian protests, defensive alliances were concluded with France and Prussia. Prusso-Swedish cooperation against Russia had been a French goal since the mid-1730s. The Russian Chancellor, Bestuzhev, accordingly laid plans in 1748 for a war to overthrow the Hats, depose Adolf Frederick and possibly establish Finland as an autonomous duchy. In 1749, the Russians revived the Nystad clause relating to the Swedish constitution. Danish, Austrian and, in particular, British unwillingness to support Russian action, which, in light of French and Prussian backing for Sweden, would cause a major war, led the Russians in August 1749 to decide not to act. Russian attempts to win the support of Denmark, successful in 1746–8, were blocked when in 1749 French good offices secured a settlement of the Holstein-Gottorp issue by which Adolf Frederick agreed to renounce his claim and to accept an exchange of the territories for Oldenburg and Delmenhorst, Danish possessions in north-western Germany. The betrothal of Adolphus's son, Gustavus, and a Danish princess followed in 1751. The Hats abandoned any idea of supporting constitutional changes on the succession of Adolf Frederick and Russia was given assurances to that effect in 1749. As a result, Adolf Frederick succeeded peacefully in 1751 and Elizabeth turned her attention to Frederick II. The avoidance of a second Great Northern War is worthy of particular attention.

Consolidating the Old System

The Duke of Newcastle, the British minister with most influence in the field of foreign affairs after the fall of Carteret in 1744, had been determined that the Anglo-Austrian alliance should survive the end of the War of the Austrian Succession, in contrast to the period after the War of the Spanish Succession. Although he had become a Secretary of State in 1724, during a period of alliance with France, Newcastle had become convinced that French power was a threat both to Britain and to European liberties, conceived of as the existing international system. Looking back to the wars of 1689–1713, he felt that Britain must intervene actively on the Continent to resist French initiatives, and he argued that the diplomatic framework of this intervention should be the Old System, a term he first used in 1748 to describe the alliance of Britain, Austria and the United Provinces. Newcastle devoted his energies in the postwar years to strengthening this system.

It is easy to overlook these efforts if attention in the mid-eighteenth century is devoted to tensions and developments that appear to prefigure the Diplomatic Revolution of 1756, but it is necessary to query any attempt to make that 'Revolution' appear inevitable. To many contemporaries, the European system in the years after 1748 was relatively stable, indeed a continuation of that of the war opposing France and Prussia to Britain, Austria and Russia. The principal departure was the Austro-Spanish alliance of 1752, the successful culmination of several years of effort on the part of Britain to separate Spain from France.

Newcastle's determined attempt to strengthen the Old System helped to lead to the failure of two other diplomatic possibilities. An attempt to improve Anglo-Prussian relations in 1748 was thwarted by Newcastle who made it clear that improved relations could only be subsidiary to Britain's alliances with Austria and Russia, a view that Frederick found unacceptable. Puysieulx, French foreign minister in 1747–51, sought better relations with Britain and hoped that Anglo-French cooperation would ease tensions whether in the Baltic or North America. Although there was no reason in 1748 to believe that an alliance with France would be negotiated as it had been three years after the War of the Spanish Succession, there was equally little reason why Anglo-French relations should not have developed as their Anglo-Spanish counterparts were to, with a commercial treaty settling outstanding differences in 1750 and good political relations in the early 1750s. France did not appear poised for war with either

Britain or Austria and her links with Frederick were not so close as to preclude better Anglo-French relations. Newcastle, however, pushed active anti-French and pro-Austrian policies. Hoping to dissuade future French aggression, Newcastle sought to have the Barrier in the Austrian Netherlands restored and actively sponsored the Imperial Election Scheme, a plan for the election as King of the Romans, and therefore next Emperor, of Maria Theresa's son Joseph, the future Joseph II. The support of most of the Electors was obtained, in part through the payment of British subsidies, but unanimity could not be secured, in large part due to the opposition of Frederick, and Newcastle was hesitant about the idea of a majority election. He was not helped by a lack of enthusiasm on the part of Maria Theresa who objected to the idea of obtaining votes by concessions. The plan collapsed in 1752, and an attempt to revive it in 1753 was unsuccessful. Similarly, the attempt to recreate an effective Barrier in the Austrian Netherlands failed, in large part because Austria did not accept British priorities, while excessive Russian financial demands hindered a British attempt to create an alliance that could prevent Frederick from threatening Hanover.

Despite these failures, Newcastle's system was still in place in 1754. Although it was affected by serious disagreements and the United Provinces was weak, it had been strengthened by the Italian settlement of 1752 and neither France nor Frederick was in a position to challenge it. Suggestions such as those of the Crown Princess of Sweden, Frederick's sister, in April 1749 that a counter-league of Prussia, Sweden, France, Spain, Sardinia, Denmark, Turkey and Saxony be created proved unrealistic. Frederick was reduced in 1752 to asking for French pressure on the Turks to declare war on Austria or Russia. International relations were of course unpredictable, as Frederick noted in July 1752 when explaining why he did not wish to make plans for the succession to the healthy Augustus III of Saxony-Poland, but a striking feature of the correspondence of the period is the sense that, between them, Britain, Austria and Russia dominated Europe. Frederick felt that he was having to respond to apparent threats such as the Imperial Election Scheme, or, in 1752–3, the prospect that Maria Theresa's brother-in-law, Charles of Lorraine, would become next King of Poland and make it a hereditary kingdom to the great benefit of Austria.[8] Newcastle's system was to collapse in 1755–6, in large part because he sought to use and extend it without considering sufficiently the views of his allies, but this clash of interests should not detract from its apparent strength in 1748–54, nor

from the fact that the War of the Austrian Succession was not imme-
diately followed by a diplomatic realignment as the Spanish and Polish
Succession wars and, to a lesser extent, the Nine Years' War and the
War of the Quadruple Alliance had been.

In Italy, as in the Empire, an attempt was made to settle possible
problems. In the first 'diplomatic revolution' of the 1750s, a treaty of
defensive alliance based on Aix-la-Chapelle was signed between Austria, Sardinia and Spain. The preliminary articles, signed at Madrid on
14 April 1752, contained reciprocal guarantees for the territorial
integrity of Tuscany, Milan, Naples, Sicily, Parma and Sardinia. In
the definitive treaty, signed at Aranjuez on 14 June 1752, Austria,
Sardinia and Spain guaranteed each other's Italian possessions, the
Emperor, Maria Theresa's husband, Francis I, in turn guaranteeing all
their possessions as Grand Duke of Tuscany.

This settlement ended the Italian Question and ensured that Italy
was mostly peaceful until the early 1790s. Spain and Austria, their
Italian interests secured, were able to turn their attention from Italy,
Austria to conflict with Prussia, a partitioning role in Poland and, in
the 1780s, renewed conflict with Turkey, Spain to oceanic struggles
with Britain. The Italian settlement both helped to ease the path for
and was in turn consolidated by what is generally termed the Diplomatic Revolution, the Franco-Austrian alliance of 1756. This alliance
removed French interest in undermining the Austrian position in Italy.
Sardinia's expansionist aspirations were effectively muzzled by the
new territorial stability in Italy. France was unwilling to lend support
to schemes for gaining territory from the Milanese, and no power
would support Sardinia in her plans to acquire sections of the Ligurian
littoral from Genoa, the pursuit of which, in the case of the port of
Finale in the 1740s, revealed the weakness of the idea that Charles
Emmanuel might act as an impartial leader of an Italian league.

To a certain extent Italian stability represented a success for the
partitioning habit in eighteenth-century international relations. Prior
to 1748, partition schemes had been ineffective, because the three
major powers capable of intervening effectively in Italian affairs,
Austria, France and Spain, had never united to accept any territorial
settlement. After 1748, Austria and France turned their attention to
the Empire where it proved impossible to devise an acceptable partition between an Austrian and a Prussian sphere of influence.

A crucial element in the mid-century change in Italian affairs was
dynastic. Philip V's successor, Ferdinand VI (1746–59), had little
sympathy for his half-brothers, Don Carlos and Don Philip, and the

Farnese drive to fulfil dynastic claims was both satisfied by the terms of Aix-la-Chapelle and extinguished with the replacement of the meteoric and opportunistic Philip V and Elizabeth Farnese by the more cautious Ferdinand. Ferdinand had no children and his successor, Don Carlos, now Charles III of Spain (1759–88), was no longer primarily interested in Italian questions. The interrelationships of dynastic and geopolitical considerations are difficult to assess, but contemporaries had little doubt that the crucial element producing instability in Italy, and therefore affecting the diplomacy of all the powers who had interests there in the three decades after Utrecht, were the rulers of Spain.

The Diplomatic Revolution 1755–6

The crucial new developments that constituted the Diplomatic Revolution were the alliances between Austria and France and Britain and Prussia, both negotiated in 1756. Neither was completely new. George I had been allied to Frederick William I as recently as thirty years earlier. Negotiations for an alliance between the powers had been conducted on several occasions since, including in 1730, 1740 and 1748. In one sense, the alliance was an obvious consequence of the attempt to supplement or replace good relations with Austria by alliances with Prussia and Russia that had characterized British policy for a number of decades.

An Austro-French alliance was more novel, though there had been approaches for good relations over the previous 41 years, largely on the part of France. Aside from Louis XIV's probe at the end of his reign, Fleury and the Austrian Chancellor Sinzendorf developed a good working relationship at the Congress of Soissons in 1728 that, however, led to nothing because the Austrian ministry preferred Eugène's policy of alliance within the Empire and with Russia and Spain. Fleury and the Austrians cooperated from late 1735 until early 1741, and there had been a number of attempts, for example in December 1745, to settle the War of the Austrian Succession on the basis of an Austro-French understanding. From 1745, the Saxons had sought to create an anti-Prussian Austro-French alliance, just as Hanover was a source for plans for an anti-Prussian alliance of Britain, Austria and Russia. Dynastically linked to France by the marriage of the Dauphin to Augustus III's daughter, Maria Josepha, in February 1747, the

Saxons, under the extremely flexible Count Brühl, sought to turn Louis XV against his Prussian ally, a policy that was to succeed eventually in 1756. Saxon talk of the need for a Catholic alliance helped to lead to Austro-French discussions in 1748, but Maria Theresa responded to French advances by making the unacceptable suggestion that Louis abandon Frederick. The Franco-Prussian alliance was an insuperable barrier to an Austro-French understanding in 1748 and was to hinder attempts to improve relations in the following years by Count Kaunitz, Austrian envoy in Paris in 1750–3. These varied negotiations in the decades prior to 1756 indicate the extent to which it is misleading to think of the events of that year as shattering a rigid system dominated by geopolitical considerations. In 1748, Marshal Richelieu suggested to Puysieulx that better Austro-French relations would not be too difficult to achieve even though they would 'absolutely change the system of Europe'.[9]

If developments in the years immediately after 1748 scarcely suggested that Anglo-Prussian and Austro-French reconciliations were imminent, there were, nevertheless, indications that both the Old System and the Franco-Prussian alliance were under strain.[10] British determination to use her allies to limit French influence clashed with the Austrian wish to direct their attention to the reconquest of Silesia. Such tensions were, however, a feature of most eighteenth-century alliances and there is no reason to believe that the so-called Diplomatic Revolution would have occurred in the form it did but for the chain of events that began in the Ohio valley in 1754. Kaunitz did not want to break with Britain and, as late as 1755, he was still devoting considerable attention to the British alliance because he feared that his rapprochement with France would fail. Although the British did not support the idea of a war to reconquer Silesia and refused Austrian pressure to commit themselves, Anglo-Prussian animosity was more obvious in Europe in the early 1750s than its Anglo-French counterpart, and fear of Prussian aggression towards Hanover encouraged Britain to turn to Russia and Austria for promises of assistance in 1753 and 1755.

This fear was lent urgency in 1755 by the breakdown of Anglo-French relations over the frontier between the French colony of New France (Canada) and the British North American territories. The commissioners to whom disputes had been referred at Aix-la-Chapelle had failed to settle them and, as the agents of both powers jockeyed for position, each fearful that the others would gain a strategic advantage, fighting broke out. In July 1754, a force of Virginia militia under

George Washington sent to resist French moves in the Ohio region was defeated by the French. Newcastle feared that if the French consolidated their position there they would be able to drive the British from America when war resumed, as he assumed it well might. As a result he insisted that action be taken to rectify the situation in North America, though he did not want a full-scale war. Thanks to Newcastle and George II's son, the Duke of Cumberland, it was decided, in September 1754, to send two regiments to Virginia which were to drive the French from the Ohio valley in early spring and then take action in other border disputes. Newcastle trusted in the pacific nature of the French ministry and the poor state of Franco-Spanish relations but he was soon dismayed by pressure, from within the British ministry, for a wide-scale aggressive attack on the French in America.[11]

Warned by British military preparations, the French began to prepare to send reinforcements, while negotiating with the British at the same time. The British ministry was forced to consider the possibility of a war with France in general and of a French invasion of Hanover, and, in early 1755, sought promises of Austrian and Dutch assistance. Anglo-French negotiations revealed the incompatible nature of their territorial demands as preparations for war were stepped up. General Braddock with the British reinforcements sailed for America on 16 January 1755, being followed by a fleet under Admiral Boscawen that was designed to prevent the arrival of the French troops that embarked at Brest in April. In early June, Boscawen attacked the French fleet carrying the troops, though he only captured three ships in the fog.

War was not declared until May 1756, but, in the meantime, both powers committed hostile acts, the British seizing all the French ships they could find on the open seas, beginning operations in Nova Scotia in June 1755 and sending Braddock to defeat the following month. The prospect of a French attack on Hanover or mainland Britain and of action by France's ally, Prussia, obliged the British ministry to seek firm commitments of support from Britain's allies. Fear of French attack and a lack of interest in the British cause in America kept the Dutch neutral, while Kaunitz had no intention of helping Britain. Refusing to reinforce the Austrian Netherlands, he made only vague offers to protect Hanoverian neutrality.

In contrast, the willingness to offer a substantial subsidy to Russia produced an Anglo-Russian treaty on 30 September 1755. This arose from the common antipathy of both powers to Frederick and was intended by the British to prevent him from attacking Hanover, but, thanks to his fear of Russia, it helped to lead Frederick to pay heed to suggestions, made that autumn through the Duke of Brunswick, that he agree to remain neutral in any Anglo-French conflict. The Anglo-Russian treaty promised mutual assistance in case of attack, provided for British subsidies, and stipulated that, for four years, Russia was to maintain an army near the Livonian frontier from which it could threaten East Prussia. Alliance with Britain would apparently free Frederick from this threat, whereas, if he provided France with assistance, he would face Russia and possibly Austria as well. As a result, Frederick, unimpressed anyway by French policy, accepted British proposals and, by the Convention of Westminster of 16 January 1756, the two powers agreed to guarantee their respective possessions and to maintain peace in the Empire by jointly opposing the entry of foreign forces.

This was presented by the British to the Austrians as freeing Austria from any apprehension from Prussian attack and therefore allowing her to concentrate on resisting France, but the Convention destroyed the system Britain had been seeking to create and thus ensured that the war would extend to the Continent and that Britain would be vulnerable there. This was because the Anglo-Prussian rapprochement led Britain to lose the alliance of Russia, and Prussia that of France.

Tsarina Elizabeth and her Chancellor Bestuzhev had seen the British alliance as a step that would further their plans for war with Frederick. Seeing him as a challenge to their influence in Eastern Europe, they sought to revive the schemes that had existed during the War of the Austrian Succession for a joint attack by Austria, Hanover, Russia and Saxony. Austria was to regain Silesia while East Prussia would be ceded to Augustus III in return for Courland and Poland east of the Dvina and Dnieper rivers to Russia. The prohibition in the Anglo-Russian treaty of 1755 of separate negotiations with the 'common enemy' was seen as referring to Frederick, and Russian anger with the Convention of Westminster led them to refuse to ratify the treaty. Frederick's hope that the British would be able to restrain Russian hostility, of which he was well-aware, was to prove misplaced, and the Russians were taken by their animosity to Frederick and alliance with Austria towards better relations with France, a power seen correctly in St Petersburg as hitherto determined to resist Russian influence in Eastern Europe.

The Convention of Westminster also helped drive France towards Austria. Despite Kaunitz's efforts, relations between the two powers had not improved significantly. Alongside the formal diplomatic approach, Kaunitz also approached Louis through his influential mistress, Madame de Pompadour. Louis was tempted by the idea of dividing Britain from her traditional ally. He also found Frederick an irritating and presumptuous ally. However, it was not clear that Austria would be more reliable.

The situation was changed by the Convention of Westminster. Frederick does not appear to have appreciated the reaction in France, where Louis's council decided, on 4 February, not to renew the alliance with Prussia. The Convention led France and Austria, on 1 May, to sign a defensive alliance, known as the First Treaty of Versailles. It specifically excluded the Anglo-French war which had passed its phoney stage on 18 April 1756 when French troops landed on Minorca. Maria Theresa promised her neutrality in that conflict, and Austria benefited most from the defensive agreement because her position made her more vulnerable to attack than France. On the other hand, the alliance appeared to free France for war with Britain by destroying the Old System, while the treaty stipulated that if a British ally attacked France Austria would help her.[12]

The new alliance also helped Russian plans for war with Prussia as it appeared increasingly likely that such a conflict would benefit from Austro-French backing, not least crucial financial support. On 26 March 1756, the newly established Russian 'Conference at the Imperial Court' produced an extensive plan for war with Prussia. Austrian hesitation about the extent of likely French assistance, for France was not bound by the Treaty of Versailles to an offensive war to gain Silesia, led Kaunitz to persuade Elizabeth to delay the attack until 1757. However, Frederick, well-aware of Austro-Russian military preparations, decided to ignore British advice to restrict himself to defensive moves and instead to launch a preemptive strike. In order to deny a base to the gathering coalition against him, Frederick invaded Saxony on 28 August 1756. This was a dangerous move. Louis XV felt obliged to succour his heir's father-in-law and this added a powerful motive to French antipathy to Frederick. Indeed Frederick helped to precipitate both a hostile Franco-Russian rapprochement and an expansion of the Austro-French alliance. Elizabeth acceded to the First Treaty of Versailles on 30 December 1756 and concluded an offensive alliance with Austria the following month.

Frederick was increasingly desperate. He speculated about the chances of Elizabeth dying or Louis changing policy and he pressed the idea of a Protestant league, but he was fully conscious of his vulnerable position and, on 4 January 1757, wrote to his sister, the

Queen of Sweden, comparing himself to Charles XII at the beginning of his reign when three neighbouring powers had plotted his fall.

In fact serious differences still separated his rivals, including French unhappiness about Russian troops operating on Polish territory and thus limiting Polish liberties, Elizabeth's anger about France's unwillingness to drop her Turkish alliance,[13] and Austrian opposition to French determination to extend the war to Hanover. Nevertheless, the pressure of the war that was already being waged drove them together to a considerable extent, even if Austria and Russia never joined France in her war with Britain. On 1 May 1757, an Austro-French anti-Prussian offensive alliance was reached in the Second Treaty of Versailles. The Diplomatic Revolution was complete. France promised an army of 105,000 and a substantial subsidy to help effect a partition of Prussia.

The Seven Years' War 1756–63: the Prussian War

The central facts of the war were the survival of Prussia in the face of Austria, Prussia, Russia, the Empire and, from March 1757, Sweden, and Britain's successful maritime and colonial war against France and, from January 1762, Spain. The long-term significance of both was considerable. Britain became the dominant European power in North America and India, while Prussian survival ensured that control of the Empire by Austria and of Eastern Europe by Russia would not go unchallenged.

Frederick's survival was the product of good fortune and military success, not only a number of stunning victories such as Rossbach (1757) over the French, Leuthen (1757) and Torgau (1760) over the Austrians and Zorndorf (1758) over the Russians, but also the advantage of fighting on interior lines against a strategically and politically divided alliance. Russian interests centred on East Prussia and Poland, the Austrians were most concerned by Silesia and, after Rossbach and the repudiation of the Convention of Kloster-Zeven (see p. 178), the French devoted their efforts to the Westphalian conflict with the British-financed and partly-manned Army of Observation. Frederick's task was far harder than in the First (1740–2) and Second (1744–5) Silesian Wars, not only because of the number of his enemies, including crucially Russia, but also because he was very much the major target of Austrian action, as he had not been during the War of the Austrian Succession.

Thus the opportunistic diplomacy which Frederick had used so skilfully during the 1740s was of little value during the Seven Years' War. Indeed an obvious feature of the conflict in comparison with the earlier war was the lesser role of diplomacy. There were fewer combatants in the Seven Years' War and they were, for at least the first few years, relatively more determined. The issues at stake and the strength of the anti-Prussian alliance thwarted British attempts to recruit Bavaria and Sardinia. George II might hold out to the Bavarian envoy in January 1759 the idea that the Imperial crown could return to the Bavarian house,[14] but it was clear that the prospect of gaining great-power status was no longer an option for second-rank rulers, as it had been in the 1740s. There were no longer two roughly equal alliances competing nor would any partition of Prussia benefit such rulers (bar saxony) as that of Austria had seemed to offer.

Although Prussia survived the war, indeed in a better shape than Saxony whose army had been forced to capitulate on 16 October 1756, it faced serious difficulties. The summer and autumn of 1757 was a period of particular difficulty with a Russian invasion of East Prussia, a Swedish invasion of Pomerania, the French conquest of Hanover, the raising of the siege of Prague and the end of the Prussian invasion of Bohemia after the Austrian victory at Kolin (18 June), and the Austrian capture of Berlin and most of Silesia. Frederick saved the situation at Rossbach and Leuthen. In 1758, the Russians captured East Prussia, which they were to hold for the rest of the war, but Frederick's victory at Zorndorf blocked their invasion of Brandenburg. The following year the Russians defeated Frederick at Kunersdorf but failed to follow it up by concerted action with Austria. In 1760–1, the Austrians consolidated their position in Saxony and Silesia while the Russians overran Pomerania.[15]

Frederick was saved by the death of his most determined enemy Elizabeth on 5 January 1762, and the succession of her nephew Peter III, the Duke of Holstein-Gottorp. Frederick was his hero and he speedily ordered the Russian troops to cease hostilities. On 5 May 1762, a Russo-Prussian peace restored Russian conquests and obtained Prussian support for a war with Denmark to restore the position of Holstein-Gottorp. Sweden followed Russia, concluding peace on 22 May.[16] Peter's assassination in July and the succession of his wife Catherine II ('the Great') was followed by a cooling in Russo-Prussian relations and the abandonment of plans for war with Denmark, but Catherine did not wish to resume the war with Frederick. Austria, isolated, was driven from Silesia. Prussian success against Austria and the death of Elizabeth permitted a peace to be signed at Hubertusberg on 15 February 1763 on the basis of the *status quo ante bellum*, terms that satisfied both Prussia and Russia. Prussia's survival contrasted with the declining significance of Sweden and the Empire, both politically and militarily.

The British War

The war began badly for Britain with naval humiliation and the loss of Minorca to a French invading force under Richelieu in 1756, and widespread fears that the French would invade Britain itself that year. The early stages of the struggle in North America were not conspicuously successful, Louisbourg not falling in 1757, and, that year, Richelieu overran Hanover forcing the defeated Duke of Cumberland to sign the Convention of Kloster-Zeven which dissolved his army, left Hanover under French occupation and exposed Prussia's western frontier. In comparison Robert Clive's victory at Plassey in distant India on 23 June 1757, which opened the way for British dominance over Bengal, appeared a minor triumph. Prussian victories and George II's repudiation of the Convention saved the Anglo-Prussian relationship. Under a subsidy treaty signed on 11 April 1758, both powers agreed not to carry on separate negotiations, the British agreed to pay a subsidy of £670,000 and George II, as King and Elector, promised to maintain an army of 55,000 in Hanover, to cover Frederick. Under this treaty, renewed in 1759 and 1760, Britain provided valuable financial and military assistance to the outnumbered and financially exhausted Frederick. Victories such as Minden in 1759 also denied the French control of Hanover, which would otherwise have served as a bargaining counter in negotiations rather as the Austrian Netherlands had done in 1748.[17]

A more crucial triumph was the successful defeat of the French invasion plan of 1759. Choiseul, who became French foreign minister on 3 December 1758, proposed a joint attack with Russia and Sweden. Plans for Russian and Swedish forces to be transported on a Swedish fleet to Scotland were thwarted by the opposition of the two powers, but, instead, French landings of 100,000 troops in Essex and Glasgow and on the south coast were projected. Instead, British naval victories at Lagos (19 August) and Quiberon Bay (25 November 1759) destroyed the Toulon and Brest fleets and Choiseul's hopes of establishing the

Jacobites, a change that would have been as dramatic as the schemes for a partition of Prussia. These victories contrasted with the failures of the British attacks on the French coast to divert forces from the war with Frederick. Whereas Britain could be threatened by invasion with serious strategic consequences, as in 1731, 1744, 1745–6, 1756, 1759 and 1779, France was not thus affected. This reflected the greater vulnerability of Britain to amphibious attack and the smaller size of its armed forces, both the regulars and militia. Britain suffered the disadvantages of seeking to act as a great European power without possessing one of the basic requirements, a large army.

British amphibious forces were more successful outside Europe, not least because French naval weakness left them with the initiative. All the major centres of the French empire bar New Orleans were captured: Louisbourg and the West African slaving base of Gorée (1758), Guadeloupe and Québec (1759), Montreal (1760), Pondicherry (1761) and Martinique (1762). British success depended in part on Spanish neutrality but Charles III (the former Don Carlos), who succeeded his childless half-brother Ferdinand VI in 1759, was concerned about a fundamental shift of oceanic power towards Britain. His attitude helped to encourage French firmness in the face of stiff British territorial demands during abortive Anglo-French peace negotiations in 1761. On 15 August, the Third Family Compact and a Secret Convention were concluded, obliging France to support Spain in her commercial and colonial disputes with Britain, and Spain to declare war by 1 May 1762 if peace had not been concluded. Attacks on Gibraltar, Ireland and Jamaica were discussed, as was pressure on Portugal to abandon her British alliance.

William Pitt the Elder, the most influential of the two British Secretaries of State, responded to this new alliance by proposing a preemptive attack on Spain, resigning when his plan was rejected. The failure of negotiations led to a British declaration of war on 2 January 1762. The Spaniards proved far worse prepared than they had assured the French and lost Havana and Manila to British amphibious attacks in 1762. Charles III hoped that gains in Portugal would compensate him for losses elsewhere and his invading forces had some success in April and May, before a British expeditionary force stiffened the Portuguese defence.[18]

Anglo-French discussions through Sardinian intermediaries in the winter of 1761–2 reflected the financial exhaustion of both powers, their desire for an end to the war and their unhappiness with their allies. They led to preliminaries of peace, signed at Fontainebleau on 3

November 1762, and confirmed by the Peace of Paris of 10 February 1763. France agreed to restore the territory of Britain's German allies with the exception of Prussia: Hanover, Hesse–Cassel and Brunswick. They also agreed to return Minorca and to recognize Britain's gains of Canada, Senegal, Grenada, Tobago, Dominica and St Vincent. Britain returned Guadeloupe, Martinique, St Lucia, Gorée, Belle Île and Pondicherry to France and left the French a part of the valuable Newfoundland fishery. Havana and Manila were restored to Spain, but she yielded East and West Florida to Britain, receiving Louisiana from France in compensation. Spain's commercial grievances against Britain were not redressed. Ambitions that were not satisfied included the British attempt to gain New Orleans and Portuguese demands for acquisitions from mainland Spain.[19]

The terms were criticized in Britain by, among others, Pitt on the grounds that they were too generous to the untrustworthy Bourbons and indeed, in April 1763, the French began to gather information that might help in an invasion of Britain. However, the terms secured a large majority in Parliament and the success of the ministry in negotiating peace was popular. Furthermore, there was the risk that if Britain fought on she might become dangerously isolated, for the Anglo-Prussian alliance had collapsed in early 1762 amidst recriminations about unilateral negotiations. This reflected the absence of any long-term shared interest to bind the two powers together. Hanoverian security had brought them together but it became less important as an influence on British policy with the accession of George III in 1760 and was, anyway, not guaranteed by alliance to the maverick Frederick.

As with so many alliances in the century, the prospect of a negotiated peace exposed serious strains. The British ministry failed to adapt the alliance to meet the consequences of the Anglo-French peace that they needed but it is unclear whether it could have survived in a postwar world in which both powers would have sought to manoeuvre to best advantage: Frederick without being tied to Britain's animosity towards the Bourbons and Britain without being tied to his opposition to Austria.[20]

1763–83: introduction

The two peaces of 1763 ended a period of warfare that had lasted for three decades and involved most of Europe. They were followed by three decades mostly of peace in Western, Southern and Northern, though not Eastern, Europe. In part this was due to the financial exhaustion produced by the wars, though that did not prevent Russia from going to war in 1768 nor Britain, France, Austria and Prussia from doing so in the late 1770s. The stability of much of the period 1763–83 in part reflected the degree to which issues had been settled or nearly settled in the mid-century wars. The Wettins of Saxony had retained the Polish throne in 1733; the Habsburgs had survived the coalition assembled against them in 1741; the Russians had retained their dominance of Eastern Europe; the British had defeated the Bourbons in the struggle to control the oceans, had driven the French from Canada and defeated them in India; Prussia had nearly been crushed by the Austro-Russian alliance but had survived.

With the exception of Britain, these conflicts had been waged with scant reference to opinion outside the higher echelons of courts and governments. French public opinion was strongly against the Austrian alliance, but it was to last to 1791. In that year, the developing vortex of disorder and governmental weakness in France was to suggest new directions in foreign policy that would even bind Austria and Prussia together in counter-revolutionary action but, until then, international relations were largely set in their mid-century mould.

In many respects, European international relations were very stable in the period 1763–83. Despite episodic probings seeking to create better relations, both Anglo-Bourbon and Austro-Prussian enmity remained reasonably constant. Austria continued to be the leading power in the Empire, and Russia in the Baltic and Eastern Europe, though both were challenged by Prussia, and it was to be Prussia that was crucial to 1789–91 plans for a territorial reorganization of Eastern Europe to reduce their power. Italy remained under the control of the Bourbons and the Habsburgs, effectively keeping the peninsula stable and leaving Sardinia with little role in international diplomacy.

France absorbed Lorraine on the death of Stanislaus Leszczynski in 1766, and in 1768–9 purchased and annexed Corsica, the rebellious dependency of the republic of Genoa, but she had in effect abandoned earlier traditions of eastward expansion, a necessary cause and consequence of the alliance with Austria which lasted until 1791. As a result, the Low Countries were free from external war from 1748 until 1792. However, both the Austrian Netherlands and the United Provinces were affected by civil war in the late 1780s, which led to a Prussian invasion of the latter in 1787 to restore order. Similarly the

Rhineland and the western areas of the Empire were peaceful from 1763 until 1792.

Although it did not determine French diplomacy in this period, the Seven Years' War, at least from a domestic perspective, had in part discredited the monarchy. This was to weaken the ability of Louis XVI and his ministers to win backing for the reform policies they supported in the 1780s and, in the end, for the maintenance of order and stability. The war led to a crisis in French political culture that resolved itself into a shift in the relationship between state and people, specifically a move from being subjects of the monarch to becoming citizens. The war led to a rethinking of Britain as rival and example, and a newly energetic patriotism focused on opposition to her.[21]

In Eastern Europe, Russian strength was displayed in war with the Turks in 1768–74 and intervention in the Crimea in 1782–3 and led to the annexation of the Crimea and the territory east of the Dniester and the establishment of Russia as a Black Sea power. The anxious French response to the fate of the Crimea was important to the beginning of the 'Eastern Question', the acute concern of Western European powers over the apparent Russian threat to conquer the Turkish Empire. In the short term, more anxiety was aroused by the First Partition of Poland of 1772, an unprovoked despoliation of the country by Austria, Prussia and Russia that suggested that other vulnerable countries would encounter a similar fate, to the destruction of any notions of a balance of power or of international legality.

Britain's loss of the Thirteen Colonies in North America also appeared to usher in a new age. The successful rejection of the authority and power of a European colonial state and the creation of a strong republican transoceanic country inhabited by people of European descent was unprecedented and suggested that the combination of new ideologies and political mismanagement might sap traditional links and loyalties throughout the European world. France, Spain and the United Provinces had intervened in the War of American Independence to help the rebels but, though the war led to some traditional territorial changes between the European powers, Britain losing Minorca and Florida to Spain, and Tobago and Senegal to France, the major consequence of their intervention was to aid in the creation of a new state that owed nothing to the world of kings and courts.

It was unclear how far the conflict would lead to the disintegration of the British empire. There were fears that British India and Ireland would be lost. In fact British naval successes in the closing year of the American war, Bourbon financial exhaustion and the stabilizing policies of William Pitt the Younger (the son of the Seven Years' War Pitt), who was Prime Minister from December 1783 until 1801, helped to maintain the empire and to strengthen it in the postwar world so that it survived the challenge of Revolutionary France better than might have been predicted in 1780, when, in the Gordon Riots, a mob took over London.

The policies of the partitioning powers 1763–74

Eastern Europe had been dominated by four powers, Austria, Prussia, Russia and Turkey, since the defeat of Sweden and the weakening of Poland during the Great Northern War, though this dominance was dependent on the maintenance of these changes, a task essentially fulfilled by Russia in the decades after 1721. A persistent challenge was mounted by France, publicly with support for Stanislaus Leszczynski in Poland, culminating in the expeditionary force sent to Danzig (Gdańsk) in 1734, as well as for Turkish demands that Russia stay out of Poland and for Swedish wishes for *revanche* against Russia.

Privately the challenge stemmed from the *secret du roi*. This secret diplomacy of Louis XV began in the early 1740s with support for a plan that his cousin, the Prince of Conti, become next King of Poland, and it broadened out into a wish to recreate a powerful alliance of Poland, Sweden and Turkey that could serve French interests against Austria and especially Russia, which was seen in France as a disruptive alien force in Europe. These schemes had to be suspended during the Seven Years' War, when France's supporters in Poland became disillusioned by her willingness to accept Russian pretensions there, but they were to be revived after the war.[22]

Differences between Austria, Prussia and Russia were arguably more important as a challenge to the order created by 1721. When the three had cooperated, in 1726–32, Eastern Europe had been particularly stable, but Austro-Prussian and Prusso-Russian animosity had kept the situation precarious since the early 1740s. It was not precarious in the sense that major territorial changes had proved readily possible – Austria and Russia had survived the attacks of 1741, and Prussia had thwarted attacks during the War of the Austrian Succession and the Seven Years' War. However conflict seemed a constant possibility and the uneasy jockeying of the powers led them to view all developments as matters that they had to influence in their own interest. They thus ensured that domestic changes in Poland, Sweden and Turkey could not be viewed without concern, while territorial gains by one of the major powers led the others to press for equivalents. This concern remained after 1763, and was more important than the shifts in alliances between the three powers.

From Hubertusburg to the outbreak of the Russo-Turkish War 1763–8

None of the Eastern European powers had benefited territorially from the Seven Years' War and all had emerged financially exhausted and anxious to introduce domestic reforms that would revive and strengthen their states. The death of Elizabeth and the brief reign of Peter III (1762) had injected a major element of inconsistency into Russian policy and many other rulers felt that Catherine II's position was an unstable one. The first international crisis was inspired by a traditional cause, the death of a king of Poland, Augustus III, on 5 October 1763 and manoeuvres over his succession. These started before his death and related to the possibility of resisting what the French envoy in Vienna, Châtelet, termed 'the despotism that the court of St Petersburg seeks in Polish affairs'.[23] Austro-Russian relations were cool after the Russian abandonment of Austria in 1762 and, in July 1763, Kaunitz proposed united pressure by Austria, Britain and France on Prussia and Russia over Poland. That month, the Saxon envoy warned Châtelet that if measures were not taken to oppose Prussia and Russia, the Saxons would in light of their strength have to abandon their pretensions. However, Britain, seeking better relations with Russia, was not interested in opposing her over Poland, her attitude from the early 1730s until the late 1780s, while Austria and France were less determined than Prussia and Russia.[24] Seeking a pliable monarch, Catherine supported the candidature of a former lover, the Polish noble Stanislaus Poniatowski, rather than a Saxon candidate who might make the throne appear hereditary. Frederick correctly saw Catherine's anxiety about opposition as an opportunity to assuage his fears of Russia by negotiating a defensive alliance, the treaty of 11 April 1764, which was renewed in 1769 and 1777. This freed Catherine to dominate Poland while blocking any Austrian attempt to regain Silesia.

The new alliance served as the basis for the 'Northern System', advanced by Nikita Panin, who became Russian foreign minister in October 1763, a scheme that sought to maintain the Russian position in Eastern Europe and dissuade France and Sweden from revisionist efforts by creating a collective security system of alliances that was to unite Britain, Denmark, Prussia and Russia. They were to cooperate in preventing anti-Russian policies and the reintroduction of strong monarchy in Sweden, the country that appeared most to threaten the Russian status quo after the Polish election had been settled in Poniatowski's favour. Russo-Danish treaties were negotiated in 1765 and 1767, but Britain stayed out of the system as a result of Frederick's opposition and British unwillingness to meet Russian demands for subsidies and the extension of any defensive guarantee to cover a Balkan war. Thus Russian foreign policy came to centre on a Prussian alliance that satisfied Frederick's desire for security while Prussia recovered from the punishing Seven Years' War, but that offered little to Russia if her attention was redirected towards Turkey.[25]

Poniatowski was as much a disappointment for Catherine as Adolf Frederick of Sweden had been for Elizabeth; his rule prompted the idea that the Russian policy of an effective protectorate over Poland might require replacement. Catherine felt obliged to intervene to limit his independence and to block his moves to introduce reforms that might strengthen Poland. She used the position of the Dissidents, non-Catholic Poles, as an excuse and sent troops to influence the Diet of 1767–8. The Russian envoy, Repnin, behaved like a proconsul, arresting five leading politicians in October 1767 for criticizing Catherine. Russian pressure led the Diet on 24 February 1768 to approve the Perpetual Treaty, by which Poland and Russia mutually guaranteed their territories, while Poland undertook to safeguard the rights of the Dissidents and placed her 'constitution, the form of her government, her liberties and her rights' in Catherine's hands. Opposition within Poland led, however, in February 1768, to the formation of the Confederation of Bar and the outbreak of fighting. Turkey, concerned about the potential consequences of Russian control of Poland in any future war and encouraged by Choiseul, who had been pursuing a markedly anti-Russian policy since the spring of 1766, responded to the violation of her territory by Russian forces pursuing Polish confederates by declaring war in October 1768.

The First Partition of Poland and the Russo-Turkish War 1768–74

Despite initial unpreparedness, the Russians were soon beating the Turks, overrunning the Crimea, Moldavia and Wallachia and destroying the Turkish fleet at Cesmé off Chios in July 1770 with ships that had been sent from the Baltic, becoming the first Russian fleet to enter and winter in the Mediterranean. Though their attempt to use naval power to drive the Turks from the Aegean and to inspire a rebellion that would drive them from Greece was unsuccessful, Russian naval power had a serious economic effect on the Turks, while other Mediterranean states were forced to consider the possible implications of Russia spreading her power. When her warships at Zante disregarded Venetian quarantine and other regulations in 1773, observers wondered what military, political and commercial consequences might flow from Russian gains from the Turks, including a possible base in the eastern Mediterranean.

Russian success alarmed both Austria and Prussia, Kaunitz arguing in December 1768 that Austria had more to fear from Russia than Prussia, that Catherine sought a Greek empire, and that Russia could only be a safe ally when she was pushed back to her former frontiers. Austrian ministers were concerned about Russian gains in the Danubian principalities (Moldavia and Wallachia), traditionally an area of their interest, while the Prussians were anxious about both the unbalancing consequences of an excessive growth of Russian power and the possibility of Austro-Russian cooperation against the Turks. These twin fears produced warmer Austro-Prussian relations in 1769–70 and meetings between Frederick II and Joseph II at Neisse and Neustadt in August 1769 and September 1770 respectively. Frederick told Joseph at Neisse that it was necessary to stop Russia, while Kaunitz assured Frederick that Austria had renounced the idea of reconquering Silesia and that, if Russia gained Azov and the Crimea, her greater strength would threaten Prussia and Austria. Kaunitz instructed the Austrian envoy in Constantinople in November 1769 to assure Turkey of Austria's benevolent neutrality and, in early 1770, Kaunitz proposed joint Austro-Prussian mediation of the Balkan war, a mediation that was to be supported by military preparations and a demonstration of strength. As the Turks indicated a willingness to accept mediation, such a step would clearly be anti-Russian. Frederick found Catherine's demands, outlined in December 1769, intolerable. They included territorial gains, especially Azov, free navigation of the

Black Sea, Crimean independence, an Aegean base, and the occupation of the Danubian principalities for twenty-five years. The Austrians persisted with their plan for an armed mediation with Prussia and took hostility to Russia to the point of signing a defensive alliance with the Turks in July 1771 which, though unratified, led to their acquisition of the poor Turkish province of Bukovina in 1775.[26]

However, neither Austria nor Prussia really wanted war, and their ability to cooperate was compromised by distrust. Frederick's solution was an agreement to offset any threat to the balance of power posed by Russian gains by allowing Austria and Prussia a share with Russia in a partition of Polish territory, hitherto a sphere in which neither had had much influence. A settlement of Polish disputes was clearly going to have to be part of any Eastern European pacification. The French had sought to use the Polish situation to help the Turks. French agents were sent to the Confederates and in August 1770 Choiseul chose General Dumouriez as an agent charged with creating a confederate army that would, with French help, be able to assist the Turks. In common with others who had sought to turn Eastern European insurrectionary movements against Austria, Russia and Turkey, Dumouriez was disappointed to find the Confederates divided, badly armed and disciplined, and less numerous than he had hoped, but French plans lent force to the Russian desire to regain control of Poland.

A partition would ensure that the settlement was to the benefit of all three powers. A partition scheme had been sent for discussion to St Petersburg by Frederick in February 1769, but it had been dismissed as impracticable. Pursuing his anti-Russian theme, Kaunitz had suggested to Frederick at Neisse that Catherine withdraw her forces from Poland and that the three powers should jointly guarantee the peace of Poland, but Frederick became more interested in the idea of partition as the result of a favourable visit by his brother, Prince Henry, to St Petersburg. Despite Panin's opposition, Catherine, in the autumn of 1771, accepted the idea of a partition which she hoped would defuse tension with Austria and Prussia and allow Poland to be quietened.

Despite Austria's forcible annexation of the county of Zips and of three areas in the Carpathian foothills from Poland in 1769–70 there was opposition in Vienna to the idea of a partition that would benefit Prussia and which Maria Theresa regarded as a crime. When, in May 1770, Frederick had suggested to an Austrian envoy that Austria might gain Bavaria, he had been told that Austria had never usurped anyone's territory and his suggestion that she could seek

Parma and part of the Venetian republic had similarly been rejected. However, the danger that Prussia and Russia might make gains without any Austrian equivalent was sufficient to lead to a change of heart. In February 1772, Prussia and Russia agreed to the acquisition of Polish territory and precise shares were allocated by conventions signed in St Petersburg on 5 August 1772. The presence of Russian troops in Poland and the danger of further losses led the Polish Diet to accept the partition on 28 September 1773. Poland lost nearly 30 per cent of her territory and 35 per cent of her population. Austria gained Galicia and over 28 million people, Russia a more extensive but less populous area in Polish Livonia and White Russia, and Frederick obtained Polish (Royal) Prussia, which linked East Prussia to Brandenburg.[27]

The partition was greeted with outrage and fear, not least by the British and French governments. However, when Stanislaus appealed for support, George III replied that he could see no other remedy but that of divine intervention. It was feared that the partitioning powers would seize other territories, Prussia possibly acquiring Danzig and Swedish Pomerania and Russia intervening to reverse Gustavus III's Swedish coup of August 1772. One of the British Secretaries of State, the Earl of Suffolk, responded to reports that the Prussians might attack Hanover, by telling the Wittelsbach envoy, 'if the triple alliance continues one could say that these three powers are the sovereign masters of the continent and could partition it as they wish, and I am very afraid that they already have plans to achieve this'.[28] In 1773, the Duke de Broglie, formerly envoy in Warsaw and the director of the *secret du roi*, painted for Louis XV a bleak picture of the consequences of the new alliance:

> Poland will remain partitioned, the Turks defeated, Gustavus will probably be dethroned; all of Germany will only exist at the discretion of the Emperor and the king of Prussia, who will despoil the princes one by one. Italy will be threatened with oppression under the specious pretext of Imperial rights, and all of Europe will be subject to the influence of three rulers, united in order to subjugate or overturn it.[29]

As far as the Balkans were concerned, such fears were largely misplaced. Agreement over Poland ensured that Austria dropped her support for the Turks and the scale of Russian demands led to the failure of Russo-Turkish negotiations in 1772–3. When military operations were resumed in 1773, however, the Turkish empire did not collapse, not least because of the diversion of Russian forces to deal with the Pugachev rising, a widespread peasant-Cossack rising of 1773–4 that indicated the potentially serious political consequences of a brutal social regime, as the Transylvanian rebellion of 1784 was also to do.

By the Treaty of Kutchuk–Kainardji of 21 July 1774, Russia gained several Crimean fortresses and territory to the north of the Black Sea and in the Caucasus and was allowed to fortify Azov and to navigate on the Black Sea. Russia also gained the right to protect those associated with a new Orthodox Church in Constantinople, a provision that was to be extended to wide-ranging demands to protect Orthodox Christians, and obtained the independence of the Khanate of the Crimea, a move that was assumed correctly to be a preliminary to Russian annexation. Though indeed the Crimea was to be annexed in 1783, as the final stage in the destruction of the buffer zone between Russia and Turkish centres of power, assumptions about the resulting potential of Russian naval power in the Black Sea were to be proved exaggerated by the war of 1787–92, while, for the rest of Europe, the crucial aspect of Kutchuk–Kainardji was the Russian failure to obtain their earlier goals in the Danubian principalities, let alone the Aegean.

A new European system?

Arguably the best comment on the fears provoked by the First Partition was the absence of significant territorial changes in the following two decades. The Austrians did not increase their power in Italy, the Bavarian Exchange Scheme was thwarted, and Russia did not succeed in intimidating Gustavus III. In large part, however, this relative stability reflected the anticipated collapse of cooperation between the three powers which led to the War of the Bavarian Succession of 1778–9. Thus the immediate consequences of the triple alliance were short-lived. Nevertheless, both contemporaries and later commentators argued that it inaugurated a new era in international relations, one characterized by a use of strength to gain territory without consideration of even tenuous legal claims. Outrage was one response to an apparently novel situation, as can be noted readily in the diplomatic correspondence of the period. A Sardinian diplomat claimed that the partitioning powers had adopted 'new maxims' and ignored the 'solidity of the most solemn treaties'. The British envoy in Paris wrote in 1774 that the triple alliance was 'a connexion so contrary to every political principle, a connexion begun in and supported by violence... every system is unhinged... we see the wisest courts act in direct contradiction to their essential natural interests'.[30]

The existence of 'new maxims' can be questioned. Treaties had been cynically breached on many occasions, and the actual or planned despoliation of weak states by more powerful neighbours, alone or in combination, was far from novel. The remodelling of territorial control by agreement among some or all of the major powers, generally without heeding the views of their weaker counterparts, had been a characteristic of the extensive diplomacy over the Spanish succession and was a feature of the peace settlements of the period. William III had told Tallard, the French envoy, in April 1698 that they were determining the fate of countries they did not control. It is possible to present this diplomacy in an optimistic light by stressing the role of equivalents, considerations of balance, and the desire to achieve a peaceful and 'rational' solution to disputes, especially in avoiding general war. The reality was that the pretensions of the weak were overridden. In the first half of the eighteenth century, there had been numerous rumoured partition plans, such as that in 1715–16 of a league of Austria, Spain and Victor Amadeus II to redistribute the territories of Western Europe in the event of the death of Louis XV, or an anti-Austrian scheme of France, Spain and Russia in 1722, a plan to partition the Austrian Netherlands in 1724, or the possibility of cooperation between Austria, France and Spain to despoil Sardinia in 1748. The rumours indicate the extent to which partition plans were considered feasible, and a number of schemes played a major role in diplomacy, including those of the anti-Swedish coalitions during the Great Northern War, the plan of 1722 for a partition of Poland between Prussia, Russia and Augustus II, and those during the War of the Austrian Succession for partitions of Austrian and Prussian territories.

Numerous suggestions of hostile seizures of territory can be found in the diplomatic correspondence, and they were not only propounded by rulers, such as those of Russia, who had few dynastic and other legal claims that they could advance. In 1704, Frederick I of Prussia demanded Nuremberg as his price for abandoning the Grand Alliance, in the early 1740s Spain advanced plans for major territorial changes in Italy, and, in 1744, Frederick II, while suggesting major gains for Prussia and Saxony in Bohemia, argued that Charles VII could be compensated for his claims there with the archbishopric of Salzburg and the bishopric of Passau. The Baltic was a region particularly fertile in schemes for new territorial dispositions, some not intended as hostile, such as the Holstein project in 1726 for the acquisition of Russia's conquests from Sweden by the Duke of Holstein-Gottorp or the Danish wish to regain Sweden by monarchical election in the 1740s; others required war, such as those of 1744 for action against Prussia, leading to the gain of East Prussia by Poland, with Russia obtaining an equivalent in eastern Poland, and for the acquisition of Bremen and Verden from Hanover by Denmark, which was, in turn, to return Schleswig to Holstein-Gottorp.

Contemporaries had little doubt of the sweeping changes envisaged by many rulers, and diplomatic papers provide little support for claims that attitudes were characterized by stultifying conservatism and rigidity. Amelot, the French foreign minister, commented on the 'vast ideas' of Charles VII in 1743 while, in 1744, the French envoy to Charles, faced with the accusation that French policy would be seen as renewing the idea of a universal monarchy, complained that George II sought to dispose of eastern France 'like the things in his garden at Herrenhausen'. The same year, a British diplomat claimed that French support for the Jacobites 'gives a flat lie to the boasted moderation and innocence of her views and must convince every subject of the republic, as well as of England, that not only the possessions of the House of Austria, and the Balance of Power, but even our own liberties and religion, are struck at by that ambitious power'.[31]

Minor powers were particular victims of the desire for expansion. Those in the German part of the Empire, especially the vulnerable ecclesiastical principalities and Imperial Free Cities, were protected to a certain extent by respect for, and a disinclination to challenge, the Imperial constitution, supported as it was by the Imperial position of the Habsburgs and by the guarantors of the Peace of Westphalia, particularly France. In northern Italy, the situation was less favourable, and the Austrians seized the Duchy of Mantua and a number of smaller territories, with scant respect for justice. Their limited respect for legal rights was more than matched by the rulers of Savoy-Piedmont, whose expansionist schemes were conducted simply with reference to diplomatic opportunity. Frederick II told a British envoy in 1748 that Genoa had been justified in joining the Bourbons because by the Treaty of Worms her territories had been disposed of 'against all the rights of man'. Paradoxically he also revealed that he was willing to support a similarly illegal and unprovoked Hanoverian acquisition of Osnabrück and Hildesheim.[32] The fate of Genoese-owned but rebellious Corsica had also been a matter of discussion with it being provisionally allocated in the 1740s to both Don Philip and Sardinia. Francis of Lorraine had complained impotently about the fate of his duchy in 1735.

Possibly the First Partition created such a shock because Europe had been territorially stable since 1748, but it is more likely that the key elements inspiring fear were the combination and seeming apparent invulnerability of the three partitioning powers. A sense of balance was lost and that destroyed any element of predictability. It was no longer the case that schemes would be opposed by states that could hope to block them. However it would be wrong to suggest that the shock was felt all over Europe. James Harris, the British envoy in Berlin, commented in November 1772, 'the South of Europe seems to be so little concerned with what is going on in the North',[33] and, although Britain and, to a greater extent, France were worried about the actual and possible consequences, both were soon to be more interested in the fate of the maritime and colonial balance of power.

Anglo-Bourbon struggles 1763–83

Although both the Anglo-Prussian relationship and Franco-Russian good relations did not survive the Seven Years' War, both the Austro-French and the Franco-Spanish alliances did. This sustained the difficult position Britain had been in. Hopes that the Austro-French alliance would disintegrate proved misplaced and, whatever the tensions between the two powers, Austria was unwilling to cooperate with Britain against France until the era of the French Revolution. Attempts to negotiate defensive treaties with Prussia and Russia proved unsuccessful[34] and thus the British faced the prospect of renewed conflict with France without allies. Arguably more crucial was the French success in winning the support of the other major maritime powers, Spain and the United Provinces, although the latter was a declining naval power. In the Seven Years' War, the Dutch had been neutral and their complaints about the British attempt to prevent their handling of French trade had been a major grievance.[35] It helped to lead to Dutch support for France and, during the War of American Independence, in 1780, this caused a British attack that was misguidedly intended to provoke a crisis that would sweep William V of Orange into power, as his predecessors had been in 1672 and 1747. The Fourth Anglo-Dutch War (1780–4) led to major Dutch losses of shipping but it helped to worsen Britain's relative naval position.

Spain was more important as a naval power and nearly constant poor relations from 1759 to 1790 posed a serious problem for Britain. They contrasted with the situation earlier in the century when, despite British concern over the consequences of the Bourbon succession in Spain, relations between France and Spain had often been poor, in large part because of Spanish expansionist interest in Italy. The Anglo-Spanish conflict of 1718–20 had arisen as a direct result of this interest and Philip V and his wife were more interested in fighting Austria in 1741 than Britain in 1739. They were willing to satisfy British commercial demands for the sake of support in Italy in 1729 and 1731 and the Austrians feared that the British would make a similar offer in 1741.

In the second half of the century, however, the Spaniards displayed a greater concern with the transoceanic position. This reflected the threat apparently posed by the British, who now appeared as conquerors rather than interlopers, as well as Charles III's determination to obtain more substantial economic benefits from the empire, and the stability of Italy and the western Mediterranean, where the unsuccessful Spanish attack on Algiers in 1775 did not indicate any intention to conquer North Africa. However, there was nothing inevitable about Spanish support for France and the Franco-American alliance of 1778. Charles III was unhappy about the idea of helping American rebels, and offered Britain neutrality in 1778 in exchange for Gibraltar. It was the unacceptable nature of the British response to the Spanish offer to mediate, rather than any immutable consequences of the Family Compact, that led Spain to help France. The Spaniards insisted on French assistance to regain Florida, Gibraltar and Minorca from Britain, and that the two powers mount a joint invasion of Britain in order to force a quick end to the war, an attempt that the weather helped to make an expensive mistake in 1779.

If Spain was an important ally to France in the American war, with colonial and commercial grievances of its own against Britain, it was, nevertheless, France that was Britain's prime opponent in Europe, on the oceans and in the colonial world. Readjustment of Britain's Continental foreign policy in the 1730s, so that it centred on finding allies against France, a policy that had been given greater force by the Duke of Newcastle after 1748, was not reversed, even though

George III and his ministers were less interventionist in European diplomacy than his grandfather, George II, and his ministers had been. There was concern in London and, to a far greater extent, Paris, about events in Eastern Europe and this led to suggestions of cooperation, but they were less important than the continued reality of rivalry. In both Britain and France it was assumed that the peace negotiated in 1763 would not last. The British used gunboat diplomacy in 1764–5 to defend their position successfully in colonial disputes in West Africa and the West Indies. However, domestic stress, associated especially with the Wilkesite troubles, ministerial instability and a maladroit handling of diplomacy, helped to produce a confused and weak policy in the later 1760s which encouraged the assertive schemes of Choiseul and led in particular to an irresolute response to the French annexation of Corsica in 1768.[36]

The Falkland Islands crisis of 1770, in which Britain threatened hostilities when Spain expelled a British settlement, led France to the brink of war in support of her ally. The Falklands were seen as a staging post to the Pacific, an area of Spanish commercial monopoly that the British were increasingly keen to penetrate. Louis XV's unwillingness to fight, which led to Choiseul's fall on 24 December 1770 and to the notification to Charles III that France needed peace, defused the crisis and persuaded Spain to accept an agreement on 22 January 1771. By this, Spain restored Port Egmont to a British garrison, in return for a secret verbal assurance that it would eventually be abandoned, as it was, largely on the grounds of cost, in 1775.

D'Aiguillon, Choiseul's successor as foreign minister, was interested in the idea of a rapprochement with Britain, in order to resist what he saw as the threat of Russian power to the European system. He set out deliberately to make concessions in colonial disputes in order to improve relations and, in March 1772, proposed concerted pressure on Austria and Russia to dissuade them from partitioning Poland. George III, however, responded coolly and when the French-backed Gustavus III staged a coup in Sweden in August 1772, seizing power from a ministry inclined to Britain and Russia, suspicion of France increased.

Concern about the domestic response clearly played a major role in dissuading the British ministry from heeding d'Aiguillon's approaches, but there were also good diplomatic reasons for British caution. An Anglo-French understanding would have committed Britain to opposition to the most powerful alliance in Europe, fears were raised about the security of Hanover, it was pointed out that the

French could do little to help Poland, and British ministers argued that the partitioning powers would not remain united for long. It was easy for observers to suggest that Britain and France might be able to negotiate an understanding, based on France agreeing not to offend Britain in commercial and maritime matters, but British ministerial suspicion of France remained strong and, however concerned the government might be about the policies of the partitioning powers, it had no wish to allow France to commit Britain to opposition to them. It was more reasonable to hope that British relations with the partitioning powers could be improved than that a successful Anglo-French alliance could be created. Furthermore, it was possible that d'Aiguillon would be replaced by a less cooperative minister as happened in 1774 when the accession of Louis XVI led to his replacement by Vergennes. In such a situation it would be foolish to have alienated other powers simply because Britain and France had held similar views in 1772. These attitudes led the British to use threats in 1773 to dissuade the French from deploying their navy against Russia in the Baltic and the Mediterranean. However, conflict was avoided as both powers sought peace because of their domestic problems and saw no reason to fight.

It was to be the American rebellion that altered the situation. The new ministry of 1774 was less inclined than d'Aiguillon to heed British wishes, but they would not have risked war with Britain had it not been for developments in America where, in 1775, long-standing discontent and the militarization of British authority led to fighting. The rebels sought the assistance of France and declared independence in 1776. The French ministry was unwilling to commit itself publicly but ready to provide financial and military assistance. Vergennes hoped that the British would lose America and therefore that a colonial balance of power, lost in the Seven Years' War, would be restored, enabling the two powers to cooperate in limiting the influence of the partitioning states and France to redirect expenditure from the navy. Other French ministers were more interested in the simple idea of weakening Britain. Expenditure on the French navy more than quadrupled between 1774 and 1778. Tension over French aid to the rebels, specifically allowing their privateers to use French ports, interacted with British failure to suppress the revolution. This encouraged the French to intervene and led to the treaties of Alliance and Commerce of 6 February 1778 with the Americans. The notification of the Treaty of Commerce to the British government on 13 March led to the recall of the British envoy in Paris, for George III could not accept the recognition of American independence. As neither power wished to appear an aggressor to her allies, hostilities did not begin until June when the struggle to control Channel waters started.

Until French intervention, it had been feasible to imagine that British success might lead to a negotiated end to the war, but the French role made this much less likely. For France, however, the war brought major financial burdens and, in the short term, it restricted her chance to affect the Bavarian succession crisis of 1778–9. By going to war, she limited her options and mortgaged her future, as most eighteenth-century combatants did, but she did so without pressing need and failed in the long term appreciably to increase either her influence in Europe or her relative power overseas.

The British proved reasonably successful in resisting the Bourbons, but were defeated in America. Though Minorca and a number of West Indian islands were lost, Gibraltar successfully resisted an active siege and the French failed to defeat the British in India, though their squadron under Suffren and, on land, their ally Haidar Ali of Mysore each achieved considerable success. By 1782, British general superiority at sea was established and the Franco-Spanish naval effort was nearing exhaustion towards the end of the war. Rodney's victory at the Saints in April 1782 saved Jamaica from the risk of invasion. However, French superiority in American waters had forced the besieged Earl Cornwallis to surrender a British army to the French and Americans at Yorktown on 18 October 1781. The British still held much of America, including New York, Charleston and Savannah, but Yorktown produced a political crisis that brought down the ministry of Lord North, ending twelve years of ministerial stability and bringing to power the Rockingham Whigs who were determined to give independence to America and to negotiate peace. As Vergennes was anxious to direct his attention to blocking Russian expansion in the Crimea, British willingness to negotiate was matched by that of France.

Rockingham's death on 1 July 1782 was followed by the creation of a new ministry under the Earl of Shelburne who was responsible for the more far-reaching aspects of the peace. He saw American independence as an opportunity to create a fruitful commercial relationship between Britain and America that might also bring political cooperation. While retaining Canada, Newfoundland and Nova Scotia for Britain, he yielded the 'Old North West', the lands south of the Great Lakes, to the United States. Bourbon gains were more modest, France receiving Tobago, Senegal and concessions in the

Newfoundland fisheries, while Spain obtained Minorca and East and West Florida. Symbolic of the changed relationship was the abrogation of the article in the Peace of Paris giving Britain the right to maintain a commissioner at Dunkirk to prevent the rebuilding of its fortifications. The Dutch yielded the Indian port of Negapatam to Britain and the right of navigation among their spice islands (in what is now Indonesia). Britain remained isolated but France was exhausted and had failed to undermine the British empire conclusively.[37]

Division among the partitioning powers 1775–83

Predictions that the tensions between the partitioning powers would divide them became more realistic as the Polish occasion for their cooperation receded in importance. In August 1775, James Harris noted, 'I never recollect the North in such a state of tranquillity, glutted with the division of Poland the several powers seemed to be sleeping off their debauch – the moment of their awakening I have no doubt will be serious, every day may produce events, which may certainly change the present system and the smallest change in this system necessarily brings about new alliances'.[38] The principal cause of tension was Austrian concern about Russian intentions in the Balkans, which led an Austrian envoy to tell Frederick II in early 1775 that Austria would oppose any further Russian advance which would, he argued, unbalance Europe. Joseph II was increasingly adopting a more volatile attitude than his mother and co-ruler, Maria Theresa. Concerned by this, Frederick sought both to improve his relations with Catherine and to increase French concern about Austrian intentions.

Distrust ensured that the partitioning powers did not plan their policies jointly or create cooperative arrangements akin to that established in the so-called Congress System after the Napoleonic Wars. Partly as a result, differing views over the first major dispute, the Bavarian succession, led to war. Neither Maximilian Joseph of Bavaria (1745–77) nor his successor, Charles Theodore of the Palatinate, had any direct heirs and Joseph II saw this as an opportunity to gain much of Bavaria. After Maximilian Joseph's death, on 30 December 1777, Joseph II reached an agreement with Charles Theodore by which the latter ceded much of Bavaria and many of his illegitimate children were found posts in Vienna. This was opposed by Frederick II,

197

concerned about any accretion of Habsburg strength, by Charles Theodore's heir, Charles Augustus of Zweibrücken, by the Elector of Saxony, who had his own claims, and by France, which was concerned about Habsburg gains in the Empire. Unwilling to support either side militarily, not least because of her developing commitments to the American cause, France's refusal to back her Austrian ally was a serious blow to the Habsburgs, especially as Catherine gave important diplomatic support to Frederick.

Frederick attacked Austria in July 1778, but failed to win a decisive victory. The cost and stalemate of the conflict and Maria Theresa's concern for peace led rapidly to negotiations. By the Peace of Teschen of May 1779, Austria gained the Innviertel, a small but strategic area of south-eastern Bavaria, but far less than the gains stipulated in the agreement with Charles Theodore. The peace was concluded under Franco-Russian mediation, leading to an important increase in Russian prestige particularly in the Empire.

The war and a revival in concern about the Balkans led to a diplomatic realignment. Joseph's determination to destroy the Prusso-Russian alliance took precedence over earlier concern about Russian expansion against the Turks and was aided by the death on 29 November 1780 of Maria Theresa who was hostile to Catherine. Catherine gradually shifted her attention in the late 1770s from Panin and his 'Northern System', a policy essentially of defending a beneficial status quo, to ambitious anti-Turkish schemes, including the Greek Project, the plan for the expulsion of the Turks from the Balkans and the creation of an empire ruled by her grandson born in 1779 who was symbolically christened Constantine. These schemes were associated with an influential former lover, Potemkin, who was involved in the development of Russia's recent gains from the Turks. Intervention in the Crimea, in support of a client khan, Sahin Giray, and the Convention of Aynali Kavak (1779) increased Russian control of the Crimea. Catherine supported agreement with Austria in order to facilitate her plans and, though her claims to an imperial title, which Joseph found unacceptable, prevented the negotiation of a formal treaty, in May and June 1781 the two rulers exchanged letters that in practice constituted a secret treaty of defensive alliance.[39]

The alliance was to be of considerable benefit to Catherine, both in facilitating her peaceful annexation of the Crimea and in freeing her from having to fight the Turks alone later in the decade. Instability in the Crimea, where Sahin Giray proved an unreliable client ruler, led to Russian military intervention in 1782 and annexation on 19 April

1783.[40] Vergennes sought British cooperation against the step, just as in March 1777 he had written of the need for Anglo-French cooperation against measures to weaken Turkey,[41] but the British preferred to hope for improved relations with Russia. Catherine's disclosure of the secret Austro-Russian alliance that summer successfully intimidated France and Prussia. The period therefore closed with a demonstration of the consequences both of Russian power and of the Austro-Russian alignment.

In the longer term, the independence of the United States was more important. However, this had little immediate consequence for European power politics. Independent America did not develop as a major naval power until the late nineteenth century, and the Americans did not see their revolution as for export throughout the European world. Instead, there was a powerful sense of American 'exceptionalism' – of a culture and society separate from that of Europe.[42] This disengagement was further encouraged by the turmoil of the French Revolutionary period,[43] although, already prior to that, there had been a deterioration in American relations with France.[44]

Chapter 9

The French Revolutionary and Napoleonic Period 1783–1815

The political atmosphere of international relations changed in the last fifteen years of the eighteenth century. Domestic disorder was to become an increasingly important element in international relations from the late 1780s. Rebellions in the Austrian Netherlands[1] and Hungary affected Austrian conduct and Prussia sought to exploit them, just as Louis XVI had allied with the Americans against Britain. This prefigured the attempts of Revolutionary France to exploit revolutionary feeling elsewhere, but without the potent, though at times weakening, element of ideological affinity that the French sought to pursue. However, alongside new developments, traditional rivalries continued. Austria, Prussia and Russia watched each other's activities anxiously as Poland was partitioned into extinction in 1793 and 1795, while Britain, which had remained aloof from the crusade against Revolutionary France in 1792, went to war with her in early 1793 over threatened French control of the Low Countries.

Initially, however, there was scant sign in the 1780s of a new political context. With the death of Maria Theresa in 1780, Joseph II acquired sole direction of Austrian policy, but he was less successful in his projects than Catherine the Great. Compared by Frederick II in August 1781 to a chemist who kept the affairs of Europe in fermentation, he took a number of steps which increased his reputation for unpredictability and disrespect for international agreements. Uninterested in compromise or the views of others, and unwilling to honour accepted conventions and privileges, either domestically or internationally, Joseph prefigured to a certain extent the attitudes of Revolutionary France, though he proved less willing to push issues to a crisis. In 1780, the tradition that a Wittelsbach should fill the Archbishopric Electorate of Cologne and the neighbouring prince bishoprics was broken in favour of the election as successor of Joseph's younger brother, Maximilian. In 1781, Joseph expelled the Dutch garrisons from the Barrier, but French opposition led him to back down from a threatened war with the Dutch over the opening of the river Scheldt in late 1784. This would have brought prosperity to Antwerp but, as a result of pressure from the Dutch, it had been banned under the Westphalian settlement.[2]

Earlier that year, Joseph began to press hard the scheme for an exchange of the Austrian Netherlands for Bavaria but, though Charles Theodore of Bavaria was willing, his heir was not and the French, unwilling to support a measure which they saw as likely to strengthen the Habsburgs, refused to back their ally. Russia offered some diplomatic help but was unwilling to intimidate Frederick II who responded to Joseph's plan (at a time when the Emperor was already disillusioned about his prospect of success), and to Austrian pretensions in general by forming a *Fürstenbund*, League of Princes, with other German princes in July 1785. It was a measure of the suspicion aroused by Joseph that the German princes, who had traditionally supported the Emperor, or been wary of opposing him, and had tended to isolate Frederick within the Empire, were now willing publicly to form a league against him. Many of the ecclesiastical princes were also unhappy about Joseph's attitude to the Church and suspected him of being willing to support secularization. The *Fürstenbund* was more powerful than the last major league unrelated to external sponsorship, the Wittelsbach *Hausunion* of the 1720s, and it represented a revival of the alliance of 1719–26 between Hanover and Prussia that had opposed the apparent determination of Charles VI to increase imperial authority in the Empire.

The *Fürstenbund* marked the failure to weaken Prussia within the Empire, and was to be followed by growing French interest in a rapprochement with her and also by the Anglo-Prussian alliance of 1788. The *Fürstenbund* helped to bring stability to the Empire in the last years of Joseph's reign as sole ruler (1780–90) but this stability was probably more due to the unwillingness of Joseph's French and

Russian allies to provide significant support for his schemes. Just as in Italy, the last years of *ancien régime* diplomacy in the Empire were characterized by territorial stability, a marked contrast to the uncertainty and apparent volatility produced by war and confrontation in Eastern Europe. The principal threat to this stability came from Austrian hopes of benefiting from the death of Frederick in August 1786 in order to wage a war of revenge against Prussia. Such hopes were probably unrealistic, but they were to be dashed anyway by the Turkish declaration of war on Russia in August 1787.

War and confrontation in Eastern Europe 1787–95

An escalating Russo-Turkish struggle for influence in the Caucasus and Turkish anxiety about the development of Russian Black Sea naval bases at Kinburn and Sevastopol led the Turks to fear Russian attack, but it was actually they who declared war unexpectedly in August 1787, because of the rise of bellicose ministers in Constantinople and the apparent opportunities created by Russian harvest problems. Joseph II had sought to prevent a Russian attack, but the Turkish declaration of war activated the defensive side of his alliance with Catherine. Kaunitz, whom Joseph had retained as Chancellor while increasing his own role in foreign policy, argued that Austria would have to support Russia both because of her possible need for assistance against Prussia and, more particularly, to prevent a Prusso-Russian reconciliation, and in order to influence Russian conduct of the war in the Balkans. Joseph unenthusiastically could see no alternative option, and, in February 1788, Austria declared war having attempted unsuccessfully a surprise attack on Belgrade.

The war was not as disastrous initially for the Turks as many had imagined and, though Russia captured Ochakov in 1788, neither she nor her ally had much to boast of from that campaign. The conflict broadened when Gustavus III of Sweden took advantage of Russian commitments to declare war in 1788. He saw Russia as a hostile power and hoped by successfully reconquering some of Sweden's former territories to strengthen his position domestically. However, domestic opposition, especially in Finland, hamstrung his efforts and he was only rescued from action by Denmark, Russia's ally, in August 1788 thanks to Anglo-Prussian pressure, including a threatened Prussian invasion of Denmark. Gustavus signed a subsidy treaty with the Turks in July 1789, but his failure to defeat Catherine led to the signature of peace at Verela in August 1790 on the basis of the frontiers of 1788, Russian recognition of the new Swedish constitution of 1772, and a Russian renunciation of intervention in Swedish politics.

The failures of 1788 had led Joseph II to begin peace negotiations with the Turks in the winter of 1788–9, but the accession of the bellicose Selim III in April 1789 caused their failure. However, the Austrian and Russian armies fought well in that campaign, defeating the Turks and capturing Belgrade and Bender respectively. The prospect of substantial Austro-Russian territorial gains led Prussia to press for an equivalent from Poland, which, in an extensive exchange scheme, was to be compensated by regaining Galicia from Austria. The prospect of war with Frederick William II, who was already providing diplomatic support to Selim, and escalating domestic problems in the Austrian Netherlands and Hungary, where Prussia appeared willing to support rebellion, led Joseph's successor, Leopold II (1790–2), to decide to defuse the crisis soon after his succession in February 1790. The possibility of war with Prussia was lessened by a convention with her, negotiated at Reichenbach on 27 July 1790, which provided for an end to operations against the Turks and the summoning of a peace conference which produced the Peace of Sistova of August 1791 by which Austria returned her gains.

Catherine was less concerned about the anti-Russian movement of Austrian policy under Leopold than by a comparable shift in Poland. Russian control there decreased with the outbreak of war in the Balkans and the Polish reform movement that had begun after 1772 culminated in the four-year Diet that began in 1788 and saw the rejection of Russian influence and the issue of a new constitution on 3 May 1791. This changed Poland into a hereditary constitutional monarchy and instituted a number of far-ranging political and governmental reforms. The establishment of a substantial standing army was also stipulated.

Reform in Poland was supported initially by Prussia, which signed a defensive alliance on 29 March 1790, and by Britain. Both were concerned to prevent any Balkan settlement that might leave Austria or Russia too powerful and, having divided Leopold from Catherine, they saw an opportunity to reduce Russian influence in Eastern Europe. Russia was an important commercial partner of Britain and agreement, if not alliance, with her had been the goal of successive British ministries, not least because of her poor relations with France. However, relations had deteriorated for a number of years because of Catherine's hostility towards George III, whom she believed to be intriguing against her, and because the Russians, far from renewing the commercial treaty with Britain which had expired in 1786, had concluded one with France in 1787. Suspicion of Russia led to opposition to her interests in Eastern Europe. This direction was encouraged during the Regency Crisis produced by George III's severe ill health in the winter of 1788–9 during which the initiative in the Triple Alliance (Britain, Prussia, United Provinces) was increasingly taken by Prussia with its bold plans for limiting Austro-Russian power, while in British foreign policy it was increasingly taken by the anti-Russian envoy in Berlin, Joseph Ewart. William Pitt the Younger, the head of the British ministry, who was influenced by Ewart, hoped that Poland would become a larger trading partner than Russia and he sought to impose the *status quo ante bellum* on Catherine. This demand was supported by British preparations for a naval expedition to the Baltic and by an attempt to create a powerful anti-Russian alliance, a move that was weakened, however, by the Russo-Swedish peace and by Leopold's refusal to cooperate.

The crisis culminated in the spring of 1791 with the presentation of an ultimatum demanding that Russia not annex Ochakov and the territory between the Bug and the Dniester. However, serious domestic criticism in Britain, in part due to skilful action by the Russian envoy Vorontsov, and an absence of ministerial confidence and unity over the issue led to a climb-down which destroyed the Anglo-Prussian alliance and thus British influence on the Continent, and left Russia free to settle with the Turks. Further Russian victories led Selim to accept negotiations in the summer of 1791, and, by the Treaty of Jassy of 9 January 1792, the Turks recognized the annexation of the Crimea and yielded Ochakov and the territory between the Bug and the Dniester.

The failure of the confrontation with Russia led Frederick William II of Prussia to abandon the Turks and seek reconciliation with Russia. Catherine was furious at the collapse of Russian influence in Poland and worried that reform would lead Poland to radicalism. Freed of the Turkish war, she was able to concentrate on restoring her influence in Poland, a course eased by the death on 1 March 1792 of Leopold II who was unenthusiastic about intervention in Poland, and by the outbreak of war between France and Austria on 20 April 1792. Russian troops invaded Poland in mid-May under the pretext of supporting the Confederation of Targowica, a Polish noble league that Catherine had inspired. The outnumbered Poles were forced to submit in July 1792.

Catherine's concern that Poland be thoroughly controlled in order to prevent it from becoming a revolutionary base and her wish to keep Frederick William II in the struggle with France led her in December 1792 to accept his demand that he be compensated with Polish territory. By a Russo-Prussian treaty of partition signed at St Petersburg on 23 January 1793, Poland lost about 60 per cent of her territory and about half her population. Most of the gains were made by Russia, which received the western Ukraine, Podolia and the rest of White Russia, including Minsk, while Prussia gained Danzig and Great Poland, the area round Poznan. Russia forced the Diet of Grodno to ratify the treaty, to reject the constitution of 3 May 1791 and, on 16 October 1793, to accept a treaty making Poland in effect a Russian protectorate.

A Polish insurrection against the new settlement began in March 1794 but was crushed by the Russians, with Austrian and Prussian assistance, by the end of the year. Both powers intended to retain their gains in a fresh partition and, though Austria had wished to maintain a Polish buffer state and had stayed neutral, she felt obliged, by the Prussian military advance and by the need to maintain her position with respect to the other powers, to intervene. Austria and Russia agreed on their shares on 3 January 1795, and the more ambitious Frederick William II was coerced into accepting them. Prussia was too isolated and exhausted to resist.

By treaties signed on 24 October 1795, Poland ceased to exist as a state.[3] Though Russia had, in exchanging her protectorate for partition, lost influence over much territory, she had acquired the largest section of Poland, extending her frontiers considerably further west with the acquisition of Courland, Lithuania and Podlesia in 1795, so that Vilnius, Grodno and Brest-Litovsk were all brought under Russian rule. Prussia gained Warsaw and Austria, Cracow and Lublin. Russia's role in Eastern Europe was to be further enhanced by the difficulties that French success and expansion created for Austria and Prussia. Catherine II herself saw ending Polish independence as a prelude to renewed expansion into the Balkans, and Austria secretly promised to back her plan for a satellite kingdom in Wallachia and Moldavia.

British recovery 1783–90

British attempts after the American War of Independence to gain European allies were singularly unsuccessful. Both Joseph II and

Frederick II rejected British approaches and, despite British efforts, a Franco-Dutch treaty was signed in 1785. Attempts to exploit Continental crises in order to divide Austria from France also failed. The British failure to win allies reflected the low esteem Britain was held in and the extent to which French power and intentions were no longer seen as a threat by other Continental monarchs. Political turmoil in Britain led Continental commentators, such as Joseph II and Frederick II, to place a low estimate on British strength and stability. Had a neutral observer been asked which European country would experience a revolution within a decade, he would probably have replied Britain, not France.

British diplomatic rivalry with France was matched by naval and colonial competition, particularly in India where concern about French intentions focused on France's interest in developing her position in the Indian Ocean which, with the Pacific, was the great area of imperial and commercial speculation in the last two decades of the century. Distrust was endemic, understandably so in light of the experience of the American war, which suggested that France would exploit any difficulties that Britain encountered. In this context, the commercial negotiations that culminated in the Eden treaty of 26 September 1786 were of limited importance. The Peace of Versailles had stipulated such a treaty and Vergennes had been anxious for it, believing that it would help the French economy and bind the two nations together by economic links, rather as Shelburne hoped to do in the case of Britain and America. Shelburne supported the causes of freer trade and economic links between Britain and France, but, after his fall in February 1783, the proposals received little support in the British government until threatened French reprisals led them to negotiate in earnest. The abolition of certain tariffs and the lowering of others in the treaty negotiated by William Eden were contentious steps in both countries and contemporaries were divided about their economic consequences, a difficult subject to assess not least because of the economic depression in France in the late 1780s and the varied and decentralized nature of the French economy. British manufactured exports certainly harmed particular French industries, although probably far less than complaints might suggest. French colonial trade continued to grow, driving Britain from part of the prosperous trade in the reexport of colonial goods, such as sugar. Commercial links with France were defended with considerable enthusiasm by Pitt, who criticized the idea of natural enmities, but that notion was deeply entrenched in the British political nation, being expounded not only by opposition figures who criticized the treaty, but also by George III, the Marquis of Carmarthen, Foreign Secretary in 1783–91, and most British diplomats.

The Dutch crisis fused British concern about French maritime and colonial intentions with her attempt to limit French influence in Europe. The fear that France would gain control of the Dutch navy and of Dutch colonies, particularly those on the route to India at Cape Town and in Sri Lanka, made the struggle in the United Provinces between the British-supported Orangeists and the French-backed Patriots more than simply a dispute for diplomatic dominance. As in America, France helped a movement seeking to create new political arrangements. Though not democrats, the Patriots were a movement of those in the middling orders traditionally excluded from the oligarchic world of Dutch politics and, through their militia, the Free Corps, they were able to gain power in a number of areas, including the wealthiest province, Holland. The Dutch crisis became a test of Anglo-French relations in large part because of the aggressive intervention of Sir James Harris, British envoy at The Hague, who was suspicious of France and sceptical of the Eden treaty. Harris's activity and British financial support helped the Orangeist cause, but they might not have succeeded but for the long-desired Prussian intervention of September 1787. This was provoked by the arrest and humiliating temporary detention of William V of Orange's politically active wife Wilhelmina, the sister of Frederick William II. This was an affront with results comparable to the return of the Infanta in 1725 and Frederick's attack on Louis XV's Saxon relations in 1756. It led to a Prussian ultimatum to the Patriots and preparations for military intervention that were crucially encouraged by the outbreak of war in the Balkans, which tied the hands of France's ally Austria. French threats to act on behalf of their Dutch protégés were thwarted by a lack of money, an absence of diplomatic support and successful Anglo-Prussian brinkmanship. While Britain armed her fleet, Prussian forces invaded the United Provinces in September 1787, achieving a rapid and complete success.[4] William V's authority was restored, many of the Patriots fleeing to France where during the Revolution they were to press for action against him. This victory prefigured the restoration of order in the Austrian Netherlands in 1790 and the defeat of Polish irregulars by Russian regulars in 1794, but provided no precedent for Prussian action against the regular forces of Revolutionary France in 1792.

France's failure to act led to her diplomatic nullity of the late 1780s. Arguably France could not have faced Britain and Prussia alone but she had been humiliated. Possibly the Balkan crisis was to blame, but the Austro-French alliance had been devoid of much meaning in terms of cooperation and shared views for a number of years and France's inability to influence her partner was if anything masked by the Balkan crisis. Had Louis XVI acted in 1787 and the Prussians not invaded then possibly he and the French monarchy would have achieved an aura of success and prestige that would have helped to counter the complex grievances of those years. As it was, the developing domestic, financial and constitutional crisis in France led to the Assembly of Notables in 1787, and then to its failure, and to the decision, in 1788, to summon an Estates General, a national representative body that had not met since 1614 and whose decisions it was impossible to predict. In foreign policy terms, 1787 marked the beginning of the Revolution and of the first stage of Revolutionary France's international position, one of nullity and inconsequential diplomatic gestures, that was to last until 1791.[5]

French diplomatic impotence was exacerbated by the effects of the Dutch crisis. Austria and Russia paid no heed to French attempts to mediate a Balkan peace that would both enable them to confront Prussia and protect the interests of France's traditional ally Turkey. Furthermore, while moves for a Franco-Prussian rapprochement were blocked, an Anglo-Dutch–Prussian alliance system was created that lent permanence to the consequences of the crisis. Anglo-Dutch and Dutch–Prussian defensive treaties in April 1788 were followed on 13 August 1788 by an Anglo-Prussian defensive alliance, creating the so-called Triple Alliance of 1788. This alliance was to lead Britain to take an active role in Eastern European diplomacy and, in the Ochakov crisis of 1791, to confront Russia's Balkan plans. Pitt, however, had to back down in part because opposition to Russia did not command the favourable resonances in the political nation that hostility to France enjoyed.

In contrast, in 1790, Pitt's aggressive attitude towards Spain in the Nootka Sound crisis had been in tune with political sentiment. Spanish determination to control the American Pacific coast south of Russian Alaska led to a clash with British fur-traders at Nootka Sound on the west coast of what is now Vancouver Island. Pitt demanded recompense for a destroyed trading post and seized ships, and used a substantial naval mobilization to press for a wide-ranging settlement of Anglo-Spanish colonial disputes. Seeking to resist, the Spaniards asked for French assistance under the Family Compact. This produced a confused response in Paris, where factional politics led the National

Assembly to challenge the royal right to declare war, before, in August, it voted to arm a considerable fleet. Uncertainty over French intentions, justified scepticism about the ability of the French to prepare a large fleet, British pressure and the size of the British navy all led Spain to back down. A settlement in October 1790 gave Britain access to the empty coastline north of Spanish California and secured Spanish consent to British whaling in the Pacific. Two years earlier, a British penal colony had been established at New South Wales in the opposite corner of the Pacific, the basis for eventual British control of Australia. The French had been major Pacific explorers with state-sponsored expeditions under Bougainville and La Pérouse, but it was Britain that was increasingly gaining ground around the ocean's rim. Her influence was to further increase during the following quarter-century as naval mastery in the wars of 1793–1815 allowed Britain to conquer the colonies of other European powers and to dominate Europe's transoceanic trade.

The origins of the French Revolutionary War 1789–92

While events in Eastern Europe dominated the diplomatic agenda, developments in France in 1789–90 simply enhanced the extent to which the country had already been largely written off as a political force. There was concern in some foreign quarters that the Estates General, which met in 1789, might lead to the reform of French society and institutions, and thus a revival of French strength, but this was swiftly ended by the political turmoil that instead followed. Foreign governments were most interested in the state of the French armed forces and government finances, and both these deteriorated, with army mutinies, naval indiscipline[6] and an increasing loss of confidence. A loss of military morale, cohesion and force crippled royal power. The confused, factious and weak French response to the Nootka Sound crisis in 1790 appeared to epitomize the collapse of France as a power and her related unreliability and lack of value as an ally. Requests from royalist émigrés for assistance were rejected by, among others, Louis XVI's brother-in-law, Leopold II, and only the maverick Gustavus III was prepared to consider intervention. And yet, within two years, both Austria and Prussia were to be at war with France and, by the end of 1792, French forces had overrun the Austrian Netherlands, Savoy and part of the Rhineland.

This change was due to developments in France and elsewhere. In 1790, neither Austria nor Prussia was really in any state to fight France, however weak she might be. Both were principal players in the crisis in Eastern Europe and Austria was additionally challenged by rebellions in Hungary and the Austrian Netherlands. The resolution of the eastern crisis the following year enabled a shift in attention to take place. The Austro-Prussian rapprochement that followed the Convention of Reichenbach led, on 27 August 1791, to the Declaration of Pillnitz, a joint statement by Leopold II and Frederick William II expressing concern at the position of Louis XVI after his unsuccessful flight to Varennes and the wish that the European powers would act to assist him. Louis's youngest brother, the Count of Artois, who had left France after the fall of the Bastille, and his adviser Calonne were both at Pillnitz though they had little influence there or elsewhere. Though the declaration made action dependent on support by other states and was a disappointment to French émigrés, it indicated that the two monarchs were concerned about developments within France. This was more important than the actual provisions of the Declaration of Pillnitz. French radicals argued that the Revolution was under external threat and must be defended, thus ensuring the process of radicalization under real or apparent threat that is crucial to so many revolutions.

In late 1791, Austro-French relations became increasingly tense as each power sought, in an atmosphere of growing mistrust and uncertainty, to intimidate the other, both convinced that the other would respond by backing down and failing to appreciate that their measures would be taken as warlike steps. Two major areas of tension were the feudal privileges of German princes in Alsace and the protection afforded to the émigrés in the Rhineland, particularly by the Archbishop-Electors of Mainz and Trier. On 4 August 1789, the French extended the abolition of the feudal regime to the Alsatian rights of German princes which had been guaranteed by successive treaties. This was a clash between the national sovereignty of a new political order determined to enforce its decrees universally within its frontiers and the intention of other powers to retain a more variegated notion of sovereignty in which inherited privileges and corporate rights played a major role. The Imperial Diet declared its support of the princes' claim in July 1791 and Leopold's subsequent backing for it in diplomatic exchanges with Paris that winter aroused anger. Coblenz in the electorate of Trier had become the central focus of émigré activity in 1791 and, as French concern about counter-revolutionary activity and possible intervention in France increased, so more pressure was exerted by the French on the Rhenish rulers to deny the émigrés support and hospitality. This led to Leopold indicating his determination to defend the princes from any French pressure. Conventional diplomatic relationships were being compromised by pressures arising essentially from ideological fears. Radical French attitudes appeared to threaten agreements, as with German privileges in Alsace, and to suggest that sovereign rights would be challenged, as with the Rhenish rulers or the Papacy, whose enclave of Avignon within France had been annexed in September 1791.

In France, a political grouping under Brissot saw confrontation with Austria as a means to power. The cause of 'peoples against kings' was a potent one in radical circles, not least because kings seemed to be acting against peoples. Increasingly aggressive policies were advocated in Paris and Austrian demands were rejected. Leopold II, who had sought to avoid war and without whom a violent German confrontation with France was impossible, died on 1 March 1792, to be succeeded by his more bellicose son, Francis II. On 20 April, France declared war on Austria in the hope that a revolutionary crusade would defeat the enemies of the Revolution, consolidating it in France and extending the revolutionary example elsewhere in Europe. A variety of proposals for the reorganization of Europe were advanced, including the extension of France to her 'natural limits' and the division of much of Europe into small republics. Refugees from failed revolutions elsewhere in Europe, particularly from the Austrian Netherlands and the prince-bishopric of Liège, Dutch 'Patriots' and radicals from other countries, such as Britain, encouraged deceptive opinions concerning the willingness of their compatriots to rebel and to help France, and pressed strongly for French assistance in remodelling the Low Countries.

Initially the war went badly for the Revolutionaries with the failure of their offensive into the Austrian Netherlands. Frederick William II, who had signed a defensive alliance with Leopold in February 1792, declared war on France on 21 May 1792, hoping that Prussia would again reap the glory and benefit that her successful invasion of the United Provinces in 1787 had brought and be rewarded with Polish territory. Frederick William wanted to reconcile the Habsburgs to Prussian expansion in Poland and the Empire.

The early stages of the French Revolutionary War, 1792–6

A Prussian army under the Duke of Brunswick invaded France but supply problems and the lateness with which the campaign had begun encouraged him not to persevere when his forces encountered superior French forces in a skirmish at Valmy on 20 September 1792. The French then gained the initiative, invading Savoy, the Rhineland and the Austrian Netherlands. An outnumbered Austrian force was defeated at Jemappes on 6 November and their position in the Austrian Netherlands collapsed. This was to lead hitherto neutral Britain into the war. The British ministry and many French politicians did not want war but the British felt bound to respond to the threat to the United Provinces posed by the French advance, and to a number of decrees including the opening of the Scheldt and, on 19 November 1792, the offer of French help to all subjects seeking to overthrow tyrannical governments.

The autonomous French approach to diplomacy, their determination to reject the conventions and practices of *ancien régime* international relations, and the absence of any strong government that could give a clear, firm direction to policy, suggested that it would be impossible to fulfil hopes of a compromise settlement over the Low Countries, a crucial area of British interest. Tension was increased by mutual hostility towards domestic developments in the other country, moves in Britain against radical groups and the radicalization of the French Revolution: the September massacres, the abolition of the monarchy, and the trial and, on 21 January 1793, execution of Louis XVI. This led to the expulsion of French diplomats in London. Suspicious of British intentions, the French declared war on Britain and the United Provinces on 1 February 1793.

Although many of the French gains in late 1792 were to be reversed the following year, the Austrians defeating the French at Neerwinden on 18 March and driving them from Mainz in July, it was clear that the war was not going to be a quick royalist police action or a profitable restoration of order in France.[7] Britain took a major role in creating the First Coalition (1793–7) against France but, as in her earlier wars with France, she found her allies unwilling both to subordinate their strategies to British wishes and, at least in British eyes, to forget traditional animosities and interests. British radicals had a point in contrasting the Pitt ministry's opposition to the French attempt to create a new political order in the Low Countries with its willingness to accept the Second and Third Partitions of Poland.

However, the ministry's determination to influence the fate of Eastern Europe had been a victim of the Ochakov crisis and, from 1792, the British concentrated on their traditional area of prime concern, the Low Countries. They should not have been surprised that other powers acted similarly in focusing on their regions of prime concern.

Just as the outbreak of war increased the paranoia of French public culture and helped the Revolutionaries associate themselves with France, so war drove the pace of the foreign policy of the French republic. The course and goals of policy and the response of other powers both greatly reflected the fortunes of war. Thus, defeat at Neerwinden and the loss of Belgium to the Austrians in 1793 led to a more cautious approach to annexation and the spread of revolution, and to stronger interest in peace. Brissot and the Girondins fell in June 1793 and their foreign minister, Lebrun, was executed. The Jacobin coup initially gave power to Danton who sought a return to more conventional diplomacy; in contrast to the more radical domestic policies of the Jacobins. In order to get peace, Danton tried to create an alliance system. Prussia, Sardinia, Switzerland and Tuscany were offered terms designed to weaken the relative position of Austria and Britain. Danton sought a negotiated peace with Britain in late 1793, but French objectives were scarcely those that would satisfy either her or Austria.

The situation was transformed by the victories of the Revolutionary armies in Belgium in 1794, especially Fleurus on 26 June. Victory gave war prestige and discouraged compromise. Government and generals came to require continued warfare in order to fund their activities. This remained true of the Thermidorean regime that succeeded the Jacobin Terror in July 1794. Exploitation by French occupying armies generated resistance in the Rhineland, but Austria and Prussia were increasingly concerned about Eastern Europe, while, in alliances with Britain signed in March 1793 and February 1795, Russia promised only warships to the anti-French cause. Relations between Prussia and Austria had deteriorated, in part because of anger about Prussia's gains under the Second Partition of Poland, and Johann Amadeus Franz von Thugut,an opponent of Prussia, was appointed Director-General of the Chancery in 1793. Unable to fulfil her hopes of exchanging the Austrian Netherlands for Bavaria, Austria began to look for fresh gains in Poland.[8] All three of the partitioning powers sent armies to destroy the Polish rising of 1794. Although tensions between the partitioning powers were foremost, the disunity of the First Coalition was more widespread, including, in particular, major differences between Britain and Austria, and Britain and Prussia. The Prussians showed only limited interest in fighting France and, in October 1794, the British cancelled their subsidy to Prussia.

Having overrun the Low Countries in 1794–5, the French were able to negotiate peace with an exhausted Prussia. Under the Peace of Basle of 5 April 1795, Prussia accepted French occupation of the left bank of the Rhine, while France promised compensation on the right bank and accepted a Prussian-led neutrality zone in northern Germany. This abandonment of the coalition covered France's position in the Low Countries and led other powers to follow. Prussia did not fight France again until 1806.[9]

The conquered Dutch, on 16 May 1795, accepted satellite status as the Batavian Republic, as well as a massive indemnity, the cession of Maastricht, Venlo and Dutch Flanders, a French army of occupation until a general peace was negotiated and a loss of control over the navy. The creation of new sister republics, of which this was the first, epitomized the use of power to make revolutionary changes elsewhere in Europe. Natural limits and small republics had indeed been aspects of the Girondin plan for Europe, but they were to be introduced under the shadow of a dominant and exploitative France.

Although Bilbao and Vitoria were captured by the French in 1795, Spain had not been overrun. The Catalans had ignored French suggestions of a French-backed independent republic. Spain was also tangential to the principal spheres of French strategic and territorial interest. By its Peace of Basle, of 22 July 1795, Spain only ceded Santo Domingo, its half of Hispaniola, to France. The following year, Spain allied with France. As a result, the British fleet was outnumbered in the Mediterranean and withdrew from it in late 1796. These treaties improved France's position towards Austria and Britain. Although there was a peace party in Vienna, and hopes of Russian assistance were again disappointed, neither Austria nor Britain was seriously interested in accepting French gains, and their separate discussions with France in early 1796 proved fruitless. The French invaded southern Germany and northern Italy that summer. War would continue.

The foreign policy of the French Directory 1795–9

France's success led to a growing intensity in the debate among her opponents about war goals. The restoration of the Bourbons was pushed hard by counter-revolutionaries, but others argued that this was unrealistic and that it was necessary to accept the Revolution. The idea that domestic change within France could be accepted so long as she renounced foreign gains was not, however, credible, because not enough French politicians were willing to accept it and fight for it. French policy did not reveal a consistent willingness to accept limits that were acceptable to others. Instead, the continuation of the war encouraged fresh ambitions on the part of France, as well as a fearful desire for her defeat and for revenge from her opponents.

The Directory, a group of ministers who governed France from 1795 until 1799, believed war necessary in order to support the army, to please its generals and, for these and other reasons, to control discontent in France, not least by providing occupation for the volatile commanders, the views and ambitions of many of whom were not limited to the conduct of war. Interest in peace was not pursued with great energy. The Alsatian Jean-François Reubell, who was the most influential in foreign policy of the five Directors, sought a peace that would guarantee what were presented as natural and, therefore, rational frontiers: the Rhine and the Alps. Such frontiers appeared a counterpart to the redrawing of boundaries within France, as long-lasting provinces were replaced by the new *départements* and their supposedly more rational boundaries. This rationalization, however, also entailed a significant expansion of French power into Germany and the Low Countries. Reubell saw this also as a reasonable compensation for the gains made by Austria, Prussia and Russia through the Partitions of Poland.

In northern Italy, initial French victories led to pressure for further conquest, in order to satisfy political and military ambitions and exigencies. Napoleon rose to prominence through his successful operations as commander of the French Army of Italy in 1796–7, and because his successes contrasted with the failed invasions across the Rhine in 1795 and 1796. It proved difficult to fix success. The brutal exploitation of Lombardy in 1796 led to a popular rising that was harshly repressed. There was also a serious popular rising in Swabia and Franconia, evidence of the fragile basis of French gains. In Italy, however, Napoleon managed to regain the initiative, a characteristic feature of his imaginative generalship and opportunistic approach to international politics. Marching to within 70 miles of Vienna, he forced Austria to accept the Truce of Leoben on 18 April 1797.

Napoleon's victories had already destroyed the Directory's initiative earlier in the year, of peace on the basis of the gain of Belgium, with Austrian possessions in Italy returned. His victories ensured that the Directory, which was primarily interested in the annexation of the left bank of the Rhine, and saw Italian gains as negotiable in return for Austrian consent, had, instead, to accept the Leoben terms, and the accompanying French commitment to Italy. Austria agreed to cede Belgium to France, and the Milanese to a newly formed French satellite republic, the Cisalpine Republic, and was to receive the Veneto (Venice's possessions on the Italian mainland) in return. Venice would be compensated with Bologna, Ferrara and Romagna, territories seized by France from the Pope in the Treaty of Tolentino of 19 February 1797. The principle of compensating victims at the expense of others, one established in *ancien régime* international thought, but less so in practice, was now being applied with both ruthlessness and energy. Napoleon was to become a master of the technique.

The Directory, angered by Napoleon's failure to secure the left bank of the Rhine, hoped for additional gains in the Rhineland that cut across any idea of real compromise with Austria in Germany. French goals in Germany and Italy represented a major shift from her recent policy. In June 1797, Napoleon remodelled much of northern Italy into the Cisalpine and Ligurian Republics. This proactive position was increased by the coup of 18 Fructidor (4 September 1797), when the two moderate Directors – Barthélemy and Carnot – were removed by their more assertive colleagues: Barras, Reubell and La Révellière.

To avoid the resumption of war, Austria was obliged to accept the Treaty of Campo Formio on 18 October 1797. The location of the treaty's signing, at a village near Udine, in what is now north-east Italy, was a testimony to the range of Napoleon's advance. France's gain of the Ionian Islands, Venetian Albania, the major north Italian military base of Mantua and the prospect of most of the left bank of the Rhine, as well as Austrian recognition for the Cisalpine Republic, exceeded the hopes of Louis XIV and Louis XV. France was left the dominant power in Italy and Germany, although Austria received Venice, the Veneto, Salzburg, and the likelihood that it would benefit from the congress that would be held to negotiate peace between France and the Holy Roman Empire. The cession of the republic of Venice to Austria was condemned by Jacobins as a betrayal of revolutionary ideals.

The congress, held at Rastatt, agreed to the cession of the left bank of the Rhine to France, with the secular rulers compensated at the expense of the ecclesiastical states, the terms outlined by Napoleon when he visited Rastatt in November 1797. As the ecclesiastical states had been great supporters of the Imperial system, these terms augured the end of the Holy Roman Empire, and thus helped to create a vacuum beyond the Rhine. They also exemplified the process of seeking the support of the defeated at the expense of others, the technique of divide and rule that the French were to employ so successfully.

Although there was a popular desire for peace, this was not the end of French expansion. Military convenience, lust for loot, the practice of expropriation, ideological conviction, the political advantages of a successful campaign and strategic opportunism all encouraged aggressive action both before and after Campo Formio, as with the occupation of Venice in 1797, the Papal States in February 1798 and Piedmont in December 1798, and the invasion of Switzerland in February 1798.

The traditional Bourbon claim that Britain's maritime and colonial position subverted any balance was repeated. On 19 August 1796, France and Spain signed the Treaty of San Ildefonso, creating an offensive alliance aimed at Britain and her ally Portugal, and Spain declared war in October. The British sought direct peace talks with France at Lille, but their demand for a mutual return of conquests was unacceptable and in December 1796 the French brought the negotiations to a close. A French invasion force appeared off southern Ireland in December 1796, and another invasion army was prepared a year later. The Irish rising of 1798 led to the landing of a small force in western Ireland, but it was quickly defeated. French schemes to overthrow Britain included plans to invade Jamaica and instigate slave risings there. However, Britain's position improved with victories over the Spanish and Dutch fleets at St Vincent and Camperdown in 1797.

Italy was not the limit of Napoleon's range and ambition. Having decided that an invasion of England would fail, Napoleon, supported by the foreign minister, Talleyrand, pressed the case for an invasion of Egypt, in order both to retain his own military position and for France to be better able to challenge the British in India. The Directors were keen to keep Napoleon out of France. Mounted in 1798, this invasion of Egypt was a major independent initiative on the part of Napoleon. It revealed a characteristic absence of the sense of mutual understanding that is crucial to the successful operation of the international system. He assumed that the Turks, the imperial overlords of effectively autonomous Egypt, could be intimidated or bribed into accepting French action, which, indeed, followed a whole series of provocative acts. These assumptions were coupled with a contempt for Turkey as a military force. Having first easily overrun Malta, a vulnerable military target then ruled by the Knights of St John, Napoleon's army landed in Egypt on 1 July 1798. He defeated the Mamelukes, the *de facto* rulers of Egypt, at Shubra Khit (13 July) and Embabeh, the battle of the Pyramids (21 July), spectacular victories for defensive firepower over shock tactics. These gave the French control of Lower Egypt.

The Turks, however, resisted, and in alliance with Britain and Russia. The French cultural supposition of superiority and arrogance of power had led to a lack of sensitivity that caused the conflict to spread. The British under Admiral Horatio Nelson destroyed the invasion fleet in Aboukir Bay, in the Battle of the Nile on 1 August 1798. The following year, the British overran Mysore, France's likeliest ally in India, and Napoleon was repulsed at Acre by a Turkish garrison with British naval support. After Napoleon had evaded the British fleet and returned to France in the autumn of 1799, the French army left in Egypt was eventually defeated by the British in 1801.

More immediately, the French, again, as in 1741, discovered that the use of force to extend their power produced unexpected responses which France could ill afford. Furthermore, force increasingly defined their relations with other powers. Paul I, who became Tsar in November 1796, had initially abandoned his predecessor's plans to send a British-subsidized army to oppose the French in Western Europe, but he was increasingly doubtful about the willingness of the French to limit their expansion and concerned about their ideological agenda. The French occupation and then annexation of the Ionian Islands in 1797, and their occupation of Malta in 1798, accentuated Paul's doubts about both the geopolitics and the legitimacy of French power. He was unprepared to see France expand into the eastern Mediterranean.

The Egyptian expedition led in 1798 to a move by Paul I and by Ferdinand IV of Naples into the anti-French camp and, in 1799, to a Russo-Turkish capture of the Ionian Islands. As the two powers had been bitter enemies, this remarkable cooperation was a testimony to the unexpected consequences of Napoleon's aggression. The Neapolitans attacked French-occupied Rome in November 1798, although they were rapidly repulsed. Occupying Naples in December 1798, the French established the Parthenopean Republic, another satellite regime, just as they had set up the Helvetic Republic when they conquered Switzerland earlier in the year, and the Roman Republic in the Papal States. However, these new governments were unpopular and compromised by their links with expensive and meddlesome French occupation. Risings against the French in Naples and elsewhere in 1798–9 were crushed, but they were a warning about the need to find a broader base for a French system.

The War of the Second Coalition pitched Austria, Britain, Naples, Portugal, Russia and Turkey against France. Distrust, rather than the specific points at issue, proved the crucial element in leading France and Austria to renew hostilities in 1799. The Austrians also sought revenge. The French were defeated by the Austrians in Germany in March at Ostrach and Stockach and driven back across the Rhine, and also expelled from most of Italy by Austrian and, in particular, Russian forces, and from Switzerland by the Austrians. With Poland partitioned out of existence and Russia at peace with Turkey, the Russians were able to intervene effectively in Western Europe.

However, Anglo-Russian plans to overthrow the Republic and restore the Bourbons exaggerated the scope of the divided coalition's power. The Directory was able to rally French strength, helped by the failure of their opponents to disrupt seriously the French home base, but it was unpopular, discredited by division and unable to manage the army. A change seemed necessary. A coup in Paris on 18 June 1799 was followed by a more vigorous prosecution of the war that helped to exacerbate differences in the opposing coalition. Paul I and the Austrians fell out, while an Anglo-Russian amphibious invasion of Holland failed. Paul withdrew from the Second Coalition. The French were helped throughout the period by divisions among their opponents, and these divisions strengthened whether France did well, leading her opponents to fear that they would be left behind in their allies' rush for peace, or badly, causing a dispute over likely spoils. Nevertheless, the strains on France of a conflict that itself owed much to Napoleon's folly helped to provide the opportunity for his seizure of power.

Napoleon's will to dominate

Napoleon's seizure of power on 9–10 November 1799 (the coup of 18–19 Brumaire), as the Directory was replaced by the Consulate, might seem to reflect a return to *ancien régime* patterns of diplomatic activity. The inexorable scope of Napoleon's ambition and his vainglorious capacity to alienate others can be seen to repeat those of

Louis XIV. Just as Napoleon's regime marked a limitation of radicalism within France, so it can be seen as reflecting and sustaining an abandonment of Revolutionary objectives and methods in international relations, although this abandonment had begun in the mid-1790s. Open diplomacy was replaced by pragmatism, and fraternity by the restoration of slavery in Guadeloupe and Martinique in 1802 and the prohibition of entry to France for West Indian blacks and mixed-race people. This would, therefore, suggest that a fundamental divide in foreign policy came, not with the final fall of Napoleon and the Vienna peace settlement of 1815, but, rather, with his rise to be First Consul (1800) and then Emperor (1804). Such an approach can be taken further by suggesting that there was, therefore, a fundamental continuity throughout the nineteenth century: Napoleon III (President of France 1848–52, Emperor 1852–70) could, justifiably, look to the example of Napoleon I.

Such a continuity, however, did not mean that the return of France to a monarchical system under Napoleon I entailed a return to an *ancien régime* system of international relations. Instead, a characteristic feature of warfare, both in the Revolutionary/Napoleonic period and subsequently, was a degree of popular mobilization that was greater than that of the pre-Revolutionary eighteenth century and one that owed much to measures to obtain a favourable public opinion. Public opinion focused on nationalism, which can be understood as a positive force for identity and cohesion and also as a negative xenophobic response to others, whether other nation states or incorporating international forces, most obviously Napoleonic France. The need for domestic support in wartime encouraged propaganda that, combined with the contemporary emphasis on the nation, led to explanations that hinged on the defence of national interests and honour, although such a defence could well be advanced and presented in aggressive terms. The calls for national risings for liberty that, albeit often cynically, had characterized the 1790s became far less common. Napoleon called on the Hungarians to rise for independence from Austria in 1809, talked of an Italian national spirit in the Kingdom of Italy, and sought to profit from Polish nationalism in the Grand Duchy of Warsaw, but, in general, he avoided international populism.

Napoleon's foreign and military policies were not only a continuation of those of the 1790s in the reliance on the mobilization of the French public. There was also a similar unwillingness to accept compromise, a desire, at once opportunistic, brutal and modernizing, to remould Europe, a cynical exploitation of allies, and a ruthless reliance on the politics of expropriation that had led not only to gains by Revolutionary France, but also to the Partitions of Poland. A bully in negotiations, Napoleon sought agreements that were provisional in one direction: containing clauses that enabled him to make fresh demands. Thus, in 1807, Napoleon followed up the Treaty of Tilsit by continuing to occupy Prussia and by trying to make Russia invade Sweden, accept a French gain of Silesia if it seized Moldavia and Wallachia from the Turks, and grant French companies monopoly privileges. The Russian envoy in Paris, Tolstoi, saw such demands as part of an inexorable aggrandizement driven by Napoleon's personality and his reliance on his large army.

Weaker powers, whether allies or defeated, were victims, their possessions and resources to be used for the benefit of Napoleon's diplomatic and military calculations. Occupied areas, satellite states, such as Switzerland and the Ligurian Republic (the republic of Genoa until 1797; annexed by France in 1805), allies, such as Spain, and neutrals were all expected to provide troops, ships or resources to help. Once war had been renewed with Britain in 1803, Napoleon brought the Batavian and Italian republics and Switzerland into the conflict on his side. Spain was obliged to provide subsidies. The costs of such cooperation discredited alliance with Napoleon, just as they had earlier weakened the satellite republics. The burdens of war also helped to cripple reform initiatives in the territories of German allies, such as Bavaria. The army of the Kingdom of Italy grew from 23,000 in 1805 to 90,000 in 1813. The majority of those sent from it to fight in Spain, Russia and Germany died.[10] The Grand Duchy of Warsaw had to man a 30,000–strong army, much of which died in Russia in 1812. French economic control over conquests and allies was disruptive and could also be harsh.

In 1806, in his peace negotiations with Britain, Napoleon did not consult his ally Spain, even when proposing to cede the Balearic Islands to Ferdinand of Naples, and in 1808 Florida was offered to the United States as a bribe for an alliance, again without considering the integrity of the Spanish empire. The same year, the French agreed, by the Conventions of Paris and Elbing, to end their onerous occupation of Prussia, but at the cost of the cession of Magdeburg and Prussia west of the Elbe to France, the permanent occupation of the major fortresses in eastern Prussia, a massive indemnity, a network of French military roads across Prussia, the limitation of the Prussian army, Prussian support in any conflict with Austria and the free transit of French goods. Given territory at the expense of Austria in 1809,

Bavaria was obliged to cede land to Württemberg and the Kingdom of Italy.

Napoleon was happiest with force; his character, views, ambitions and ambience did not lend themselves to accommodation, other than as a short-term device. He was in a position not only to act as an innovative general, but also to control the French military system and to direct the war effort. Enjoying greater power over the French army than any ruler since Louis XIV, Napoleon was in many respects also more powerful than Louis. His choice of commanders was not constrained by the social conventions and aristocratic alignments that affected Louis, and both armies and individual military units were under more direct governmental control than had been the case with the Bourbons. Furthermore, Napoleon was directly in command of the leading French force throughout the wars of his reign. French resources were devoted to the military with a consistency that the Revolutionary governments had lacked.

In his generalship, Napoleon was fired by the desire to engage and win. He confronted grave problems, not least the number and fighting quality of his opponents, the difficulty of establishing their positions, let alone intentions, the primitive communications of the period, and the need to raise the operational effectiveness of his conscripts. In response, Napoleon developed an effective military machine, even as he undermined it by the strains of near-continuous warfare, and eventually overwhelmed it in 1813–14 by failing to end a multi-front struggle. Able, even in 1813–14, to adapt rapidly to changing circumstances, Napoleon had a remarkable ability to impose his will upon war. He won close to fifty battles in his career, including the largest, most complex engagements hitherto seen in the gunpowder age.

Napoleon's will to dominate was both personal and a continuation of that of the Revolution. It ensured that peace treaties were imposed, and that, once they were made, the French sought further benefits, while their defeated opponents felt only resentment and a determination to reverse the settlement. This, in turn, led to further conflicts. Whereas the European peace treaties of 1763 – Hubertusburg and Paris – had been followed by over a decade of peace between the former combatants, and that of Vienna in 1814–15 ushered in a longer period of peace, 1795–1814 was a great age of peace treaties, but repeatedly saw them broken.

This was not only because of the sense that the French position was unacceptable and that Napoleon could know no limits, but also because of the conviction on the part of opponents that the French could be held and even beaten: war was unavoidable and victory possible. This inspired not only the attack on France in 1792 but also subsequent coalitions. If Napoleonic France could not be incorporated into the balance-of-power politics, and could not be accepted as a hegemonic state, it had to be brought down.

Although French propaganda presented Napoleon as always in favour of peace, the Napoleonic regime celebrated power, not least the power of victory, as in Baron Gros's battle paintings. A quasi-mystical emphasis on the cult of the warrior can also be seen in the celebration of the mythical Celtic poet Ossian. As an aspect of this, Napoleon took further the increased tendency to employ soldiers in diplomatic roles, a tendency that already could be seen in the 1790s. This contributed to an increasing militarization of the conduct of French foreign policy. The use of generals was an important aspect of Napoleon's failure to appreciate that an effective diplomatic service must produce reports and ideas that might be challenging.

The settings of the Napoleonic regime were not those that might encourage moderation. Indeed, the looting of Europe's artistic treasures to glorify its new centre encapsulated the apparent benefits of aggression. The spoils of aggression were also shown by the Senate's proclamation of him as Emperor of the French on 18 May 1804. That December, Napoleon crowned himself with the Crown of Charlemagne. The following year, he followed by becoming King of Italy and crowning himself with the Iron Crown of Lombardy. His family was rewarded with kingdoms.

Napoleon's views contributed strongly not only to repeated breakdowns of compromise peace treaties but also, more generally, to a sense that he could not be trusted, a sense that, in turn, affected the attitudes of other rulers to his specific demands. Napoleon sought satisfaction, not as part of a process of negotiation and conciliation, but as something to be seized. He had no real idea of how to turn strengths and successes into lasting and acceptable solutions. As a result, he wrecked the hopes of those who had hoped for partnership, or at least cooperation, with France, such as Alexander I of Russia, in 1803 and 1807, or the Austrians, who, in March 1807, produced a plan for a general peace that would have left Napoleon in control of the Low Countries and much of Italy. Napoleon's role has been stressed in order to underline a theme of this book, the issue of personality in international affairs.

Napoleon's unwillingness to accept limits for any length of time stemmed from his personality, but also from a related assessment of a

Europe in which the hegemony of one power – himself – was unconstrained by any outside force. This was the international politics of imperial China, or of the twentieth-century USA towards Latin America. It created far more problems in Europe, with its traditions of multipolarity. There was a widespread reluctance to accept his perspective, a reluctance that reflected the strength of political identities across much of Europe. Equally, Napoleon's precarious new imperial system enjoyed only limited support, especially in Iberia, southern Italy, and Eastern Europe (with the exception of Poland), and attempts to encourage coherence and cooperation within the empire fell foul of existing attitudes, habits, practices and interests, as well as of policy contradictions. For all his egocentric ambition, Napoleon was genuinely interested in a certain kind of rational modern administration and government that he sought to promote in the Europe he controlled. He introduced some worthwhile features of government, but his ideas of rational modernity were often crude, for example, his views on economic and financial matters, and he undermined his efforts by his rapacity, militarism and neo-feudalism. The Napoleonic system and psyche required force.

Napoleon did not understand compromise, and rejected the excellent advice he received, but, even without these character flaws, he faced formidable obstacles. Napoleon initially benefited from the operational and organizational advantages that the French enjoyed over their opponents in the 1790s, but these relative advantages were eroded in the 1800s as other states imitated many of France's developments. Across much of Europe, the modernization of political structures and administrative practices was influenced by French occupation or models, or by the need to devise new political and administrative strategies to counter the French. The changes introduced in the Prussian army and society after defeat by Napoleon in 1806 are an important example, although, in that case as in others, there was also considerable continuity with the enlightened reforms of the pre-Revolutionary period.

Napoleon's policies 1799–1802

Once he had seized power, Napoleon sought triumphs in war in order to consolidate his position. Thus Napoleon did not want Austria to accept the peace he offered in February 1800 until he had had another opportunity to defeat her, as he did at Marengo on 20 June, a victory that strengthened his position in France and lessened the likelihood of a coup against him. Napoleon then successfully divided his foreign opponents. The Austrians would have preferred no peace without Britain, but further French victories, especially at Hohenlinden on 3 December 1800, led, on 25 December, to an armistice and, on 9 February 1801, to the Treaty of Lunéville with Austria. Based on the terms of Campo Formio, this included Austrian recognition of French annexation of the entire left bank of the Rhine. The earlier annexation of Belgium was confirmed, and the Emperor Francis II also recognized the French satellite republics.

France had achieved a territorial settlement that exceeded Bourbon expectations, a settlement that Austria and most of Germany and Italy were willing, albeit grudgingly, to accept; and in 1800 Paul I of Russia had abandoned his conflict with France. Britain was isolated. Early in 1801, Paul I sent a mission to Paris to discuss cooperation against Britain, only for his envoys to discover that Napoleon sought cooperation simply on French terms. Paul's assassination on 22 March ended the alliance negotiations, but a treaty was signed in Paris by the two powers in October 1801.

Napoleon had been checked by the defeat of the French army in Egypt by the British on 21 March 1801 and the British naval victory off Copenhagen over the Danes on 2 April, although the French-supported Spanish invasion of Portugal in April 1801 forced the latter to break with Britain, which became more isolated. Napoleon characteristically sought to deny any benefit to Spain and succeeded in alienating her support. Although France could not defeat the British at sea, the latter had to accept French hegemony in Western Europe by the Treaty of Amiens (25 March 1802).

Lunéville and Amiens were followed on the part of Napoleon not by any serious attempt to control disputes, but by military consolidation and political aggrandizement, including an attempt to regain control of St Domingue in the West Indies, that were rightly perceived by the British as threatening. Napoleon broke treaties as and when it suited him; for example, the clause of the Treaty of Amiens in which he had agreed to respect the neutrality of the Batavian Republic, formerly the United Provinces. This was crucial to Britain, given the strategic importance of the Dutch colonies, especially the Cape of Good Hope, which the British had returned at Amiens, as they had also all their colonial gains from France. It was also foolish to alienate the British, because they had accepted French dominance of the Continent. This removed from the equations of Continental power politics the paymaster of opposition to France, and these subsidies were needed by Austria, Prussia and Russia in order to sustain their war efforts.[11]

The end of peace 1802–5

Napoleon needed to command. Thus, he rapidly ignored the limits agreed with Austria at Lunéville in 1801, and quickly violated the assumptions on which Russia made peace at Tilsit in 1807, while, although the terms of Amiens included a provision for the French evacuation of Egypt, Napoleon sent Colonel Horace Sebastiani to report on the possibility of a reconquest. The French gain of Louisiana from Spain in 1801, their creation of a new pro-French political system in Switzerland in 1803, their attempts to acquire Florida and to build up their navy, and moves to increase their presence in Algiers and Muscat also worried the British. This was not the conduct of a ruler willing to accept territorial or procedural limits on his hegemony, and it exacerbated British distrust, leading to a Russian-backed British refusal to evacuate Malta despite having agreed to do so. On 18 May 1803, Britain declared war on France.

Tsar Alexander's peace plan of 1803, a plan produced in response to Napoleon's request for mediation of his differences with Britain, was curtly rejected by Napoleon, because it would have required France to evacuate Hanover, Italy, Switzerland and the United Provinces. Alexander and his ministers were offended by the contemptuous way in which they were continually treated and concerned by the onward march of French policy. They were anxious about France's views for the Ionian Islands and worried about French intentions in the Balkans. The kidnapping from Baden of the Duke of Enghien, a Bourbon prince believed to be conspiring against Napoleon, and his trial and execution in March 1804, led to a marked deterioration in relations. France rudely rejected the Russian protest and relations were broken in August 1804. The Russians then stepped up their efforts to persuade Austria to take a prominent role in an alliance against France, efforts that had already led to refusals in December 1803 and April 1804. Napoleon meanwhile wooed Prussia. The Russians allied with Britain in the spring of 1805, but Alexander sent a peace mission to Paris, only to abandon it when Napoleon annexed Genoa in June.

In the early 1800s, the Austrian government sought to accommodate itself to French power, and adopted a conciliatory approach towards extensions of Napoleon's power in Germany and, in particular, Italy where Napoleon annexed Elba and Piedmont in 1802 and had himself elected President of the Italian Republic (as the Cisalpine Republic was now called). Despite this, in 1805, Napoleon demanded that Austria demobilize and formally declare its neutrality, in other words, surrender its capacity for independent action. This drove Austria to cooperate with Britain and Russia. Austria declared war on France and invaded her ally Bavaria, beginning the War of the Third Coalition.

War with Austria, Russia and Prussia 1805–7

The War of the Third Coalition opposed Austria, Britain, Naples and Russia to Napoleon. Having invaded Bavaria, the Austrians halted and were successfully counterattacked by the French. Decisive victories at Ulm (20 October) and Austerlitz (2 December) completely changed the situation. The French had benefited from the years of peace on the Continent from 1801 in order to train their infantry, increase their artillery and cavalry, and produce better balanced corps. The earlier years of war had provided experienced troops and an officer corps sifted by merit. In 1805, the Austrians were preparing for an attack from the west through the Black Forest, but they were outmanoeuvred by the rapid advance of the French from the middle Rhine to the Danube in their rear. The overly cautious Austrian response left an army bottled up in Ulm and, after it surrendered, Napoleon overran southern Germany and Austria, before defeating an Austro-Russian army at Austerlitz.

Austria left the war by the Treaty of Pressburg of 26 December 1805. This cost her Venetia, Istria, Dalmatia, the Voralberg and the Tyrol, and a massive indemnity, terms that subsequently made it difficult to support good relations with Napoleon in Vienna other than on the basis of expediency and necessity. Germany seemed securely under French leadership. Frederick William III of Prussia had initially refused to support the Third Coalition and, instead, by the Treaty of Schönbrunn of 15 December 1805, secured Hanover from Napoleon. However, Napoleon's exploitative treatment of Prussia, French bullying, threats, infringements of the Prussian neutrality zone and Prussian opportunism led to war in 1806. Prussia had entered the Third Coalition by a treaty signed at Potsdam on 3 November 1805, only to discover that Austerlitz fatally weakened the coalition, and encouraged Napoleon to a series of aggressively opportunistic steps that offered Prussia no choice other than client-statehood or war. The poorly-commanded and outmanoeuvred Prussians were rapidly defeated by the French at Jena and Auerstädt on 14 October 1806, and Frederick William III fled to Memel. Jena persuaded the Danes that Napoleon could not be resisted; and led the Sultan, Selim III, to move towards a French alliance and to declare war on Russia on 24 December 1806.

In a politics of trickery and bullying, meanwhile, neutral powers were exploited and attacked by Napoleon. Peace became war by other means. Naples and Hanover, potential allies of Britain, were both occupied in 1803, the Hanseatic cities and much of the Papal States following in 1806, and Rome in 1808. The French position in the Baltic was strengthened when the Swedish German possessions of Stralsund and Rügen were seized in 1807. Etruria (Tuscany and Parma) was annexed in 1808, Rome in 1809. This was the culmination of a process of bullying that led to Napoleon's excommunication by Pius VII, a step countered by the arrest of the pope. Switzerland lost the Valais, which was annexed by France in 1810, while the canton of Ticino was occupied. The Kingdom of Holland was annexed to France in 1810, as were Hamburg, Lübeck, Bremen and Oldenburg. Having intervened in Spain in 1808, Napoleon allocated Spain north of the Ebro to four military governorships, as a stage towards annexation. Opposition within Napoleonic Europe was repressed, 48,000 troops being committed to suppress the rebellion that began in Calabria in 1806.

Once Austria had been defeated, Napoleon reorganized Germany, creating in July 1806 an institutional basis for French intervention, the Rheinbund or Confederation of the Rhine. This league linked France and sixteen south and west German states, the largest of which were Bavaria, Württemberg and Baden. Territorial gains helped make these rulers allies. Napoleon was to be their Protector. This alliance was designed to limit Austrian and Prussian influence, represented a rejection of the Russian intervention in German politics under the Peace of Teschen of 1779 that Russia had mediated in order to end the War of the Bavarian Succession, and was intended to give Napoleon control over the forces and resources of the members of the Confederation. All the Rheinbund backed Napoleon against Prussia later in 1806. He had the Emperor, Francis, dissolve the Holy Roman Empire, so that Francis now became only Emperor of Austria, a title he had assumed in October 1804. The Austrians were forced to accept this when Napoleon moved the entire Grand Army into Upper Austria. They even handed over the imperial crown.[12] In 1806, Napoleon also had Saxony made a kingdom, part of his strategy of building up an ally in east-central Europe capable of opposing Russia.

Control over Germany was a crucial prelude to the continued prosecution of the war with Russia. This conflict, brought to an end by the Treaty of Tilsit of 7 July 1807, was punishing, but it further vindicated the quality of the French military machine. The fighting of 1805–7 had indicated the superiority of the French corps and divisional structure over the less coherent and less coordinated opposing forces. French staff work, at army and corps level, was superior to that of both Austria and Russia, and this helped to vitiate the numbers France's opponents put into the field. The quality of French staff work enabled Napoleon to translate his wide-ranging strategic vision into practice, and to force what might have been a segmented war into essentially a struggle in one major theatre of operations where he could use the Grande Armée effectively.

War with Britain, Spain and Austria 1806–9

No serious effort was made to settle differences with Britain, foolishly so, as the resources of worldwide British trade financed opposition to France, while, at Trafalgar, on 21 October 1805, Nelson had defeated the Franco-Spanish fleet. Negotiations in 1806 were designed by Napoleon only to isolate Britain, preparatory to an eventual new French attack. The British were prepared to accept French hegemony in Europe west of a Russian sphere, but Napoleon was not ready to make such hegemony even vaguely palatable. While peace was not on offer, war was to be total. The Berlin decree of 21 November 1806 – its place of issue under French occupation since 25 October – decreed a blockade of Britain, the confiscation of all British goods and the arrest of all Britons. The decree was for France's allies as much as France. The former were pressed to develop their navies for use against Britain.

The assault on British trade – Napoleon's Continental System, launched in 1806 and expanded by the Edict of Fontainebleau (1807) and the two Decrees of Milan (1807) – was a unilateral policy formulated and executed without consultation with client states, allies and neutrals. It hit long-established trades, infringed sovereign rights and created enormous hostility. An economic policy centred on French interests meant that Napoleon's effort to anchor his new dynasty in Europe found few popular roots. Alliance with France was revealed as costly and humiliating.[13]

Believing that everything was possible for him, Napoleon pressed on regardless. Portugal was invaded in 1807, despite its attempts to appease Napoleon, because he insisted on closing it to British trade and saw its conquest as a way to increase the French military presence in Iberia. Once conquered, there was no attempt to conciliate the Portuguese. Increasingly imperious and unwilling to listen to critical advice, Napoleon dismissed his experienced, independent-minded foreign minister, Talleyrand, in August 1807. In 1808, Napoleon used the disputes between Charles IV and Crown Prince Ferdinand – who succeeded Charles as Ferdinand VII – in order to replace the Bourbon monarchy in Spain by a Bonapartist one, that of his brother Joseph: an alliance amounting to indirect control was not enough, and Charles and Ferdinand were tricked and bullied into handing over the kingdom to Napoleon.

However, a nationalist rising in Spain (from 2 May 1808) and Portugal led to the Peninsular War, creating a military and political problem that was to challenge Napoleon for the remainder of his period of office. British troops were sent to Portugal in 1808 and, after several years campaigning, eventually overcame the French in Spain in 1813, winning a major success at Vitoria on 21 June.[14] In the meanwhile, France also had to fight Spanish regulars and guerrillas, operations that absorbed large numbers of troops. Spanish naval strength had also been lost to France, greatly limiting Napoleon's post-Trafalgar attempt to rebuild his navy in order to challenge Britain anew. The invasion of Spain also gave Napoleon a new war aim. Under the treaty with Alexander signed at Erfurt on 12 October 1808, that essentially confirmed Tilsit, no treaty was to be made with Britain unless she recognized the Bonapartist position in Spain, terms that would have entailed French dominance of Latin America.

Such terms were impossible for Britain as they would have revived France's transoceanic position. In practice, Latin America was sheltered from French power by the British navy, but the French invasion of Spain helped undermine the Spanish position in Latin

America, and, after the Napoleonic Wars, Ferdinand VII was to be unsuccessful in his attempt to restore royal power there.

The Bonapartist coup in Spain gave an edge to Napoleon's bullying of Austria. In December 1808, the Austrian government again decided on war, because it felt its safety threatened by French policy, which included a demand for disarmament, and because it feared a recurrence of the coup method already staged against Spain. Once armed, the finance minister warned that the armaments could not be long sustained, thus increasing the pressure for action. There was a sense that there was no choice, that French policy anyway threatened to impose the consequences of defeat, and that war was the sole alternative.

Austria got both war and defeat in 1809. Francis declared war on 9 April, and Napoleon found Austria a tougher opponent than in 1805, although the Austrians were handicapped by poorly-conceived war aims, inadequate and divided central leadership, and a foolish strategy. At Aspern-Essling (21–22 May 1809), Napoleon's bold attack on a superior Austrian force was repelled and he had to abandon the battlefield in the face of a serious Austrian advance and better Austrian generalship. At Wagram on 5–6 July, however, Napoleon proved the better general and the French corps commanders were superior to their Austrian counterparts, although this battle of attrition was no Austerlitz.

The Austrians received no help from Frederick William III of Prussia or the other German rulers, and the diversionary British attack on Walcheren was both too late and unsuccessful. Now allied with France and pursuing its own interests, Russia offered no support to Austria and, instead, attacked her. The Treaty of Schönbrunn of 14 October 1809 not only awarded Austrian territory to France and Bavaria, but also left the Duchy of Warsaw, the French client state created under the Tilsit agreement, in what had been Prussian parts of Poland, with gains from Austria. Austria lost about 3.5 million people and was left landlocked, with an indemnity of 200 million francs and with its army limited to 150,000 men. In 1810, having failed to obtain a Russian princess, Napoleon married the Archduchess Marie-Louise, a spoil of war designed to cement Austria's new relationship with France. Until the summer of 1813, Austria, which went bankrupt in February 1811, sought a peaceful partnership with Napoleon. In 1810, Austria rejected a Russian approach for an alliance. The rivalry and mutual distrust of Austria and Russia were important to Napoleon's success.

Relations with Russia, 1807–12

By the Treaty of Tilsit of July 1807, Alexander I had reached an agreement that left Napoleon dominant in Western and Central Europe. This was an acceptance of French hegemony that previous tsars had refused to signal. Indeed in 1735 and 1748 Russian armies had moved into Germany in order to put pressure on France. Such an acknowledgement was especially important, given the rise of Russian power in the closing decades of the eighteenth century. Signature at Tilsit, on the Russo-Prussian frontier, was a testimony to the range of Napoleon's power. Russia gained a small portion of Poland round Bialystok, that had been acquired by Prussia under the Third Partition, and her policy was now intertwined with that of Napoleon. Alexander agreed not only to deliver his Mediterranean base, the Ionian Isles, to France, but also to join with her in offering Britain peace terms. If these were rejected, Alexander was obliged to go to war with Britain and to coerce Austria, Denmark, Portugal and Sweden into doing the same. Frederick William III was abandoned by his Russian ally: Prussia was to lose her territory west of the Elbe, lands that contained nearly half Prussia's population, while other Prussian territories became part of the Grand Duchy of Warsaw. In return, France agreed to fight Turkey if she rejected the peace with Russia that Napoleon was to seek to obtain. If so, the Turks would lose most of the Balkans, thus creating the need for a Franco-Russian *entente* over the fate of what would be a fatally weakened Turkish empire.

Yet, despite his experience of Russian fighting quality at the battles of Eylau (8 February 1807) and Friedland (14 June 1807), Napoleon could not sustain this accommodation and these mutual guarantees, and thus concentrate his forces against Britain, let alone turn Tilsit into a strong partnership. His development of the Grand Duchy of Warsaw as a French client state, nominally ruled by the pliable King of Saxony, challenged Russia's position in Eastern Europe. For over 250 years, Polish weakness had been a condition of Russian strength. Napoleon's refusal to accept a draft convention, negotiated in January 1810 by his ambassador to Russia, guaranteeing that the Kingdom of Poland would not be revived, greatly increased Russian distrust about Poland and much else, and ensured that French actions were viewed through this prism. There was no true peace, and the French were unenthusiastic about supporting Russian ambitions in the Balkans. Matters were made worse in December 1810 by the French annexation of the north-west German Duchy of Oldenburg, which had dynastic links with the Romanovs and had been guaranteed at Tilsit.

In December 1810, Russia left the French economic camp, when it abandoned the Continental System which was proving ruinous to the Russian economy. New regulations were announced for neutral shipping. Such a unilateral step threatened the cohesion of the French system and challenged Napoleon's insistence on obedience and his treatment of allies as servants.

Napoleon responded to Russian independence, first with bluster, but also by greatly stepping up the military preparations for possible war, preparations already begun in October 1810 – although, at this stage, they were designed for intimidation, not conflict. He did not respond positively to Russian diplomatic approaches the following spring. From October 1811, French military preparations were accelerated and, in January 1812, France's position in the Baltic improved with the occupation of Swedish Pomerania.

Having assembled a powerful coalition against Russia, forcing an isolated Prussia to accept an offensive alliance treaty against Russia on 24 February 1812, Napoleon invaded on 24–5 June, the logic of his system demanding the curbing of his victim. Napoleon's closest advisers opposed the invasion, which was as unnecessary diplomatically as it was foolish militarily. But for the invasion, the French might well have been able to send more troops to Spain, have beaten their Spanish opponents, and then been better placed to defeat the British expeditionary force.

As with his earlier attacks on Austria, Prussia and Spain, and his planned invasion of Britain in 1805, Napoleon resolved to strike at the centre of his opponent's power, thus gaining the initiative and transferring much of the logistical burden of the war to his enemy. He invaded with half a million men, most of whom were allied troops, principally German, Italian and Polish. The Russians, however, fell back, denying Napoleon a decisive battle. Although there was interest among some of the nobility in a restored independent Grand Duchy of Lithuania, that was free of Poland as well as Russia, Napoleon found little local support. He considered proclaiming the freedom of the serfs, but did not do so: such a move did not accord with his limited goal of forcing Alexander to reenter the Continental System.[15]

Like the Germans in 1941, the French were not prepared for the nature of their task. Russian scorched-earth and guerrilla activity hit supplies, and the French lost men through hunger, disease and fatigue. Finally, at Borodino on 7 September, the Russians sought to stop the advance on Moscow. In a battle of attrition, that involved 233,000 men and 1227 cannon, the Russians resisted successive attacks and, when finally driven back, did so without breaking. Russian casualties were heavier, but Napoleon lost a quarter of his army. Napoleon followed up Borodino by entering an undefended Moscow on 14 September, but the city was set ablaze, probably by the Russians. The enormity of the task, logistical problems and Russian endurance had defeated Napoleon militarily before the difficulty of securing any settlement could thwart him politically. He had no terms to propose, faced an opponent who would not negotiate, and could not translate his seizure of Moscow into negotiations.

This was equally true once he had retreated from Russia with very heavy casualties. Due to heavy snowfalls, supply breakdowns and Russian attacks, the retreat had turned into a nightmare. Thereafter, there was no real attempt to accept the military verdict and offer Russia terms that would assuage its hostility. Napoleon could conceive of neither a new ethos in French foreign policy nor a new system in Eastern Europe. This greatly contributed to Russia's determination to implement the decision in December 1812 to press on against France, and thereby put Prussia, which Napoleon had instructed to raise another 30,000 men, in the front line. Russia's position had been strengthened in May 1812 by the Peace of Bucharest with Turkey. Although Russia did not gain Moldavia, Wallachia or an alliance with Turkey, as had been hoped, she gained both Bessarabia and an end to the war. However, there was still interest among Russian policy-makers in stirring up the Balkan Slavs against both Turkey and Austria, and tensions continued with both powers.

Defeat in Germany 1813

The states that Napoleon had bullied into providing troops and resources were to abandon him, although some, such as Austria – which sought peace – took a while before attacking France. A wave of francophobia in the army and parts of the populace in early 1813 led Prussia to declare war on Napoleon in March, beginning the collapse of his grip on Central Europe where he had long struggled to establish dominance and had come close to succeeding in 1809–12. In January 1813, Napoleon had harshly rejected Prussian terms and ordered the continuation of exactions. On 27–8 February, Prussia negotiated an alliance with Russia at Kalisch and Breslau and this was followed, on 19 March, by a convention at Breslau in which the two powers agreed on the liberation of Germany.

Napoleon fought back hard in Germany, aided by concerns about Russian and Prussian intentions among the German rulers, specifically their support for a mass insurrection; while the Prussians themselves were concerned about Russian plans for Poland. Napoleon rebuilt his army, but the new recruits were more like the fresh troops of 1792 than the veterans of his earlier campaigns, and, unlike in 1792, France's opponents were not outnumbered. However, new levies, both French and German, helped Napoleon drive his opponents out of Saxony in May 1813, winning victories at Lützen (2 May) and Bautzen (20–21 May), and north Germany did not rise against him as had been anticipated. Saxony rallied to Napoleon in May, and Denmark in July.

Concerned about their intentions, Austria refused to join Russia and Prussia but, instead, stopped fighting Russia, became neutral, mediated the armistice of Pleswitz on 4 June 1813, sought to mediate peace, and proposed an independent central Europe, neutral towards both France and Russia. Prince Clemens von Metternich, the Austrian foreign minister, was hostile to Prussia and Russia and hoped to reach an agreement with Napoleon, in order to obtain a partnership that would secure Austrian interests and reestablish Habsburg influence in Germany. In particular, Metternich saw a powerful France as a counterweight to Russia. He sought stability rather than territorial expansion. Metternich offered Napoleon the left bank of the Rhine, co-guarantorship of a neutralized Rheinbund, non-interference over Spain and diplomatic support over colonial concessions from Britain.

The response was unhelpful. Napoleon declared all France's annexations inalienable and began military preparations against Austria. Defeat had not curbed his instinctive bellicosity. Napoleon's refusal to negotiate peace, or to understand that it entailed compromise, delivered in person by an angry Emperor to Metternich in Dresden on 26 June, led Austria finally to join the anti-French camp: she declared war on 11 August.

The league of the partitioning powers had been recreated, but, unlike in 1772, their target was a France that refused any limitations on its power. The French were also heavily outnumbered. Austrian, Prussian, Russian and Swedish forces exceeded 600,000, while Napoleon's total field army was only 370,000. Only at Dresden (27 August) was Napoleon victorious. Threatened with Austrian invasion, Bavaria, long a stalwart of French interests, allied with Austria in October, repeating their alignment of 1745. On 16–19 October, in the major battle of the year, the heavily outnumbered Napoleon was defeated at Leipzig. Germany was lost. Napoleon was no longer in a position to assist and exploit Frederick August of Saxony, whose territories were now occupied by Prussia and Russia. The Rheinbund collapsed.

Both then and in 1814, Napoleon failed to offer terms that would divide his assailants, despite the fact that Austria distrusted Russia and Britain and would have liked to retain a strong France, while the Russians sought a strong France in order to balance Britain. Their definitions of strength included a France territorially more extensive than in 1789 and, at least initially, they were willing to accept a continuance of Napoleon's rule, but his instinctive refusal to accept limits or half-measures wrecked such schemes. Furthermore, repeated French assaults on other states for two decades had led them to adopt reforms that enhanced their ability to mobilize their resources. Thus, Napoleonic policies helped to close the capability gap between France and other states and to end the subservient acceptance on which his imperial rule depended.

The collapse of the Napoleonic Empire 1813–14

There were also changes in the international system in response to Napoleon. If Napoleon was immensely destabilizing in terms of established notions of international relations, he also represented a culmination of the politics of 'grab' exemplified by the Partitions of Poland. Indeed, Tilsit was in some respects another partition treaty with a different cast. Partly in reaction to the chaos and incessant conflict of such 'diplomacy', a concept and culture of international relations emphasizing restraint developed. It was seen in operation in the negotiations that led to and accompanied the anti-French coalition in 1813–15, in the Congress of Vienna, and in the postwar attempt to maintain peace and order by the Congress System. Napoleon could not be encompassed in this new system, and, once defeated, his system and methods were made redundant by it.

He was abandoned by former allies in 1813–14, losing for example Württemberg and Naples to Austrian alliances in October 1813 and January 1814, although the lesser states did not abandon

Napoleon as speedily as is sometimes thought. Napoleon accepted the loss of Spain and made a peace treaty with Ferdinand VII, but refused to surrender the Kingdom of Italy, the Rhineland and Holland as the price of a more general peace and, instead, planned to invade Italy. However, the French forces abandoned Holland in November 1813, and Napoleon's attempts to divide the alliance, for example, his response to the Austrian proposals of November 1813, failed. In France, Napoleon was affected by falling tax revenues, widespread draft avoidance, a serious shortage of arms and equipment, and a marked decline in the morale and efficiency of officials. The economy was in a parlous state, hit by British blockade and by the loss of Continental markets.

In early 1814, the Allies invaded France. Initially successful – so that Napoleon discovered a willingness to negotiate, abandoning his earlier demands for a Rhine frontier and much of Italy – the Allies were checked in mid-February, as Napoleon manoeuvred with skill in order to destroy the most exposed Austro-Prussian units. He then returned to his demands of the start of the year. These, however, were unacceptable to Austria, the power most willing to negotiate and to leave Napoleon in power. The Allies agreed at Chaumont on 9 March not to conclude any separate peace with Napoleon and, instead, to continue the war and then join in maintaining the peace. Metternich was still interested in peace with Napoleon, but the Emperor's last proposals were unacceptable and Metternich rallied to his allies. As the Allies advanced on Paris, Napoleon's control over both regime and army crumbled. Paris surrendered on 31 March. A provisional French government deposed Napoleon and, with his marshals unwilling to fight on, Napoleon abdicated unconditionally on 6 April, having failed, as he had hoped, to do so on behalf of his son.

Louis XVIII, brother of Louis XVI, returned to France on 24 April, the only option for the government of France that did not appear to require allied military support. Already, under the Treaty of Fontainebleau of 11 April, Napoleon had been given the title of Emperor, the small Mediterranean island of Elba as a principality, and a revenue from the French government. Under the armistice signed on 23 April, the Allies agreed to withdraw from France and the French to evacuate their forces elsewhere. The armistice seemed the best way to consolidate Louis's position.

German hopes of regaining Alsace were not fulfilled in the Peace of Paris of 30 May 1814, which followed the first Paris peace conference. Instead, France got her frontiers of January 1792, with some important and favourable border rectifications. She kept Avignon, Montbéliard and other former enclaves within France. She also received back all her colonies, bar Tobago, St Lucia and the Seychelles, all of which went to Britain. These were generous terms designed to help Louis.

The Congress of Vienna

The settlement of other issues was referred to a peace congress that met at Vienna from September 1814 until June 1815. The congress established a *barrière de l'ouest* designed both to reward powers and to limit France. The Kingdom of Sardinia was strengthened with the acquisition of Genoa. Opportunities for French expansion or influence in northern Italy were further lessened with Lombardy and Venetia becoming Austrian territories, and Parma and Tuscany a Habsburg secundogeniture. In the short term, this put paid to liberal agitation for Italian unity or for Lombard independence. The Papal States were reestablished.

The Austrian Netherlands and the United Provinces were joined as the Kingdom of the United Netherlands under the pro-British William VI of Orange, who became William I of the new kingdom. Until 1830, this ended hopes of Belgian independence. William, however, did not gain the expansion in the Rhineland he had sought. Prussia regained the German territories it had lost under Napoleon, and gained much of Westphalia and the lower Rhineland, including Cologne, Coblenz, Münster and Trier, a major extension of Protestant rule over Catholics. These gains helped to create the Austro-Prussian dualism in Germany sought by the Prussians, but the Austrians were the predominant partner. The Holy Roman Empire was not recreated, but the German Confederation, founded on 8 June 1815, a permanent union of sovereign princes and free cities, was placed under the permanent presidency of Austria, which regained the lands it had lost to Bavaria and France, such as Tyrol and Dalmatia, although the Black Forest possessions lost in 1805 were not regained. Baden and Württemberg were both strengthened. Hanover, which had ceased to exist during the wars, being gained first by Prussia and then by France, before part of it was granted to the Kingdom of Westphalia, was restored, enlarged and became a kingdom. This was a testimony to British power. Hanover and Britain remained under the same monarch until 1837. Bavaria lost some of its Napoleonic gains, particularly the Tyrol and Salzburg, but it kept others, especially Ansbach-Bayreuth and Regensburg, and now added Würzburg and part of the Palatinate. Geneva and the Valais became Swiss cantons, and a new Swiss constitution was agreed, in order to create another stable state as a barrier to French expansion. In the Mediterranean, Britain was left in control of Malta and the Ionian Isles. The Duchy of Warsaw was partitioned, but Russia gained more than it had done in the partitions of 1772–95, with Prussia being in effect compensated in western Germany and Austria in northern Italy. The part of the Duchy that Russia gained became the Congress Kingdom of Poland, with the Tsar as King. Norway's transfer from Denmark to Sweden in 1814 was not reversed.[16]

These territorial changes helped mark the end of an era. Unlike Louis XIV, Napoleon left a smaller France, and one with fewer opportunities for further expansion. The congress also helped set a new agenda for the next century down to 1914. This agenda was initially built partly around the Congress System of settling disputes, but, over the longer term, owed much in Western Europe to a slow realization of French decline and to the replacement of Britain by Germany as the major French enemy. French relative decline owed much to French politics, specifically the heavy loss of life in the French Revolutionary and Napoleonic Wars. Over a million Frenchmen died as a result. The Revolution itself was less bloody, but a combination of civil war and emigration both led to heavy losses and disrupted family life and peacetime reproductive strategies. Partly as a consequence, France's population grew by less than 50 per cent in 1750–1850 while that of England nearly tripled. This contrast can in part be attributed to a fall in the French birth-rate arising from the spread of birth control in the late eighteenth century, but repeated choices for war were also important.

As in 1667, 1678, 1713, 1735, 1748 and 1783, peace offered an opportunity for new alignments. Russia sought cooperation with France against Britain, but Louis preferred an informal relationship with the British, designed to ensure that France played a role in settling German and Italian issues. Talleyrand took a prominent role at Vienna in opposing Russo-Prussian pressure for the Prussian annexation of Saxony. Initially, Metternich had hoped for an alliance of Austria, Britain and Prussia in order to check both France and Russia. As a result, he had been willing to see annexation as the price of Prussian cooperation against Russia. However, when Frederick

William III of Prussia rejected this policy of his minister Hardenberg, Metternich changed tack. On 3 January 1815, Austria, Britain and France concluded a Triple Alliance agreeing to oppose, if necessary by force, Prussian ambitions in Saxony and those of Russia in Poland. Supposedly secret, the terms of the treaty were deliberately leaked to the Russians. They led to a resolution of differences by means of a Prussian and Russian backing down. Each accepted less than they had sought, although, by the partition treaty of May 1815, Frederick William was still ceded about 58 per cent of Saxony. Talleyrand's cooperation with Austria and Britain on the issue was designed to replace the alliance that had defeated Napoleon, the continuation of which would have left France with only a limited role, by a new diplomatic order in which France could have greater influence in Europe, as well as specific benefits on her frontiers.

From Elba to Waterloo 1815

Louis, however, was overthrown when Napoleon returned from Elba. Landing in southern France on 1 March 1815, he was able to reimpose his authority relatively easily. Napoleon promised to observe existing treaties and affirmed peace with the rest of Europe, but his rhetoric within France was hostile and bellicose. Caulaincourt, again Napoleon's foreign minister, was ordered to create a new league with the lesser powers, including Spain, Portugal, Switzerland and the minor German and Italian states, a testimony to Napoleon's lack of realism.

Napoleon's return united the powers. On 25 March 1815, they renewed their alliance to overthrow the restored Emperor. Had he not been defeated by British, Dutch and German forces at Waterloo on 18 June, other Allied armies would probably have rapidly defeated him. At Waterloo, defensive firepower beat off successive French frontal attacks. The arrival of Prussian forces on the French right spelled the end.

France was then invaded and occupied. Napoleon surrendered to the captain of a British warship and was exiled to distant St Helena, a British possession in the South Atlantic, to return to France only as a corpse. Louis XVIII, in contrast, returned to Paris on 8 July. The Second Treaty of Paris, of 20 November, stipulated an occupation of northern France for five years, a large indemnity of 700 million francs, and the cession of Beaumont, Bouillon, Saarlouis and Landau. The loss of the Saar and Sambre coalfields has been seen as a serious blow to France's industrial development. By the Quadruple Alliance of 20 November 1815, the four great powers – Austria, Britain, Prussia and Russia – renewed their anti-French alliance for twenty years, a step designed to limit the chances of France disrupting the peace. Napoleon had failed, totally. In his place had come an attempt to develop a practice of collective security through a Congress system, and Tsar Alexander's Holy Alliance of Christian monarchs, or at least those of Russia, Austria and Prussia, designed to maintain the new order.[17]

Napoleon and the loss of overseas empire

In European terms, Napoleon failed. He did not create a lasting dynasty, his empire collapsed and, under the terms of the Treaty of Vienna, France was constrained territorially, especially with the establishment of Prussian power on her German frontier. The acquisition of Belgium by the House of Orange and its restoration in the Netherlands was designed to create a powerful pro-British state on France's northeastern border, and to provide a reliable axis linking Britain with the Continent. Napoleon III, the reviver of Bonapartist monarchy, had to attempt to overthrow a European order that provided no opportunities for French expansion.

There was also a failure of France as a global power. In the 1780s, British politicians had worried about France's global ambitions, but France's transoceanic empire, trade and possessions were hit from 1793 as the British captured many French imperial bases. Napoleon I got these possessions back under the Treaty of Amiens of 1802, and the treaty was followed by a revival in France's Atlantic trade, including the slave trade, both of which had been badly hit by war and British naval mastery in the 1790s. However, this revival was cut short by the resumption of war with Britain in 1803. This resumption also hit transoceanic French diplomacy. General Bernadotte had been appointed envoy to the United States in January 1803, but, due to British naval power, was unable to assume that duty. Instead, he commanded I Corps of the Grande Armée in the Ulm–Austerlitz campaign of 1805.

Like the Revolutionaries before him, Napoleon also failed to hold on to the French world. He could not, despite initial successes, recapture St Domingue/Haiti, losing large numbers of troops to yellow fever; he had to accept the collapse of French hopes in the Middle East; and he was unable to prevent the British defeat of the Marathas in India in 1803. Mysore, the state in southern India most ready to look to France, had already been conquered in 1799, and the Nizam of Hyderabad's French-trained force had been disarmed by the British the previous year. Indeed, fears about Napoleon helped to drive a British forward policy in India, and the success of this policy made Britain the dominant power there and, more generally, in South Asia.

Furthermore, benefiting from their naval power and their skill in amphibious operations, the British took the leading French bases – Guadeloupe (1810), Martinique (1809), Réunion (1810) and Mauritius (1810) – after war resumed in 1803, as well as the bases of France's client states, such as Cape Town (1806) and Batavia, now Djakarta (1811), from the Dutch, although they were unsuccessful when they attacked Buenos Aires (1806 and 1807). In addition, having gained Louisiana from Spain in 1800 by the Treaty of San Ildefonso, Napoleon sold what was then France's most extensive overseas possession to the Americans in 1803, thus ending France's options in North America. Having persuaded Charles IV of Spain to hand over his territories in 1808, Napoleon planned to take over the Spanish empire, not only in the New World, but also the Philippines. These hopes were thwarted by Spanish resistance, and would, anyway, have been inhibited by British naval power.

Napoleon's global ambitions essentially arose from seeking to thwart Britain, a power that opposed him in Europe. Partly due to their failure, he pursued his colonial plans within Europe, although – like Hitler – his world view, anyway, was largely focused on Europe, especially on territories to the east. After the Egyptian expedition of 1798, Napoleon's interest in, let alone commitment to, the world outside Europe was episodic. Furthermore, it essentially arose from interest in harming European rivals, rather than from any sense of France's role in an expanding Western world.

British influence rested in large part on trade. This was true not only of Asia but also of the New World, with relations with both the newly independent United States and the Iberian colonies. Napoleon did not greatly understand either how to further trade or the dynamics of commercial activity and its relation with public finances. This failing, serious enough for France within Europe, was of even greater consequence beyond the bounds of French military power. Napoleon's replacement by Louis XVIII in 1814 was greeted with enthusiasm in the leading trading ports, such as Bordeaux and Marseilles.

   The Napoleonic legacy was not only a weaker France in Europe, and a European international system that left few options for France, but also a European overseas world dominated by Britain. France's colonies in 1815 were only those allowed them by Britain, such as a number of now inconsequential bases in India. Britain dominated the Western world and France was in a weaker transoceanic position, both absolutely and relatively, than had been the case both before and after the peace treaties signed in 1697, 1713, 1748, 1763 and 1783, and indeed than in the nadir of Revolutionary weakness, division and defeat in 1793. Despite imperial expansion from 1830, especially in North Africa (Algeria) and, later, West Africa and Indochina, France was never to reverse that loss. Britain's dominance of the nineteenth-century world was one of the major legacies of the period of international relations covered in this book.

Chapter 10

Conclusions

A detailed examination of international relations subverts easy formulations and simple accounts of the relationship between such relations, states, societies and warfare. Much scholarly work undermines any simplistic narrative of modernity in terms of a turning point at the supposed transition from medieval to modern. This is true whether the turning point is held to be the 1490s and the outbreak of the Italian Wars,[1] the Reformation crisis of the early sixteenth century, the Westphalian settlement of 1648, or the supposed novelty of the international relations of the 1710s and 1720s with peace congresses and the search for collective security. Instead, it is possible to point to continuities that question the depiction of any of these as marking a major turning point, and thus to postpone what is generally understood as modernity. This can lead, instead, to a focus on changes arising from the French Revolutionary Wars or later in the nineteenth century.

This post-dating of modernity in part involves a repositioning of scholarly focus that can take a number of forms. For example, in place of a focus on a process of, in effect, baton exchange from one leading power to another – the rise and fall of the great-powers approach – it is possible to emphasize developments in societies and states not generally seen as at the forefront. Such an emphasis can be seen in much recent work. For example, Christopher Storrs demonstrated the increased sophistication of military administration in Savoy-Piedmont in 1690–1720 and probed the growing integration of individual provinces and communities, but he was wary of any simplistic account of state formation:

It is questionable whether Victor Amadeus really wanted to create a uniform state. If the years between 1690 and 1713 saw an apparently more determined drive to extend central control and impositions at the expense of local liberty and exemptions it was the result less of a ducal blueprint for 'absolutism' than of a desperate search for money and men to wage wars.[2]

From another direction, Peter Wilson emphasized the value of the collective security arrangements offered by Imperial institutions and German political culture, and questioned the emphasis on Prussia and Prussianization as the course and cause of modernity. Indeed, Wilson stressed the continued value of long-established Reich institutions on the eve of their dissolution: 'No *Reichstag* decision was blocked by religious controversy during 1792–1801; on the contrary, the institution acted promptly and effectively on many issues. The *Kreis* structure also displayed resilience. What stifled these positive signs was the coincidence of the revolutionary threat with Austro-Prussian rivalry.'[3]

In the case of France, frequently seen as central to the process of change, Guy Rowlands explicitly contested conventional theories of modernization:

> Historians must be wary of attributing too many modern notions of governmental and military efficiency to Louis XIV's management of his armies, for if efficiency were the principal criterion for administration then some of Louis' actions were clearly counter-productive. In fact, Louis was always principally concerned with the future of the dynasty, which ultimately required the support of the *grands*. Accordingly, the King himself was prepared to sacrifice much 'rational' and centralised efficiency in order to satisfy the aspirations of the senior *noblesse* and to enhance his own *gloire*, and thereby to safeguard the future of the monarchy through the careful nurturing of loyal and contented sentiment.[4]

Noting the persistence of practices and ideas that are not regarded as 'modern' but, instead, as traditional, if not anachronistic, invites the question whether this is equally pertinent throughout the period. It is certainly clear that much that was important in the seventeenth can also be seen in the following century. Just as the importance of seventeenth-century thinkers for eighteenth-century thought is readily apparent whether Jansenism, the German Natural Law tradition, Lockean psychology, Newtonian physics, international law, Deism or aristocratic constitutionalism is considered, so also there is a need to note continuities in political and administrative history and in international relations. This is but part of a more general problem, the compartmentalization of the eighteenth century and the creation of a chronology that treats its early years as the concluding period of the era of Louis XIV, and then, after a period much of which is in shadow, focuses on Maria Theresa, George III and the 'enlightened despots': Frederick the Great, Catherine the Great, Joseph II and Charles III. The nature of this chronology, and the extent of this period of shadow, varies by country and subject; but it is certainly true that we know less of the Portugal of John V than of that of Joseph I and Pombal, less of the Spain of Philip V and Ferdinand VI than that of Charles III, less of the Russia of Catherine I, Peter II, Anna and Elizabeth than of that of Peter the Great and Catherine the Great, less of the War of the Austrian Succession than of the Seven Years' War, and so on. As a result, it is difficult to establish what was novel about the 'enlightened despots'. Nevertheless, despite this the notion of a unity, at least down to the French Revolution, whether termed *ancien régime* or not, may well be inappropriate. If century-long units are to be adopted, then the first half of the eighteenth century in many respects sits more comfortably with the second half of the seventeenth, and change can be seen from mid-century.

This notion of a transforming period of change, whether in the mid-eighteenth century or in the French Revolutionary period, or later, which can be related to a discussion of international relations, has to be considered alongside the argument that we need a more dynamic understanding of the entire 'early-modern' period. The very linguistic connotations of the term *ancien régime*, with their suggestions of rigidity and conservatism, create problems, but if the emphasis, instead, is rather on a more dynamic, fluid or 'plastic' *ancien régime* or early-modern period,[5] then it is less necessary to focus on change or the causes of change in the late eighteenth century. Instead, the French Revolution can be seen as an extreme example of the variations present within early-modern international relations.

The degree of novelty of French Revolutionary foreign policy and of the international relations of the Revolutionary period are important, related but different, questions that can be approached in a number of lights. These can be simplified to objectives and methods, although a new method of conducting foreign policy was itself one of the objectives of the Revolutionaries. Furthermore, abstract goals became less important than the pressures created by the volatile and emotional ideas and atmosphere of Revolutionary Paris. They combined to produce a context within which it was difficult to conduct not just diplomacy as conventionally understood, but also any negotiations in which mutual understanding and concessions were to play a role. To a degree, the alarming or invigorating energy, if not fanaticism, of Revolutionary foreign policy can be seen as similar to the 'Enlightenment' view of such episodes as the Crusades or the post-Reformation Wars of Religion, because the *philosophes* had argued that religious fanaticism had enslaved and aroused the people.

Some of the central aspects of confessional international relations also characterized the Revolutionary phase. Both the Wars of Religion and the French Revolution witnessed universalist, utopian and sometimes millenarian aims, a paranoid style, fanaticism, a degree of popular participation and mobilization; and a rejection of limited means and goals, of a traditional legal and institutional framework for the formulation, conduct and discussion of international relations, and of a diplomacy of compromise, exigency and expediency.[6] There is also a parallel between the interaction, tension and clash of the universalist message of individual religions creeds, or of revolutionary programmes, widely seen as subversive of all order, with the specific, generally more local and localized, requirements and policies of particular groups in both contexts. The tendency to see modern revolutions in secular terms, which is the view of revolutionary theorists and of most revolutionaries, has led to an underrating of their shared structural characteristics with confessional violence, not least such violence aimed at overthrowing established structures, and attacking either the established faith, or the faith of an important section of the community. Thus, the radical ideas and institutions of the Catholic League of France in the 1580s and 1590s prefigured those of the Revolution. In addition, the Revolutionary–Napoleonic crisis led to an intensification of religious identity and the exacerbation of confessional violence, both within and outside France.

The extent to which early-modern confessional activity prefigured subsequent revolutionary movements is less true of foreign policy than of domestic developments, because the success of such groups in gaining control of the central institutions of the state was limited, although the foreign policy of the Rump Parliament in 1649–53 represented an obvious example. Its policy, like that of Oliver

Cromwell, can be seen in 'secular' terms, primarily mercantilist at the expense of the Dutch and strategic at that of Spain, but an alternative view would stress ideological, particularly religious, factors.[7]

The revolutionary crisis of the late eighteenth century as a second general crisis akin in some respects to the Reformation might appear fanciful, but it is less so if the continuities between the 'Middle Ages' and the 'early-modern period' or the *ancien régime* are considered, and also if the religious dimensions of the Age of Revolutions are appreciated. They are readily apparent in the American Revolution, and in the hostile response evoked by the French Revolution across much of Europe, a major rallying to Church and Crown. Edmund Burke highlighted similarities between the Reformation and the Revolution in his *Thoughts on French Affairs* (1791), as did Novalis, the German Romantic poet and writer Friedrich Leopold, Freiherr von Hardenberg, in his essay *Die Christheit oder Europa*, written in 1799, when he discussed what he termed 'a second Reformation', and the German philosopher Johann Gottlieb Fichte.

In the Austrian Netherlands, Naples, the Tyrol, Portugal, Russia and Spain, opposition to the French was to take on the aspect of a crusade. The Revolutionaries themselves were also inspired by a quasi-religious zeal, not so much for the new religion that they invented as for the utopian possibilities that they appeared to be creating for mankind. This zeal made diplomatic compromise not practical politics in the winters of 1791–2 and 1792–3 as Western Europe moved towards all-out war; but this zeal can be seen not so much as a new force in international relations, but, rather, as a revival, in a new form, of the politics, policies and paranoia of zeal last seen so urgently in the maelstrom of Reformation confessional violence. Parallels between the sixteenth and early seventeenth centuries and the 1790s are very striking in terms of rhetoric and mentalities. In addition, the Wars of Religion did not preclude alliances that were fundamentally explicable only in terms of mutual political interest, such as those of Henry II of France and the German Protestants in the 1550s or Richelieu's France and the Swedes in the 1630s. These had their pendant in the eventual accommodation of Revolutionary France and, even more, Napoleon with some *ancien régime* states, for example the south German princes.

The Revolution released, energized and directed French resources,[8] so that the country was able and willing to play a more forceful role in international relations, but many aspects of the Revolutionary period were traditional. The technological and organizational changes summarized by the phrase 'Industrial Revolution' were still restricted in their impact. The major transformations in theoretical and applied science and technology in most fields, whether warfare, transport, the generation and distribution of power, medicine, contraception or agricultural yields, were yet to come, as was the possibility of mass politicization presented by universal education, widespread literacy and the creation of a more intense political world thanks to the rapid and frequent communication of ideas. The national politics that these changes, as well as the ideology of nationalism and widespread migration to the towns, were to permit, was rather a creation of the nineteenth century than of the Revolutionary period.

Nevertheless, even if the 1780s and 1790s reveal many aspects of continuity of the tensions of the early-modern period, and even if parallels can be found in the Reformation, the Revolution still represented a break from *ancien régime* diplomacy. Revolutionary zeal inhibited (although it did not prevent) the compromises that had characterized this diplomacy. The Revolutionaries thought of themselves as acting in a new fashion, an important aspect of novelty in response to a culture that was primarily reverential of, and referential to, the past. The claim that treaties entered into by rulers could not bind people was subversive. Foreign policy and the foreign minister were subordinated to control by a committee of a popular assembly.[9] Avignon became French and the position in Alsace altered not in response to international treaty, but as a result of what were held to be popular will and natural rights. Particular episodes over the previous century prefigured some of the experience of the Revolutionary period, but the Revolution was different. Its radicalization was unprecedented for a country the size of France, while the French Revolutionary Wars involved and affected all of Europe, although support for the Revolution outside France proved ephemeral.

The Revolution and Napoleon, however, both failed to effect any permanent change in the geopolitics of Europe. The defeat of Napoleon led to a reversal of the trend which had culminated in 1810–12 with much of Europe, including the Low Countries, Hamburg, Lübeck, Genoa, Tuscany, Savoy-Piedmont, the Papal States, Trieste, Dalmatia, and Catalonia, being part of France, while client states, such as the new kingdoms of Bavaria, Italy and Westphalia, were similarly engorged. Instead, in 1813–15, Europe returned to the situation that distinguished it from so many of the other heavily populated regions of the world, multiple kingship.

Geopolitical continuity in this sense, nevertheless, did not imply no important changes, both in geopolitical and in other terms. The Prussian acquisition of the Rhineland and Westphalia in the Vienna settlement led to a fundamental reorientation of Prussian policy westwards.[10] This had a substantial influence on the geopolitical situation as Prussia, rather than the Old Alliance or, more particularly, Austria, now represented the barrier to French eastward expansion. Prussia was thus cast in the role of champion of German national integrity against France. This shift had been prefigured by Prussia's role in the Dutch crisis of 1787, but it represented a major shift from the priorities of Prussian policy in the eighteenth century. The Revolutionary–Napoleonic period also led to crucial internal changes in German states that had been occupied or influenced by France. French hegemony produced reform and secularization.

British maritime and Russian land power were both enhanced by the sustained conflicts of the period. This was crucial to the essential geopolitical continuity of the period from Peter the Great's victory at Poltava in 1709 until German unification in the 1860s: Britain was the leading European maritime power, Russia its (less dominant) land counterpart, and Europe was divided among a number of rival sovereign powers, able to thwart hegemony but unable and unwilling to create any permanent system of effective cooperation.

Of the islands lying off the European mainland, only Britain was both independent and a major power. This allowed her to concentrate on her naval forces, unlike her Continental counterparts – France, Spain and the Dutch – who were maritime powers, but who also had to maintain significant armies. This concentration was crucial to Britain's success in defeating the Bourbons in the struggle for oceanic mastery in 1739–63 and in surviving the attempt to reverse the verdict during the War of American Independence. By the late 1780s, Britain had emerged clearly again as the strongest naval power in the world, the European state best placed to project her power across the globe. The foundation of a colony in Australia in 1788 and the challenge to Spain's position in the Pacific in the Nootka Sound crisis of 1790 were but consequences of this inherent strength. The distinctive feature of the post-medieval European maritime empires was their desire and ability to project their power across the globe: by the late eighteenth century, Britain was clearly most successful at doing so.

The Revolutionary–Napoleonic period dramatically accentuated this relative strength, giving Britain clear maritime and transoceanic commercial superiority. In territorial terms, Britain made extensive gains. Some of these were achieved at the expense of other European powers. They were mostly the islands that European maritime powers had been best placed to seize: the Seychelles, Mauritius, Trinidad, Tobago, coastal Sri Lanka and the 'land-islands', isolated from the interior, of Cape Colony and Guyana. Others, such as much of India, were gains at the expense of non-European rulers.

At the same time, the other European empires were being swept away or suffering major losses. This was true, and even so by 1830, of the French, Spanish, Dutch and Portuguese empires. Aside from losses to Britain, the Spanish and Portuguese empires were dramatically affected by the successful independence movements in Latin America. The gain of West and East Florida from Spain by the United States and its earlier purchase of Louisiana from France in 1803 were early indications of America's dynamic expansionism. During the wars, British naval strength emasculated the French, Spanish and Dutch empires as military and strategic threats and commercial rivals. British naval power had helped to make French control of Louisiana redundant. Napoleon's sale of it in 1803 was an apt symbol of the Eurocentrism that was such a characteristic feature of his policies after the failure of his Egyptian expedition; although the sale was also an attempt to bring the United States into conflict with Britain.

It was largely thanks to the British navy that in 1815 so much of the transoceanic European world outside the New Hemisphere was ruled by Britain. Largely due to successful rebellions in Latin America, by 1830 the vast majority of European possessions abroad were British. Some of the others, especially the Dutch East Indies and, later, the Portuguese colonies in Africa, were, in part, dependent territories. This situation was not to last and, in 1830, the French occupied Algiers, the basis of what was to be a major African empire. Nevertheless, the unique imperial oceanic position that Britain occupied in the Revolutionary, Napoleonic and post-Napoleonic period was to be of crucial importance to the political, economic and cultural development of the state in the nineteenth century. France was to become a great imperial power again; Portugal and the Dutch were to make gains; Germany, Italy, Belgium and the United States were to become imperial powers; but for none of these was empire as important, as central a feature of public culture, or elite careers, as it was for Britain.

Russia was similar to Britain, the two powers prefiguring the position of the United States and the Soviet Union in 1917–90, in that both were outside Europe, able to protect their home base or centres of power from other European states, yet also able to play a major role in European politics. This isolation should not be overstated. The British Isles were threatened with invasion, including in 1692, 1696, 1708, 1719, 1733, 1744, 1745–6, 1759, 1779, 1795, 1798, and 1805, while Russia was invaded, by Sweden in 1708–9 and Napoleon in 1812, attacked by Sweden in 1741 and 1788, and threatened by Prussia in 1791. Nevertheless, the strategic position of Britain and Russia was different to that of other European states; they were to see off Napoleon, and thus thwart the last attempt before the age of nationalism to new-model the European political space. The Vienna settlement left Russia dominant in Eastern Europe and Britain on the oceans, and with no balance of power in either sphere.

The Revolutionary–Napoleonic period secured the triumph of Britain and Russia. Both powers were heavily involved in the conflicts between France and her neighbours, but also able to pursue a policy of territorial gains that simultaneously ended real or apparent threats and established their hegemony. Heavily committed to her Continental position, France was unable to stop Britain, while a French-led coalition was unsuccessful in defeating Russia.

This was a continuation of the pre-Revolutionary position. Russia had dominated Eastern Europe since playing the leading role in overthrowing Charles XII and the Swedish empire. The Prussians had scant wish to repeat the punishing experience of Russian attack during the Seven Years' War. Although the Turks did not collapse as readily as had been anticipated, and Russian gains from them in peace settlements in 1700, 1739, 1774 and 1792 were less than had been anticipated, Russian expansionism was the dynamic force in Eastern Europe. Strength was demonstrated by her ability to fight Sweden and Turkey simultaneously in 1788–90, and, in the Ochakov crisis of 1790–1, by Catherine II's accurate conviction that she could resist Anglo-Prussian pressure over the terms on which she should settle with the Turks. If the French Revolutionary Wars provided the Russians with the opportunity to destroy Poland, Russia had already frequently displayed an ability to dominate the country. As another aspect of continuity, if the French Revolution in part arose from the failure to define and pursue a workable foreign policy,[11] then this was to be repeated by the Revolutionaries and by Napoleon.

Nevertheless, alongside the emphasis on continuity, it is also pertinent to note new developments in the Revolutionary–Napoleonic period, specifically the revival of the 'Western Question'. This involved three related issues: the question of whether any power was to dominate Western Europe and, if so, which; the response to France of her neighbours; and the particular issues of France's expansion east into the Empire, south-east into Italy, and north-east into the Low Countries.

As a result of the economic, political and military problems that affected Spain in 1640–1714, more particularly from 1665, and of the accession of a branch of the Bourbons to the throne of Spain, this 'Question' had ceased to be the issue of Spanish power as it had been since the Habsburgs under Charles V took over the Spanish throne. Instead, the revival of French strength under Louis XIV, his ambition and energy, and the size of the French army, had all led the Question to become one of French power. This led to Western European international relations being articulated around the axes of support for, or hostility to, France. The latter led to the 'Old Alliance' or the 'Old System', the fusion of Anglo-Dutch and Habsburg-led German energies in a common struggle against France, and this had conditioned the attitudes and aspirations of a large number of ministers and polemicists.

The defeat of Louis XIV in the War of the Spanish Succession, the relative passivity of the Orléans regency (1715–23) and of French ministries until 1733, and the rise of Austrian and Russian assertiveness and power all led to a different diplomatic agenda in which French intentions and power were not major issues. They became more prominent again in 1733–48, years of French victories and diplomatic successes, but were, in turn, relegated by defeat during the Seven Years' War, by France's relative postwar quiescence, and by the strength, resilience and independence that Austria, Prussia and Russia demonstrated in the war and in subsequent postwar diplomacy. France was not only relatively weaker, but she also acted as a 'satisfied' power. These changes made the 'Old System' redundant and also undercut the British strategic thesis that France could be weakened as a maritime enemy by the efforts of Britain's Continental allies. They also made it possible for French ministers to discuss the advantages of cooperating with Britain in Continental diplomacy.

The Revolution did not revive the 'Western Question' for several years, for France was obviously weak in 1789–90, although British anxiety in late 1789 about French intentions towards the Austrian Netherlands was an augury for the future. If French policy in 1791–2 played a major role in causing war with Austria, it was not the threat posed by French power that was foremost in the minds of the rulers and ministers of Austria, Prussia and, indeed, Britain, although

France's weaker neighbours, such as Trier, were more worried about the situation. France was invaded with at least as much confidence as Britain and Prussia had shown in planning war with Russia in 1791, if not with far more. She appeared obviously weaker than Russia, and was certainly more divided, accessible and vulnerable to invasion.

France's unexpected successes in September–November 1792 altered the situation dramatically and forced the European powers to appreciate the strength, energy and unpredictability of French power. They led directly to the entry into the war of Britain and the United Provinces. There were to be other dramatic French advances in the 1790s. The frontiers of Italy, the Rhineland and the Low Countries had been stable for the half-century after 1748; now, Europe was to be remoulded, new political spaces created, frontiers redrawn. France's auxiliary republics of the 1790s became the ancillary kingdoms of the 1800s. France became an empire; the Holy Roman Empire came to an end.

It is possible to emphasize continuity in the Revolutionary period and to argue that the pursuit of power was the consistent theme, with ideological considerations playing a minor role. Continuity can also be stressed if an effort is made to distinguish between Revolutionary ideologies and actual policies. However radical the speeches made by Revolutionary orators, many of the presuppositions underlying government policy were traditional. Ideas about France's customary allies, notably Turkey and Poland, were largely as they had been under the *ancien régime*. The hostility of the Revolutionaries to the Austrian alliance had deep pre-Revolutionary roots; and the tendency to look to Prussia as a possible or likely ally went back to the 1740s. The idea of closer relations with the German states, other than Austria and Prussia, was also revived. It can, therefore, be argued that, though Revolutionary emotion altered much of the tone of French policy, it had much less effect on its substance, and thus that the situation after 1792–3 was one of the pursuit by greatly expanded means of aims which were not in themselves essentially new.

Against this must be set the new element of distrust in international relations that the Revolution introduced, a distrust that was paranoid, that linked alleged domestic and foreign threats, and that echoed the fevered anxieties of international relations during the Reformation and Counter-Reformation. This distrust affected the content and character of policy and relations. Louis XIV had aroused considerable distrust, but posed less of a threat to the internal stability of other states than was the case with Reformation and Revolutionary counterparts. Despite the similarities discerned between *ancien régime* and Revolutionary policy, in terms of both French goals and the application of reason, Revolutionary ideals and the logic of domestic politics pushed France towards war in a fashion that was totally different from the impact of domestic pressures elsewhere. It had proved possible to avoid war over the Scheldt and the *Fürstenbund* in 1784–5, and to negotiate peace settlements in Eastern Europe in 1790–2. Such a process of compromise was not possible in the case of Revolutionary France.

The thesis of the interrelationship of domestic and foreign threats, a theme reiterated frequently in both France and her neighbours from the outset of the Revolution, and one that became more potent from 1791, made the sort of compromise sought by the British government unacceptable to many rulers and politicians. The idea that domestic change within France could be accepted as long as she renounced proselytism was not one that enough French politicians were willing to accept and fight for in 1792–3 to make it credible. Equally, it was not a notion that was welcome to most European rulers.

Alongside the stress on developments in international relations arising from the French Revolution, both the revival of the Western Question and the new role for ideological factors, it is important to attach due weight to developments in Eastern Europe. These were of greater long-term consequence for the period saw both the underlining of Russian mastery and the beginning of a new stage in Turkish decline. The popular revolt that began in Serbia in 1804 was to lay the basis of a new situation in which Turkish power declined in the face of internal rebellion and the development of independent Balkan states, rather than simply as a consequence of the advance of Austrian and Russian power. The resulting multipolarity of the Balkans played a major role in challenging the stability of twentieth-century Europe, particularly in the early 1910s and in the 1990s.

Whatever the changes in France, most powers in the early 1790s were governed by the same ruling groups, if not rulers and ministers, as in the pre-Revolutionary period. The question remains how best to conceptualize the international relations of the period. There are obvious contrasts between the language of system and clear national interests beloved by contemporaries and by many historians, and the confused and confusing manner in which developments occurred, the often kaleidoscopic nature of alliances, and the short-term character of so many alignments and speculations. For the modern scholar, the starkest problem is not only the customary challenge of how best to describe, in a relatively small number of words, the complexity of the past, but also how to make sense of, and at the same time move away from, the detailed level of short-term changes, without destroying the character of thought and action in this period by subsuming it into a level of schematic abstraction centring on a systemic approach. There is the related problem of lacunae in the sources, and the difficulties in establishing and assessing both sources and methodology created by a wider conception of foreign policy than one that focuses mostly on diplomatic activity.

The alliances and alignments of the period could be, and were, rationalized in systemic terms, most obviously through the discussion of national interests and the balance of power, but both had a some-what spurious precision. At the same time, an apparently precise and mechanistic language could be employed in a flexible fashion, permit-ting various frequently contradictory interpretations. Alongside flexi-bility in interpretation, it is also important to emphasize the role of change, chance and opportunism in the conceptualization of inter-national relations. Stressing the role of contingent circumstances re-stores to the individuals concerned some of the responsibility that a systemic perspective is apt to underrate. Arguing that the international system should be seen as inherently volatile and unpredictable in its development necessarily focuses attention on the episodic, not the structural, aspects of relations. These help to explain why the three states to emerge to great-power status in 1683–1725 – Austria, Britain and Russia – were far from constant in their interactions. In their search for advantage and security, rulers were willing to change pol-icies and allies frequently and unilaterally, while simultaneous contra-dictory negotiations were commonplace. This emerges clearly from a narrative account of the period, as does the strong contemporary sense of uncertainty over present and future developments. The nature of the historical and literary imagination of this period, with its stress on the role of individuals and the play of circumstances, is in large part vindicated as far as its international relations are concerned.

Notes

(Unless stated otherwise, all books are published in London.)

Chapter 1: Introduction

1 For stimulating recent accounts, G. Modelski and W. R. Thompson, *Leading Sectors and World Powers. The Coevolution of Global Politics and Economics* (Columbia, SC, 1996) and Thompson, *The Emergence of the Global Political Economy* (2000).

Chapter 2: What Was at Stake?

1 For a valuable theoretical dimension, H. Kleinschmidt, *The Nemesis of Power* (2000), esp. pp. 114–70, and 'Systeme und Ordnungen in der Geschichte der internationalen Beziehungen', *Archiv für kulturgeschichte*, 82 (2000), pp. 433–54. I have been greatly influenced by Kleinschmidt's work. For the importance of a consensus agenda, A. Osiander, *The States System of Europe 1640–1990. Peacemaking and the Conditions of International Stability* (Oxford, 1994).

2 M. Hughes, *Law and Politics in Eighteenth-Century Germany: The Imperial Aulic Council in the Reign of Charles VI* (Woodbridge, Suffolk, 1988).

3 G. Savage, 'Favier's Heirs: The French Revolution and the *Secret du Roi*', *Historical Journal*, 41 (1998), pp. 225–58.

4 J. Dewald, *Aristocratic Experience and the Origins of Modern Culture. France, 1570–1715* (Berkeley, Calif., 1993), p. 207.

Notes

5   P. Wilson, *War, State and Society in Württemberg, 1677–1793* (Cambridge, 1995).

6   J. P. LeDonne, *The Russian Empire and the World, 1700–1917: The Geopolitics of Expansion and Containment* (Oxford, 1997); D. Kirby, 'Peter the Great and the Baltic', in L. Hughes (ed.), *Peter the Great and the West. New Perspectives* (2001), pp. 178–85.

7   L. Bély, *La Société des Princes: XVIe–XVIIIe siècles* (Paris, 1999).

8   AST. L M. Autriche 63.

9   W. R. Ward, *Christianity under the Ancien Régime 1648–1789* (Cambridge, 1999), p. 225.

10 D. F. Allen, 'Charles II, Louis XIV and the Order of Malta', *European History Quarterly*, 20 (1990), pp. 324–5.

11 N. Aston, *Religion and Revolution in France 1780–1804* (2000), pp. 284–6.

12 AN. KK. 1393.

13 HHStA. England Varia 8.

14 M. C. Jacob and W. W. Mijnhardt (eds), *The Dutch Republic in the Eighteenth Century: Decline, Enlightenment, and Revolution* (Ithaca, NY, 1992).

15 *Polit. Corresp.* VI, 197; PRO. SP. 91/72 fol. 102.

Chapter 3:   How Did International Relations Operate?

1   For a valuable case study, L. Wolff, *The Vatican and Poland in the Age of Partitions. Diplomatic and Cultural Encounters at the Warsaw Nunciature* (New York, 1988).

2   For a subtle account of relations between a minister and a monarch, J. Hardman and M. Price (eds), *Louis XVI and the Comte de Vergennes: Correspondence, 1774–1787* (Oxford, 1998).

3   H. Kamen, *Philip V* (New Haven, Conn., 2001).

4   Instructions to Feraty de Valette, 17 Apr. 1725, Dresden, Hauptstatsarchiv, Geheimes Kabinett, Gesandschaften 2797.

5   M. S. Anderson, *The Rise of Modern Diplomacy, 1450–1919* (Harlow, 1993).

6   D. R. Headrick, *When Information Came of Age. Technologies of Knowledge in the Age of Reason and Revolution, 1700–1850* (Oxford, 2001).

7   P. Sahlins, *Boundaries: The Making of France and Spain in the Pyrenees* (Berkeley, Calif., 1990).

8   J. Lukowski, *Liberty's Folly. The Polish–Lithuanian Commonwealth in the Eighteenth Century* (1991).

9   G. Rystad (ed.), *In Quest of Trade and Security: The Baltic in Power Politics 1500–1990. I: 1500–1890* (Lund, 1994).

10   C. Storrs, 'Machiavelli Dethroned: Victor Amadeus II and the Making of the Anglo-Savoyard Alliance of 1690', *European History Quarterly*, 22 (1992), pp. 374–5.
11   Bedford, County Record Office, Lucas Papers 30/13/410/4; Munich, Bayr. Ges. London, 24 June.
12   AE. CP. Espagne 470 fol. 49.
13   Munich, Bayr. Ges. London 251.
14   T. E. Kaiser, 'Who's Afraid of Marie-Antoinette? Diplomacy, Austrophobia and the Queen', *French History*, 14 (2000), pp. 241–71.
15   J. Flammermont, *Les Correspondances des agents diplomatiques étrangers en France avant la Révolution* (Paris, 1896), pp. 102–3.
16   A. E. Lund, *War for the Every Day. Generals, Knowledge, and Warfare in Early Modern Europe, 1680–1740* (Westport, Conn., 1999), p. 198.

Chapter 4: Wars and the Military

1   AST. LM. Spagna 64, 30 May 1732.
2   L. Hughes, *Sophia, Regent of Russia 1657–1704* (New Haven, Conn., 1990).
3   R. Harbison, *Reflections on Baroque* (2000), p. 131; C. Mukerji, *Territorial Ambitions and the Gardens of Versailles* (Cambridge, 1997).
4   P. Sonnino, *Louis XIV and the Origins of the Dutch War* (Cambridge, 1988).
5   C. J. Ekberg, *The Failure of Louis XIV's Dutch War* (Chapel Hill, NC, 1979).
6   D. Showalter, *The Wars of Frederick the Great* (Harlow, 1996), p. 355.
7   J. D. Tracy, 'Introduction', to Tracy (ed.), *City Walls. The Urban Enceinte in Global Perspective* (Cambridge, 2000), p. 14.
8   J. Glete, *Navies and Nations. Warships, Navies and State Building in Europe and America, 1500–1860* (Stockholm, 1993), and *Warfare at Sea, 1500–1650: Maritime Conflicts and the Transformation of Europe* (2000).
9   J. Pritchard, *Louis XV's Navy, 1748–1762: A Study of Organization and Administration* (Kingston, Ontario, 1987).

Chapter 5: Europe and the Outer World

1   J. R. Jones, *The Anglo-Dutch Wars of the Seventeenth Century* (Harlow, 1996).
2   D. A. Baugh, 'Withdrawing from Europe: Anglo-French Maritime Geopolitics, 1750–1800', *International History Review*, 20 (1998), pp. 1–32.
3   B. Lenman, *Britain's Colonial Wars 1688–1783* (2001), p. 8.

Notes

Chapter 6: The Late Seventeenth Century 1648–99

1 D. Croxton, *Peacemaking in Early Modern Europe: Cardinal Mazarin and the Congress of Westphalia, 1643–1648* (Selingsgrove, Pa, 1999).

2 K. J. Holsti, *Peace and War: Armed Conflicts and International Order 1648–1989* (Cambridge, 1991), p. 39. For a recent example of the widespread application of the term, F. H. Lawson, 'Westphalian Sovereignty and the Emergence of the Arab States System: The Case of Syria', *International History Review*, 22 (2000), pp. 529–56.

3 R. A. Stradling, *Philip IV and the Government of Spain 1621–1665* (Cambridge, 1988).

4 L. Williams (ed.), *Letters from the Pyrenees. Don Luis Méndez de Haro's Correspondence to Philip IV of Spain, July to November 1659* (Exeter, 2000), p. xiii.

5 R. I. Frost, *After the Deluge. Poland-Lithuania and the Second Northern War* (Cambridge, 1993).

6 A. Arkayin, 'The Second Siege of Vienna (1683) and its Consequences', *Revue Internationale d'Histoire Militaire*, 46 (1980), pp. 114–15.

7 The extensive literature includes R. Hatton and J. S. Bromley (eds), *William III and Louis XIV* (Liverpool, 1968); Hatton (ed.), *Louis XIV and Europe* (1976); J. T. O. Connor, *Negotiator out of Season. The Career of Wilhelm Egon von Fürstenberg* (Athens, 1978); L. Bély, *Les relations internationales en Europe, XVIIe-XVIIIe siècles* (Paris, 1992); A. Lossky, *Louis XIV and the French Monarchy* (New Brunswick, NJ, 1994).

8 C. Storrs, 'The Army of Lombardy and the Resilience of Spanish Power in Italy in the Reign of Carlos II, 1665–1700, part 2', *War in History*, 5 (1998), pp. 20–1.

9 A useful corrective to the accustomed francocentric approach is offered by J. P. Spielman, *Leopold I of Austria* (1977).

10 K. H. D. Haley, *An English Diplomat in the Low Countries: Sir William Temple and John De Witt, 1665–72* (Oxford, 1986).

11 S. C. A. Pincus, *Protestantism and Patriotism: Ideologies and the Making of English Foreign Policy, 1650–1668* (Cambridge, 1996).

12 R. Hutton, 'The Making of the Secret Treaty of Dover, 1668–1670', *Historical Journal*, 29 (1986), pp. 297–318.

13 J. A. H. Bots (ed.), *The Peace of Nijmegen, 1676–1679* (Amsterdam, 1979).

14 J. R. Jones, 'French Intervention in English and Dutch politics, 1677–88', in J. Black (ed.), *Knights Errant and True Englishmen: British Foreign Policy, 1660–1800* (Edinburgh, 1989), pp. 1–23.

15 R. Place, 'Bavaria and the Collapse of Louis XIV's German Policy, 1687–1688', *Journal of Modern History*, 49 (1977), pp. 369–93.

16 C. Boutant, *L'Europe au Grand Tournant des Années 1680. La Succession palatine* (Paris, 1985).

17 Storrs, 'Machiavelli Dethroned: Victor Amadeus II and the Making of the Anglo-Savoyard Alliance of 1690', *European History Quarterly*, 22 (1992), pp. 347–81.
18 B. Whelan (ed.), *The Last of the Great Wars. Essays on the War of the Three Kings of Ireland, 1688–91* (Limerick, 1995).
19 H. Duchhardt (ed.), *Der Friede von Rijswijk, 1697* (Mainz, 1998).
20 M. A. Thomson, 'Louis XIV and the Origins of the War of the Spanish Succession', in Hatton and Bromley (eds), *William III and Louis XIV*, pp. 140–61; W. Roosen, 'The Origins of the War of the Spanish Succession', in Black (ed.), *The Origins of War in Early-Modern Europe* (Edinburgh, 1987), pp. 151–75.

Chapter 7: Conflict and Diplomacy in the Early Eighteenth Century 1700–40

1 AE. CP. Prusse 73 fol. 51.
2 R. M. Hatton, *Charles XII* (1968).
3 An excellent recent guide to the war can be found in R. Frost, *The Northern Wars 1558–1721* (2000), pp. 226–300.
4 M. Roberts, *The Age of Liberty. Sweden, 1719–1772* (Cambridge, 1986).
5 For example, L. Hughes, *Russia in the Age of Peter the Great* (New Haven, Conn., 1998), pp. 441–2.
6 H. Ragsdale (ed.), *Imperial Russian Foreign Policy* (Cambridge, 1994).
7 AE. CP. Suède 172 fol. 223.
8 BN. naf. 6834 fol. 58.
9 K. A. Roider, *The Reluctant Ally: Austria's Policy in the Austro-Turkish War, 1737–1739* (Baton Rouge, La., 1972).
10 BN. naf. 486 fols. 78, 89.
11 AE. CP. Ang. Sup. 4 fol. 156.
12 Bolingbroke to Shrewsbury, 17 Feb. 1713, New York, Montague Collection vol. 10.
13 G. H. Jones, *Great Britain and the Tuscan Succession Question, 1710–1737* (New York, 1998).

Chapter 8: From Frederick the Great to American Independence 1740–83

1 *Polit. Corresp.* I, 90.
2 *Polit. Corresp.* I, 91.

Notes

3   PRO. SP. 105/282 fol. 29.

4   *Polit. Corresp.* I, 411. The best recent introduction to Frederick's impact is H. M. Scott, 'Prussia's Emergence as a European Great Power, 1740–1763', in P. G. Dwyer (ed.), *The Rise of Prussia 1700–1830* (2000), pp. 153–76.

5   Munich, Bayr. London 205, Charles VII to Haslang, 19 Aug., Charles to William of Hesse, 20 Sept. 1742.

6   AE. CP. Espagne 488 fols. 65, 139–41.

7   M. S. Anderson, *The War of the Austrian Succession, 1740–1748* (1995); R. Lodge, *Studies in Eighteenth-Century Diplomacy, 1740–1748* (1930).

8   *Polit. Corresp.* IX, 161; AE. CP. Prusse 171 fols. 112–13.

9   AN. KK 1372, 8 July 1748.

10 R. N. Middleton, 'French Policy and Prussia after the Peace of Aix-la-Chapelle, 1749–1753: A Study of the Pre-History of the Diplomatic Revolution of 1756' (PhD, Columbia University, New York, 1968).

11 T. R. Clayton, 'The Duke of Newcastle, the Earl of Halifax and the American Origins of the Seven Years' War', *Historical Journal*, 24 (1981), pp. 571–603.

12 J. C. Batzel, 'Austria and the First Three Treaties of Versailles, 1755–1758' (PhD, Brown University, Rhode Island, 1974); L. Schilling, *Kaunitz und das Renversement des Alliances* (Berlin, 1994).

13 Munich, Bayr. London 235, Haslang to Preysing, 18 Jan. 1759.

14 L. J. Oliva, *Misalliance: A Study of French Policy in Russia during the Seven Years' War* (New York, 1964).

15 C. J. Duffy, *The Military Life of Frederick the Great* (1986); D. Showalter, *The Wars of Frederick the Great* (1995).

16 C. S. Leonard, *Reform and Regicide: The Reign of Peter III of Russia* (1993).

17 F. Doran, *Andrew Mitchell and Anglo-Prussian Diplomatic Relations during the Seven Years' War* (New York, 1986); K. W. Schweizer, *England, Prussia and the Seven Years War* (Lewiston, New York, 1989).

18 R. Middleton, *The Bells of Victory. The Pitt–Newcastle Ministry and the Conduct of the Seven Years' War 1757–1762* (Cambridge, 1985).

19 Z. E. Rashed, *The Peace of Paris 1763* (Liverpool, 1951).

20 Schweizer, *Frederick the Great, William Pitt, and Lord Bute: The Anglo-Prussian Alliance, 1756–1763* (New York, 1991).

21 E. Dziembowski, *Un nouveau patriotisme français, 1750–1770. La France face à la puissance anglaise à l'époque de la guerre de Sept Ans* (Paris, 1998).

22 E. Boutaric (ed.), *Correspondance secrète inédite de Louis XV sur la politique étrangère* (2 vols, Paris, 1886); M. Antoine and D. Ozanam (eds), *Correspondance secrète du comte de Broglie avec Louis XV, 1756–1774* (2 vols, Paris, 1956–61).

23 AE. CP. Autriche 295 fol. 8.

24 H. M. Scott, 'France and the Polish Throne, 1763–64', *Slavonic and East European Review*, 53 (1975).

25 H. M. Scott, 'Russia as a European Great Power', in R. Bartlett and J. M. Hartley (eds), *Russia in the Age of Enlightenment* (1990) and 'Aping the Great Powers: Frederick the Great and the Defense of Prussia's International Position, 1763–86', *German History*, 12 (1994), pp. 226–307.

26 K. A. Roider, *Austria's Eastern Question, 1700–1790* (Princeton, NJ, 1982).

27 J. Lukowski, *The Partitions of Poland 1772, 1793, 1795* (1999), pp. 52–91.

28 Munich, Bayr. London 250, Haslang to Beckers, 29 Dec. 1772.

29 Boutaric (ed.), *Correspondance secrète*, II, pp. 497–8.

30 AST. LM. Ing. 79, 9 Ap. 1773; PRO. SP. 78/294 fol. 209.

31 AE. CP. Bavière 102 fol. 78, 110 fol. 71; PRO. SP. 84/402 fol. 90.

32 *Polit. Corresp.* VI, 100–1.

33 Bedford CRO. L30/14/176/10.

34 H. M. Scott, *British Foreign Policy in the Age of the American Revolution* (Oxford, 1990).

35 A. C. Carter, *The Dutch Republic in Europe in the Seven Years War* (1971).

36 T. E. Hall, *France and the Eighteenth-Century Corsican Question* (New York, 1971).

37 J. R. Dull, *A Diplomatic History of the American Revolution* (New Haven, Conn., 1985).

38 Bedford CRO. L30/14/176/22.

39 I. de Madariaga, 'The Secret Austro-Russian Treaty of 1781', *Slavonic and East European Review*, 38 (1959–60), pp. 114–45.

40 A. W. Fisher, *The Russian Annexation of the Crimea, 1772–1783* (Cambridge, 1970).

41 J. M. Black, *British Foreign Policy in an Age of Revolutions, 1783–1793* (Cambridge, 1994), p. 68.

42 P. and N. Onuf, *Federal Union, Modern World: The Law of Nations in an Age of Revolutions, 1776–1814* (Madison, Wisconsin, 1993).

43 J. Klaits and M. Haltzel (eds), *The Global Ramifications of the French Revolution* (Cambridge, 1994), p. 53.

44 P. P. Hill, *French Perceptions of the Early American Republic, 1783–1793* (Philadelphia, Pa., 1988).

Chapter 9: The French Revolutionary and Napoleonic Period 1783–1815

1 J. L. Polasky, *Revolution in Brussels 1787–1793* (Hanover, New Hampshire, 1987).

2 For a critical view, T. C. W. Blanning, *Joseph II* (1994).

3 J. Lukowski, *The Partitions of Poland 1772, 1793, 1795* (1999), pp. 165–74.

Notes

4 M. Price, 'The Dutch Affair and the Fall of the *Ancien Régime*, 1784–1787', *Historical Journal* (1997), pp. 875–905.

5 B. Stone, *The Genesis of the French Revolution: A Global–Historical Interpretation* (Cambridge, 1994); O. T. Murphy, *The Diplomatic Retreat of France and Public Opinion on the Eve of the French Revolution, 1783–1789* (Washington, DC, 1998).

6 W. S. Cormack, *Revolution and Political Conflict in the French Navy, 1789–1794* (Cambridge, 1995).

7 P. Griffith, *The Art of War of Revolutionary France 1789–1802* (1998).

8 K. Roider, *Baron Thugut and Austria's Response to the French Revolution* (Princeton, NJ, 1987).

9 B. Simms, *The Impact of Napoleon: Prussian High Politics, Foreign Policy and the Crisis of the Executive, 1797–1806* (Cambridge, 1997).

10 F. Schneid, *Soldiers of Napoleon's Kingdom of Italy. Army, State, and Society, 1800–1815* (Boulder, Colo, 1995).

11 T. C. W. Blanning, *The French Revolutionary Wars 1787–1802* (1996).

12 E. E. Kraehe, *Metternich's German Policy. I: The Contest with Napoleon* (Princeton, NJ, 1963).

13 S. Woolf, *Napoleon's Integration of Europe* (1991).

14 C. Hall, *British Strategy in the Napoleonic War, 1803–1815* (Manchester, 1992); R. Muir, *Britain and the Defeat of Napoleon 1807–1815* (New Haven, Conn., 1996).

15 J. M. Hartley, 'Russia in 1812. Part I: The French Presence in the *Gubernii* of Smolensk and Mogilev', *Jahrbücher für Geschichte Osteuropas*, 38 (1990), pp. 179–82.

16 Kraehe, *Metternich's German Policy. II: The Congress of Vienna, 1814–1815* (Princeton, NJ, 1983).

17 P. W. Schroeder, *The Transformation of European Politics 1763–1848* (Oxford, 1994) is the best guide to scholarship on this period.

Chapter 10: Conclusions

1 M. S. Anderson, *The Origins of the Modern European State System 1494–1618* (1998).

2 C. Storrs, *War, Diplomacy and the Rise of Savoy, 1690–1720* (Cambridge, 2000), p. 312.

3 P. H. Wilson, *German Armies. War and German Politics 1648–1806* (1998), p. 340.

4 G. Rowlands, 'Louis XIV, Aristocratic Power and the Elite Units of the French Army', *French History*, 13 (1999), p. 330.

Notes

5   J. M. Black, *Eighteenth-Century Europe*, 2nd edn (2000).
6   L. and M. Frey, ' "The Reign of the Charlatans is Over". The French Revolutionary Attack on Diplomatic Practice', *Journal of Modern History*, 65 (1993), pp. 706–44.
7   S. C. A. Pincus, *Protestantism and Patriotism: Ideologies and the Making of English Foreign Policy, 1650–1685* (Cambridge, 1996).
8   H. Brown, *War, Revolution and the Bureaucratic State. Politics and the Army Administration in France 1791–1799* (Oxford, 1995).
9   B. Rothaus, 'The War and Peace Prerogative as a Constitutional Issue during the First Two Years of the Revolution, 1789–91', *Proceedings of the Western Society for French History* (1974), pp. 120–38.
10 P. G. Dwyer, 'Prussia during the French Revolutionary and Napoleonic Wars, 1786–1815', in Dwyer (ed.), *The Rise of Prussia 1700–1830* (2000), p. 258.
11 B. Stone, *The Genesis of the French Revolution: A Global–Historical Interpretation* (Cambridge, 1994).

Select Bibliography

It scarcely needs pointing out that such a section could easily run to several volumes, and, anyway, dates very rapidly. Given the constraints of space, I have adopted the following rules. First, I concentrate on works published from 1990 on the grounds that earlier studies can be tracked down through their bibliographies and notes. Second, given the likely linguistic skills of most readers, I have cited works published in English with the exception of those by Bély and Duchhardt, through which other literatures can be approached. As many books span the topics covered in individual chapters, I provide an undifferentiated list. Those who wish to keep up with the subject are encouraged to read the articles and reviews in the leading specialist journal, the *International History Review*. Unless otherwise stated, all books are published in London.

M. S. Anderson, *The Rise of Modern Diplomacy 1450–1919* (1993).

M. S. Anderson, *The War of the Austrian Succession 1740–1748* (1995).

D. Beales, *Joseph II. I. In the Shadow of Maria Theresa 1741–1780* (Cambridge, 1987).

L. Bély, *Les relations internationales en Europe, XVIIe–XVIIe siècles* (Paris, 1992).

J. M. Black, *From Louis XIV to Napoleon. The Fate of a Great Power* (1999).

T. C. W. Blanning, *Joseph II* (1994).

T. C. W. Blanning, *The French Revolutionary Wars 1787–1802* (1996).

M. Broers, *Europe under Napoleon 1799–1815* (1996).

R. Butterwick, *Poland's Last King and English Culture. Stanislaw August Poniatowski 1732–1798* (Oxford, 1998).

P. Contamine (ed.), *War and Competition Between States* (Oxford, 2000).

S. Conway, *The War of American Independence 1775–1783* (1995).

A. Cross, *Peter the Great through British Eyes. Perceptions and Representations of the Tsar since 1698* (Cambridge, 2000).

D. Croxton, *Peacemaking in Early Modern Europe. Cardinal Mazarin and the Congress of Westphalia, 1643–1648* (1999).

A. Cunningham, *Anglo-Ottoman Encounters in the Age of Revolution* (1993).

B. Downing, *The Military Revolution and Political Change. Origins of Democracy and Autocracy in Early Modern Europe* (Princeton, NJ, 1992).

H. Duchhardt, *Balance of Power und Pentarchie 1700–1785* (Paderborn, 1997).

J. R. Dull, *A Diplomatic History of the American Revolution* (New Haven, Corn., 1985).

R. I. Frost, *The Northern Wars 1558–1721* (2000).

D. Gates, *The Napoleonic Wars 1803–1815* (1997).

J. Glete, *Navies and Nations. Warships, Navies and State Building in Europe and America, 1500–1860* (Stockholm, 1993).

C. D. Hall, *British Strategy in the Napoleonic War 1803–15* (Manchester, 1992).

G. Hanlon, *The Twilight of a Military Tradition. Italian Aristocrats and European Conflicts, 1560–1800* (1998).

R. Harding, *Seapower and Naval Warfare 1650–1830* (1999).

J. Hardman and M. Price (eds), *Louis XVI and the Comte de Vergennes: Correspondance, 1774–1787* (Oxford, 1998).

N. Henshall, *The Myth of Absolutism: Change and Continuity in Early Modern European Monarchy* (1992).

K. J. Holsti, *Peace and War: Armed Conflicts and International Order 1648–1989* (Cambridge, 1991).

M. Howard, *The Invention of Peace* (2000).

L. Hughes, *Sophia, Regent of Russia 1657–1704* (New Haven, Conn., 1990).

L. Hughes, *Russia in the Age of Peter the Great* (New Haven, Conn., 1998).

M. Hughes, *Law and Politics in Eighteenth-Century Germany: The Imperial Aulic Council in the Reign of Charles VI* (Woodbridge, Suffock, 1988).

C. W. Ingrao, *The Hessian Mercenary State. Ideas, Institutions, and Reform under Frederick II, 1760–1785* (Cambridge, 1987).

C. W. Ingrao (ed.), *State and Society in Early Modern Austria* (West Lafayette, Indiana, 1994).

J. Israel, *The Dutch Republic. Its Rise, Greatness, and Fall 1477–1806* (Oxford, 1998).

J. R. Jones, *The Anglo-Dutch Wars of the Seventeenth Century* (1996).

D. Kaiser, *Politics and War. European Conflict from Philip II to Hitler* (Cambridge, Mass., 1990).

H. Kaplan, *Russian Overseas Commerce with Great Britain During the Reign of Catherine II* (Philadelphia, Pa., 1995).

J. Klaits and M. Haltzel (eds), *The Global Ramifications of the French Revolution* (Cambridge, 1994).

H. Kleinschmidt, *The Nemesis of Power. A History of International Relations Theories* (2000).

L. D. Langley, *The Americas in the Age of Revolution 1750–1850* (New Haven, Conn., 1996).

B. Lenman, *Britain's Colonial Wars 1688–1783* (2001).

J. Lukowski, *Liberty's Folly. The Polish–Lithuanian Commonwealth in the Eighteenth Century* (1991).

J. Lukowski, *The Partitions of Poland 1772, 1793, 1795* (1999).

J. Lynch, *Bourbon Spain 1700–1808* (1989).

J. A. Lynn, *The Wars of Louis XIV 1667–1714* (1999).

D. McKay, *The Great Elector* (2001).

D. McKay and H. M. Scott, *The Rise of the Great Powers 1648–1815* (1983).

P. J. Marshall, *The Oxford History of the British Empire. II: The Eighteenth Century* (Oxford, 1998).

C. Mukerji, *Territorial Ambitions and the Gardens of Versailles* (Cambridge, 1997).

R. Oresko, G. C. Gibbs and H. M. Scott (eds), *Royal and Republican Sovereignty in Early Modern Europe* (Cambridge, 1997).

A. Osiander, *The States System of Europe 1640–1990. Peacemaking and the Conditions of International Stability* (Oxford, 1994).

Select Bibliography

H. Ragsdale (ed.), *Imperial Russian Foreign Policy* (Cambridge, 1994).

K. A. Rasler and W. R. Thompson, *The Great Powers and Global Struggle 1490–1990* (Lexington, Kentucky, 1994).

G. Rystad (ed.), *In Quest of Trade and Security: The Baltic in Power Politics. I 1500–1890* (Lund, 1994).

P. W. Schroeder, *The Transformation of European Politics 1763–1848* (Oxford, 1994).

H. M. Scott (ed.), *Enlightened Absolutism. Reform and Reformers in Later Eighteenth-Century Europe* (1990).

H. M. Scott, *British Foreign Policy in the Age of the American Revolution* (Oxford, 1990).

H. M. Scott, *The Emergence of the Eastern Powers, 1756–1775* (Cambridge, 2001).

D. E. Showalter, *The Wars of Frederick the Great* (1996).

B. Simms, *The Struggle for Mastery in Germany, 1779–1850* (1998).

S. Smith, K. Booth and M. Zalewski (eds), *International Theory: Positivism and Beyond* (Cambridge, 1996).

W. M. Spellman, *European Political Thought 1600–1700* (1998).

J. Spielman, *Leopold I of Austria* (1977).

B. Stone, *The Genesis of the French Revolution: A Global–Historical Interpretation* (Cambridge, 1994).

C. Storrs, *War, Diplomacy and the Rise of Savoy, 1690–1720* (Cambridge, 1999).

D. A. Sylvan and J. F. Voss (eds), *Problem Representation in Foreign Policy Decision Making* (Cambridge, 1998).

G. Symcox, *Victor Amadeus II. Absolutism in the Savoyard State 1675–1730* (1983).

W. R. Thompson (ed.), *Great Power Rivalries* (Columbia, South Carolina, 1999).

J. Tracy (ed.), *The Political Economy of Merchant Empires. State Power and World Trade 1350–1750* (Cambridge, 1991).

J. A. Vasquez, *The War Puzzle* (Cambridge, 1993).

J. A. Vasquez, *The Power of Power Politics. From Classical Realism to Neotraditionalism* (Cambridge, 1998).

I. Wallerstein, *The Modern World-System. II: Mercantilism and the Consolidation of the European World-Economic, 1600–1750* (New York, 1980).

J. M. Welsh, *Edmund Burke and International Relations* (1995).

J. S. Wheeler, *The Making of a World Power. War and the Military Revolution in Seventeenth Century England* (Stroud, 1999).

J. E. Wills, *1688. A Global History* (2001).

P. H. Wilson, *German Armies. War and German Politics 1648–1806* (1998).

P. H. Wilson, *Absolutism in Central Europe* (2000).

Index

Index